Gothic NZ

Gothic NZ

The Darker Side of Kiwi Culture

Edited by
Misha Kavka, Jennifer Lawn, Mary Paul

OTAGO

Otago University Press

Published by Otago University Press
PO Box 56/Level 1, 398 Cumberland Street, Dunedin, New Zealand
Fax: 64 3 479 8385
email: university.press@otago.ac.nz
www.otago.ac.nz/press

First published 2006

ISBN 10: 1 877372 23 4
ISBN 13: 978 1 877372 23 0

Cover image by Rachel Ahmad-Hall

Printed in New Zealand by Spectrum Print Ltd, Christchurch

Contents

Acknowledgements

A number of the pieces gathered in this collection were first presented at the Antipodean Gothic symposium held at Massey University's Auckland campus in 2002. We thank the numerous people who gave their goodwill and talent to support the symposium, and the agencies which provided financial and administrative assistance: the School of Social and Cultural Studies at Massey University; the Department of Film, Television, and Media Studies at the University of Auckland; and Creative Communities, North Shore City.

We acknowledge the kind permissions of the artists and film-makers whose images are reproduced in this volume. In particular we are grateful to the following organisations and individuals:

- Otago University Press for permission to reprint Martin Edmond's essay 'The Abandoned House as a Refuge for the Imagination' from *Landfall* 208 (November 2004);
- *New Zealand Photography* for permission to reprint David Craig's essay 'Gothic Inversions and Displacements' from issue 58 (2005);
- Dunedin Public Art Gallery for permission to reprint 'Picnic at Woodhaugh c. 1863' (unknown artist), Saskia Leek's 'Picnic at Woodhaugh' from *Ghost Painting*, and an abridged version of 'Charmed', Justin Paton's essay on *Ghost Painting* (Dunedin Public Art Gallery, 2000);
- Rachel Ahmad-Hall for permission to reprint her photograph on the cover;
- Land Transport NZ for permission to reprint road safety advertisements;
- Bill Manhire for permission to reprint 'Picnic at Woodhaugh' from *What to Call your Child* (Auckland: Godwit, 1999).

The excerpts from 'Tiger Country' by Jack Ross have previously appeared as follows:

- 'Disorder and Early Sorrow' and 'Last Night at the Party' first appeared on the *Auckland Poetry* website (http://www.aucklandpoetry.com/poems.htm);
- 'Tiger Country' was first published in *JAAM* 18 (2002), p. 91;
- Lines 5–6 of 'Breast Cancer Doesn't Just Affect Women' are

quoted from Robert Frost's 'Into My Own' (1913) in *Collected Poems, Prose, & Plays*, ed. Richard Poirier and Mark Richardson (New York: Library of America, 1995), p. 15;

- The 'Ishtar' and 'Inanna' passages in 'Goodbye Love' were adapted (respectively) from *Poems of Heaven and Hell from Ancient Mesopotamia,* trans. N.K. Sandars (Harmondsworth: Penguin, 1971) and *The Ancient Near East: An Anthology of Texts and Pictures,* ed. James B. Pritchard (Princeton, NJ: Princeton University Press, 1971);

Finally, the editors thank Massey University's School of Social and Cultural Studies and the University of Auckland's Department of Film, Television, and Media Studies for financial support.

MK, JL, MP

Introduction

Warping the Familiar

Jennifer Lawn

Strangely, it is both too early and too late to write of a New Zealand gothic. The first book-length publication on the topic, *Gothic NZ* arrives precipitately in the sense that no critical consensus has yet emerged around what New Zealand gothic is, how it relates to the nation's cultural mythologies, or whether it even exists: as recently as 2005 Lydia Wevers could comment that our literature, for example, has 'almost no gothic'.[1] Flick the angle of vision just a fraction – itself a gothic shift – and the opposite picture appears: gothic is revealed as endemic to New Zealand's self-representation, already too profuse to allow generalisations about its influences and effects, and fractured between forms that are either too global or too intensely regional in their ambits to be pinned to a national rubric. In presenting a range of gothic zones and energies as we find them today in New Zealand visual and verbal arts, we thus have the dual sense of both starting a new conversation, and joining a rising hubbub – often as contradictory, inventive and hyperbolic as its subject matter.

The question 'where is gothic?' is elusive enough in any location. Gothic slides, it insinuates; its split time-space and structures of displacement leave us with the sense that the given scene is not the whole picture. How would we then begin to address the question 'where is gothic here?' in (around, under) these South Pacific islands at the antipodes of Western Europe? Could gothic's intimations of deep time find any place in a former colony whose dominant settler pragmatism privileged realist modes and restricted historical consciousness to what Stephen Turner calls a truncated, 'short history'? How might gothic play out through the postcolonial uncovering of colonial injustices that challenge Pakeha myths of settlement, 'releasing strange demons from the deep' as they do so?[2] Shift the frame again to postmodern New Zealand, where the country transforms itself into fantasy spaces (Middle-Earth, Narnia, Skull Island) that feed the latest enthusiasms of the global entertainment industry. Can gothic find purchase on the slick façade of the branded nation – except as one of New Zealand's niche cultural exports, like our quirky/self-ironising brand of cinema?

The contributions to this volume each take distinctively local angles on such matters of gothic migrations and mutations, while also drawing on the multiple taproots of gothic. Various genealogies are conjectured for New Zealand gothic, in part because the visual and narrative gothic arts reach back to different imputed origins: gothic art and architecture emerge in Europe's high medieval period in the early twelfth century, while English-language gothic literature conventionally dates from the publication of Horace Walpole's novel *The Castle of Otranto* in 1764, during the height of the Gothic Revival in architecture.[3] This tug-of-war between archaic pressures and new social formations is itself a conspicuous gothic theme, as gothic renews itself through an upwelling of the past. We have given preference for inclusion to contemporary pieces that convey a sense of deep time and which emphasise local appropriations of national or international influences. So the artists and writers represented here are all travellers in time and space, journeying from ancient Mesopotamian mythology, Augustinian theology, and medieval pilgrimage through to such intimate locales as abandoned houses in provincial Ohakune, the boutique fashions of Auckland's K' Road, or images of Rangitoto Island as the backdrop for an antipodean Ophelia wandering out of the frame.

The collection juxtaposes a wide range of art forms, which we hope will generate new sympathies as well as divergences between autobiography, architecture, poetry, fiction, photography, cinema, public service advertising, and television. Many of the contributions are original works published here for the first time, while we regard others as 'contemporary classics' deserving to be reprinted and distributed to as wide an audience as possible. This selection is by no means intended to be exhaustive or fully representative. Even if gothic could, in principle, be exhausted, its practice varies so extensively in New Zealand from colonial times to the present that any sample must necessarily remain seductively incomplete. We offer these pieces to tantalise and give pleasure, as well as to inform. The images are integral to the composition of the book, and many of the essays can also be enjoyed as performances in their own right, with their tone ranging from the discursive through to the whimsical and speculative. At least from the Gothic Revival period onwards, gothic has teetered between high seriousness and self-parody, and this book likewise will instruct, amuse, and delightfully bemuse.

Where is gothic here?

Introductions often assume the task of 'surveying the terrain', as the idiom goes, but in the case of gothic the boundary pegs constantly shift: gothic seems equally to happen nowhere, anywhere and everywhere at the same time in New Zealand. New Zealand literature and cinema, for example, offer 'almost no' gothic if the term is confined to the particular repertoire of images and effects associated with Gothic Revival literature: fantastical tales involving entrapped heroines, the supernatural, sublime raptures, and Catholic depravity.

In this narrow sense of the fantastic, Pakeha texts targeted for an adult audience appear very mono-dimensional, scarcely breaching the threshold of the material world to the beyond. Science fiction and fantasy scripts have rarely made it past the gatekeepers of book publishers and film producers. Ghosts are commonplace in Maori cosmology but rare in Pakeha texts, where such things still seem to need explaining, sometimes through a helpful Maori informant: 'Spirits, mate. The old people. I'll bet you a case of grog it's the spirits – a tapu on the place'.[4] Our slasher tradition is rich enough, if we allow media stories of P-addicted men rampaging with machetes. Of the most enduring gothic monsters, only the zombie has made much inroad, being an automaton peculiarly well-suited to the narcotising rounds of lawn-mowing (Peter Jackson's *Braindead*) and rural parties (Greg Page's *The Locals*). Vampires, who tend to favour a more cosmopolitan environment, have recently arrived in Elizabeth Knox's *Daylight,* Ngahuia Te Awekotuku's succubus version of Hine nui te Po in *Ruahine*, and Glenn Standring's vampire brotherhood in *Perfect Creature.* As yet we have no South Pacific Frankenstein monster, except by analogy (genetic engineering, non-Christian immigration, neoliberal economic policy – insert here your version of a nightmare-run-amok).

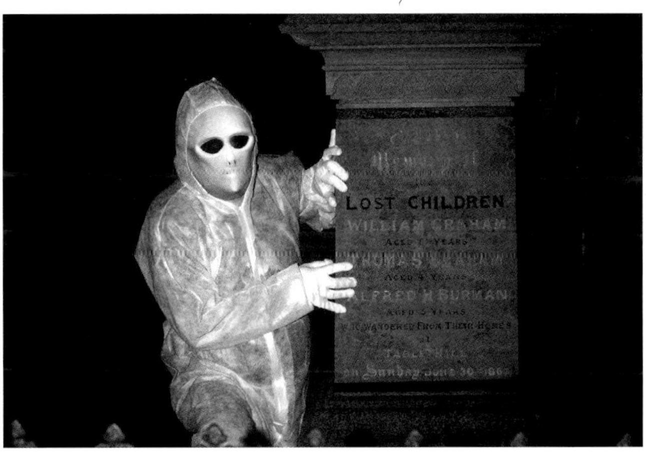

Ronnie van Hout, 'No Exit part I' 2003, Production still for DVD loop

Look from a different place, one not so focused on the supernatural, and gothic is everywhere. William Schafer deems a sense of 'sinister and unseen forces' to be endemic in modern New Zealand culture.[5] Fashion designer Karen Walker virtually sees gothic emanating from the soil: 'there's a heavy, ominous, slightly restrained kind of feel and I think that comes from our culture and our landscape and just the personality of the country. There's a heaviness to it'.[6] New Zealand literature and film churn out a welter of what we might term 'gothogenic' zones: the farm shack, with Curnow's dog dragging his chain and the evacuated land stripped of native bush (and people); the suburban bungalow with the manicured front lawn; the Scarfie flat; the beach, the bach, the gravel pit; abandoned freezing works and rotting meat; the roadside crosses looming in the headlights; and the child: the sacrificial child, the mute child, the beaten child, the good boy, the God boy. As one such beleaguered child, Elsdon Bird, would say, 'All this stuff going on … it makes you feel like going out and getting shickered'.[7]

Look through the arch-shaped window and you will find gothic expression permeating contemporary visual arts, from queasy echoes of unease, as seen in the 2005 Artspace exhibition 'Uncanny: The Unnaturally Strange', to the full-blown schlock parody of Ronnie van Hout. Contemporary artists work self-referentially, as in the demonic self-fashioning of van Hout or the colonial dress-ups of Lisa Reihana, eerily lasered onto tombstone-like granite slabs in her sequence *Native Portraits.* Saskia Leek's *Ghost Painting* (Dunedin Public Art Gallery, 2000) conveys a fragility of colonial presence: in one work a sheeted ghost sits at a formal table setting, with an empty place set for the viewer to occupy; in another, minutely penned picnickers hover around a table, dwarfed by encroaching native bush. In this volume Justin Paton discusses the work as a kind of palimpsest of a painting dating from c. 1863 which Leek reconstructs, as if by ghostly promptings, through the mediation of a poem by Bill Manhire. As Leek's Dunedin-based compositions suggest, gothic regionalisms are powerful in the New Zealand imaginary, and the dark side of Cantabrian decorum was explored in a multi-artist exhibition at the Christchurch Art Gallery in 2004/05: 'Coming Home in the Dark', named after one of Owen Marshall's most sinister and pitiless short stories. Other artists allude more to Early Modern, medieval and archaic referents. Simon Kennedy's oil paintings transfer the death's head so pervasive in allegorical Renaissance art into a *memento mori* for modernity, looming over a sublime landscape reminiscent of the Transcendentalists or, more commonly, over a still life of discarded domestic hardware. The interpenetration of the sacred and the profane fascinates other artists: in *Doomed, Doomed, All Doomed* (Artspace, 2005), Francis Upritchard relates death to ornamentation in the practices of Egyptian burial rites, producing votive fingers, funeral urns, and mummified casts; and Christopher Braddock's photographs of tattooed torsos, in this volume, make the body surface the point where the finitude of the fleshly meets the infinity of the sacred.

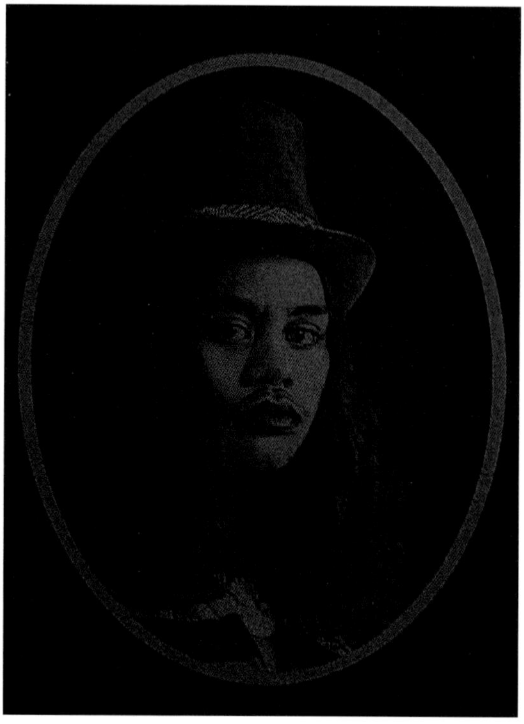

Lisa Reihana, 'Top Hat' 2003, Lasered granite, 600 x 400 mm

Yet to say that 'gothic appears everywhere' seems somehow smug; when gothic becomes a generalised condition it loses its capacity to ambush us. Gothic is too mobile and unstable for that. Perhaps the best way to describe gothic's location, then, is to say that it *could be* anywhere. This means treating gothic as a mode, not a genre: a way of doing and seeing, adaptable across dislocations of culture, time, and space, rather than a substantive category. By virtue of its fascination with the borders between categories – life/death, sanity/madness, domesticity/monstrosity – gothic troubles definitions and spawns a proliferation of hybridisations, transplantations, hyphenations. One cannot say what gothic *is*, in the sense of a positive entity, a definitive catalogue of artists and texts, or finite set of scenes and effects. Gothic works in a manner more akin to a shifting warp of the familiar. In this it shares qualities with its close relative, erotics: just as any part of the body may be eroticised, so any content, location, moment, or frequency may be perversely and unpredictably 'gothicised'. Gothic touches upon and skews the ordinary-world dimensions of domesticity, decorative form and psychological balance; it troubles them with aberration, with something that ought not be there.

Modern Habitats

Internal spaces, and the architectural façades that belie these spaces, remain a powerful and familiar domain for the concentration of gothic energies. This feature of gothic phenomenology not only survives migration to the new world, but if anything intensifies through unflinching depictions of domestic life and the sick nuclear families associated with it. 'Home' is a dangerous sign, in part because mythologies of security, safety, and fulfilment continually work overtime to obscure their own fragility: intimate relationships both sustain us and strip us bare; a thin border separates safe enclosure from entrapment; and, as Olivia Macassey's poems in this volume imply, transmissions flow secretly and seemingly uncontrollably from one generation to the next. The volatile entailments of 'home' apply also to its metaphorical extensions in other modern institutions that are imagined as ideally safe, bounded spaces: the psychiatric ward, mentioned by David Craig in his exposition of gothic as grotesque mimicry of 'home', and the white settler nation, discussed in the essays by Misha Kavka, Sarah Shieff, and Mark Jackson.

David Craig's essay 'Gothic Inversions and Displacements' theorises this tenuity of the natural, scaled, domestic world in which the grotesque hovers 'at one duplicitous ... remove from classical notions of quality and decorum'. In his account, gothic is a fundamentally modern mode, the necessary obverse to bourgeois domesticity and conventional aesthetics: gothic is simply normality with a twist. A trick of the light, a figure tantalisingly unfocused, a pose held too still, a lowered angle of perception, mistiming, a touch of hyperbole, a shade too much pressure – all are ways of 'escaping or getting beyond the core orthodoxies and hegemonies of time, public place, scale and aesthetic gender'. Gothic thus disrespects proprieties of scale, in the sense that a mere tweaking of the picture can produce wrenching distortions. It can seep through, or hover around, scenes of apparent normality – or slap us fully in the face in scenes of outrageous perversion, rampant monstrosity, or claustrophic horror. If gothic's compass swings from the subtly skewed to the blatantly fantastical, that is because in a gothic worldview these qualities are not poles apart but rather immediately adjacent.

Craig builds his argument as a reading of architectural photographs by Allan McDonald, Ann Shelton and Gavin Hipkins in which the ruins of private or public buildings evoke discarded lives. But readers familiar with New Zealand's narrative art forms will also make wider connections. The 'telescoped social order' of domestic gothic recurs persistently in settler representation: the Pakeha family is stripped to its elemental units and isolated from the relativising commerce of the wider social world in Jane Campion's film *The Piano,* Vincent Ward's *Vigil,* Garth Maxwell's *Jack Be Nimble,* Christine Jeffs' *Rain,* Peter Jackson's *Heavenly Creatures* (with double family trouble), Mike Johnson's novel *Dumb Show,* Maurice Gee's *In My Father's Den,* and Janet Frame's metaphysical treatment *Scented Gardens for the Blind.* And Craig's representation of gothic as the secret material history of modern idealisms can also be seen in the structural logic of a film such as Gaylene Preston's *Perfect Strangers,* which relies on an unstable flickering between a conventional script of seduction and the psychopathology that so neatly mirrors it. All the elements of true romance are there: the stranger with a past, the hideaway, the rescue, the candlelit dinner and luxury bath, the rival, the change of heart, the proposal, the declarations of undying love. But the hideaway is a prison, the stranger a weird fetishist; the candlelit bath suggests an elaborate pre-sacrificial ritual, the proposal miscues, eternal love needs the help of a freezer, and conventional marriage proves viable only because the bride conjures a profound fantasmatic compensation. Here the gothic mode is not only a fantastical escape from reality, but also a fuller engagement

Still from Perfect Strangers *(Gaylene Preston, 2003)*

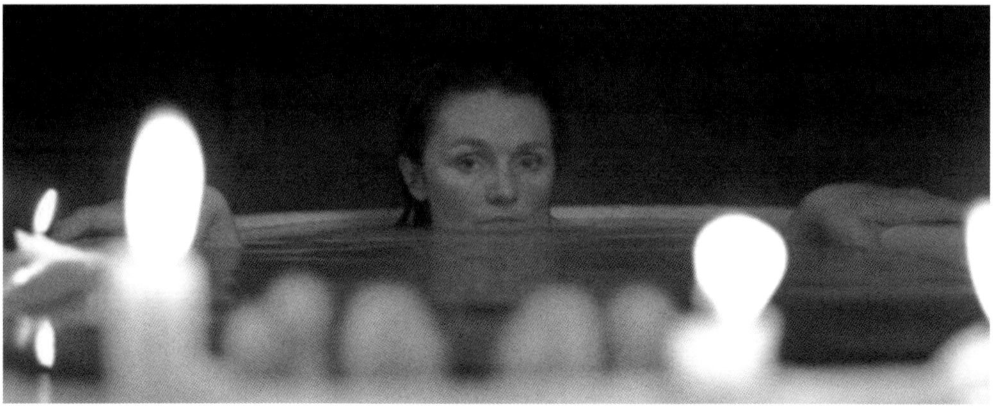

with the psychic complexities that underpin it. A similar doubling of bourgeois modernity with terror can be found in Robert Sarkies' film *Scarfies*, where a group of student flatmates create a grotesque simulacrum of the modern state, revealed to be a form of legitimised class warfare.

In this volume, Yvonne Todd's portraits also work a fine tension between the conventional and the creepy. In their most immediately local address, her works speak of the North Shore's Pakeha middle class and the tribulations of hyper-feminine debutante culture. The portraits present adolescent girls and women, often with glossed lips and lidded eyes bruised with heavy mascara or peacock-blue eyeshadow. It is always a special day; she is dressed immaculately, often sporting the signs of success in the pursuits of feminine competitive beauty: a sash suggesting a beauty pageant, a lace extravagance, a flowing white bridal gown, shades of Romantic couture. But something is subtly awry: the pose is held a little too frigidly and the manicured or gloved hands clutch a talismanic decorative object, evoking a palpable vulnerability that Gwynneth Porter has described as an underlying hysteria in Todd's vision. This is portraiture as still life or *nature morte*, a hybrid that Frances Hodgkins experimented with to very different effect in her paintings 'Self Portrait: Still Life' (c. 1935) and 'Still Life: Self Portrait' (c. 1933). But where Hodgkins depicts cluttered metonymies of the painter's playfully adopted feminine persona, Todd veers toward a more literal take, in which the subject of the photographic portrait appears to *be* the still life through the subtlest hints of death-like perfection and stasis. Here cosmetician meets mortician with a threatening sumptuousness reminiscent of David Lynch's compositions.

Misha Kavka opens her commentary on suburban gothic with a reminder that there are sociological and climatic reasons why home preoccupies New Zealanders; after all, it is a banal but material point that Kiwis spend endless hours renovating the weatherboard homes that provide so little relief from the pervasive damp of the climate. In 'Out of the Kitchen Sink' Kavka observes the incursions of nature, including vegetative roots, into domestic spaces gendered as feminine territory. But as she points out, anxiety about roots carries a double meaning. The geographical imagination of settler culture tends to foreshorten history, and legitimate occupancy of territory becomes asserted through the trope of a natural origin in the new land. To maintain this fiction, violence against Maori and appropriation of their land has to be disavowed, which partly explains why we find colonial father-figures killed off in settler gothic novels such as Fiona Kidman's *Mandarin Summer* or Dorothy Eden's romance *An Important Family*. In exposing anxieties of the domestic home, settler gothic can be read as an allegory of historical injustices and anxious permeations in the national home within 'nature'. These instabilities are not eradicated, for all our efforts to make hurried repairs – whether these refer to Kiwis' love of do-it-yourself shows, or to the endings of films, such as *The Piano*, which so unconvincingly restore the compromised institution of the settler family.

The strategies of displaced racism in nation-building are also investigated in Sarah Shieff's 'Well-laundered Elves: Purity and Degeneration in *The Lord of the Rings*'. Shieff points out how a morally-laden scale differentiates the races in Middle-Earth, from the pure cleanliness of the Elves to the foul pits of Mordor. The films' most gothic moments are also the most anti-semitic, seen in the teeming earth-births of the Uruk-hai and the cupidity of Gollum. But the racial isolationism reinstated at the end of *The Return of the King* becomes even more sinister beyond the story frame, in the context of the trilogy's production. A full-saturation branding effort accompanied the production, selling to New Zealanders and the rest of the world not only an idea of the films, but an idea of New Zealand itself. Such an epic campaign required recourse to two of our most corrosive mythologies, both hangovers from colonialism: hard primitivism, foregrounded in the casting of Maori actor Lawrence Makoare as the Uruk-hai leader Lurtz, and the projection of the land as unsullied paradise, reflected in the 'New Zealand: 100% Pure' tourism campaign which was launched during the production period. This may seem remote to gothic concerns, but Shieff shows how the 'clean green image' functions as an alibi: it displaces and partially masks the 'racialised theology' and politics of purity operative not just in Tolkien's world but also in our own.

Counteracting such racial mythologies are overtly political appeals to the supernatural in recent Maori writing. The term 'gothic' requires much circumspection when applied to a Maori context. Whereas the ghost *ought not to be there* within a Western rationalist perspective, spiritual presences are expected and socially acknowledged in the Maori lived-world, through the intertwining of past, present and future in every moment. Thus in Patricia Grace's novel *Baby No-Eyes* it is regarded as natural that an unborn child killed in a car accident would return to her mother for some time, for 'you don't expect her go away [sic], join her ancestors, foof, just like that'.[8] Likewise, the twelve orders of darkness in Maori cosmology allow a confluence of zones between light and dark. In Western modernity's elevation of 'enlightenment', darkness tends to hold more oppositional purchase and so excites a more phobic repudiation of death. Nonetheless, Maori writers do conspicuously activate the spirit world against colonial and neocolonial injustices through syncretic borrowings from Western traditions of the living dead. Grace distinguishes between the natural attendance of spirits in death and the troubled spirits provoked by the aberrations of Pakeha violence, and Tiri, the protagonist of Witi Ihimaera's play *Woman Far Walking*, likens herself to a vampire. Combining the admonitory force of the Ancient Mariner with the emblematic suffering of the Pietà, it is Tiri's curse, and her mission, to live on as an embodiment of Maori grief, until her self-abjection can be redeemed by the politically active remembrance of future generations. Perturbations of the spirit world also galvanise those estranged from Maori culture in Hone Kouka's play *Waiora* and many of the episodes in the popular television series *Mataku* (South Pacific Pictures), signalling an emergent discourse that challenges the settler nationalist paradigm.

Old world rituals

Other pieces in this volume reach back in time, beyond modernity, to relate contemporary gothic to its medieval and archaic antecedents. Modern gothic functions in an essentially reactive mode; it continually reveals the self-defeating action by which the Rational Man strives to repel death and its cognates (unreason, superstition, inefficiency, sexualised femininity), only to find that such threats redouble their force by this process. In this reactive sense, gothic can overtly relate to religion only as yet another form of self-defeat: the vampire's transubstantiation of blood into life shows how Catholicism generates its own demonic inversion; or closer to home, constipated settler Calvinism strips the world of wonder and makes penance not just a defined period of time but life itself. By contrast, Mark Jackson, Chris Braddock, and Jack Ross work in the domain of a more sacral gothic which restores something profound and ecstatic to the truncated bounds of modern human experience. In doing so, they also move beyond the established signs of 'New Zealandness' and into a philosophical and even theological engagement with death.

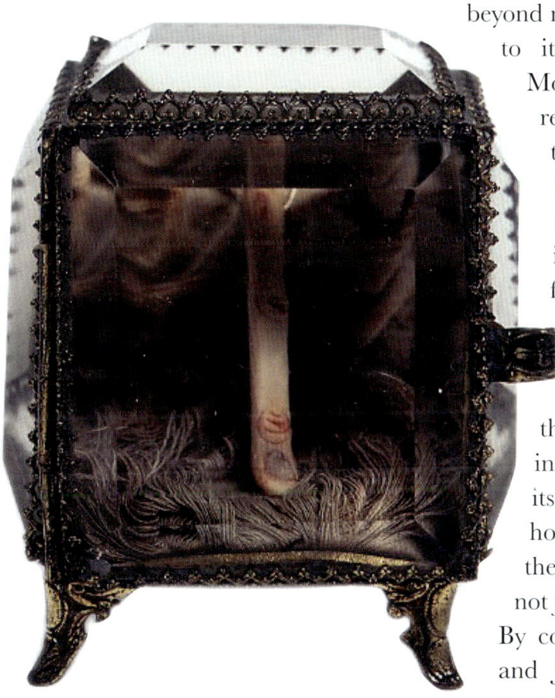

Francis Upritchard, 'Votive Finger' 2004, modelling material in glass box, 70 x 80 x 70 mm (Courtesy of Kate MacGarry, London)

Jack Ross' poem 'Goodbye Love' cross-cuts between the perturbations of the petty cosmopolitan, stalked by the seeming shallowness of his own breath, and ancient Mesopotamian exotics of primal sacrifice and cosmic disintegration. Here sacred ritual provides an ordering structure to existence, one which is inimical or at least indifferent to human affairs and which neither comforts nor bends to appeasement. In this poem, as in his fiction works *Nights with Giordano Bruno* and *Trouble in Mind,* Ross explores a pure well of malevolence and shows himself to be one of very few writers in New Zealand who convey the palpability of evil.

Chris Braddock's photographs display an expanse of flesh, torsos cut off from the head and legs and from any other contextualising or identifying features. Sacred heart and crucifix motifs appear enticingly close to conventional erogenous zones: buttock, nipple, navel, pubes. But the smooth contours of skin also slide into declivities that remind us of the body's excretory functions: the anus, the armpit. In 'Aaron' we see a pierced nipple, reminding us of what the tatooist does: cut into the skin, rather than decorate its surface. From these images, Mark Jackson develops a condensed theory of gothic as a continuation of the Augustinian doctrine of manifestation. Under this theology, divine reason can only be made manifest through the evidence furnished by the senses, that is, through the profane. But this sacred became thin when it capitulated to modern psychology, when the 'soul' became the 'psyche'. Gothic takes the place of this evacuated sacred by returning to that zone between the sensual and the sacred that so disgusts the modern Western subject.

Less speculatively, both Elizabeth Hale and Ian Lochhead document how medieval patterns re-emerge in New Zealand settings. Hale points out that the Antipodes was part of Europe's theological-geographical imagination long before any European ever set foot in the South Pacific. In the artistic visions of Vincent Ward and Maurice Gee, Auckland becomes a purgatorial underworld, a place of suffering and dislocation that is yet capable of being purged. Lochhead reminds us of the remarkable conversion of Gothic ecclesiological principles from medieval Catholicism to nineteenth-century Protestantism and Anglicanism. The aesthetic theories of John Ruskin and A.W.N. Pugin were transplanted to the new colony via figures such as Bishop Selwyn and Benjamin Mountfort. English architectural values were inventively adapted to 'low' materials such as corrugated iron, helping to explain the pervasiveness of Gothic style in colonial and Victorian architecture, from the magisterial Christchurch Cathedral to the droll little church in St Bathans, Central Otago.

I have left until last the very first essay in this collection, Martin Edmond's reminiscence 'The Abandoned House as a Refuge for the Imagination'. Edmond also inhabits the fallen and corrupt world, but he transforms it through reflection into a meditative place to 'restore to existence something which has been lost'. In a classic provincial scenario, Edmond recalls childhood summers spent roaming free of adults through the quarter-acre sections, beaches, and semi-rural farmlets of small-town New Zealand. The essay is counterpointed by a selection of period photographs showing the blank eyes of Ohakune buildings; in one, single-storey houses are distributed in single file to the vanishing point of bush and snow. For gothic kids, these lonely facades both entice and forbid entry into their dark interiors. Once inside, they thrill to the strange alchemy by which preserved objects become imbued with the longings of owners who have since passed on. Edmond is attended in his meditations by the memories of artist Philip Clairmont and novelist R.H. Morrieson, men who lived, and expressed in their work, severe tortures of the mind.

Edmond dwells in the abandoned house, attending to the unfolding patterns of personal association, aesthetic resonance, and sympathetic imagination. This book, too, offers a space for ruminative wandering, an exhibition in words and images to prompt new connections and open new conversations. Like the objects on a curious dressing table, these pieces will draw out associations and are presented for readers to pick up, absorb, rearrange. Some contributions, such as Ian Lochhead's exposition of colonial gothic architecture, tell their archives plainly; others, like Macassey's 'Nocturnes for an Only Daughter', work allusively, hinting at stories behind their stories. But in each case, what Edmond terms 'the occult properties of the mundane' can be felt: gothic infuses everyday habitats, from tattoos to television advertisements, with intimations of deep time and partially-grasped realities. And perhaps, too, Edmond offers the simplest, most intuitive answer to the question 'where is gothic?': it's in your neighbourhood, just around the corner.

Simon Kennedy, 'American Beauty' 2005, oil on canvas, 700 x 750 mm

Haunted Habitats

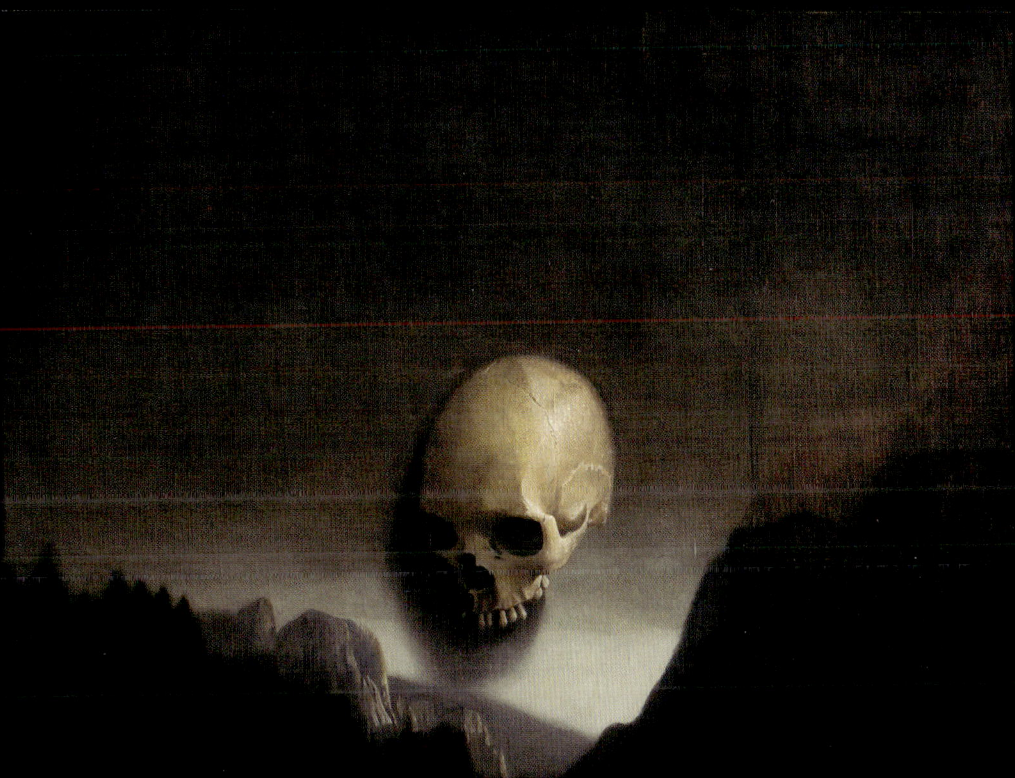

The Abandoned House as a Refuge for the Imagination

Martin Edmond

Driving in New Zealand, you pass through countryside littered with empty, wooden, decaying houses, many of them overlooked by their replacements, brand new brick and tile homes with immaculate gardens, well-cut lawns, TV aerials, satellite dishes. These new houses look like something out of a David Lynch movie and it's hard to believe there are not scary things going on in some of them just like in, say, *Twin Peaks*. In the double spectre of these differently haunted houses, the colonial dream reaches apotheosis yet leaves behind a nightmare, a paradise lost. At the new house, where people sleep, eat and watch TV, imagination seems like an optional extra no-one subscribes to any more, while down below, as the old house rots back into the soil, it is monstrously alive, conjuring ghosts, dramas, mysteries. Out of these two kinds of horror, it was always the old house I was drawn to explore, and, from quite a young age, I used to do so whenever I could.

Some of these incursions were memorable. One was into a house on the opposite corner from ours in Spring Street, Freemans Bay, in 1971. An old man lived there; he'd gone to hospital and never

Seddon Street, Raetihi, 1916 (Alexander Turnbull Library)

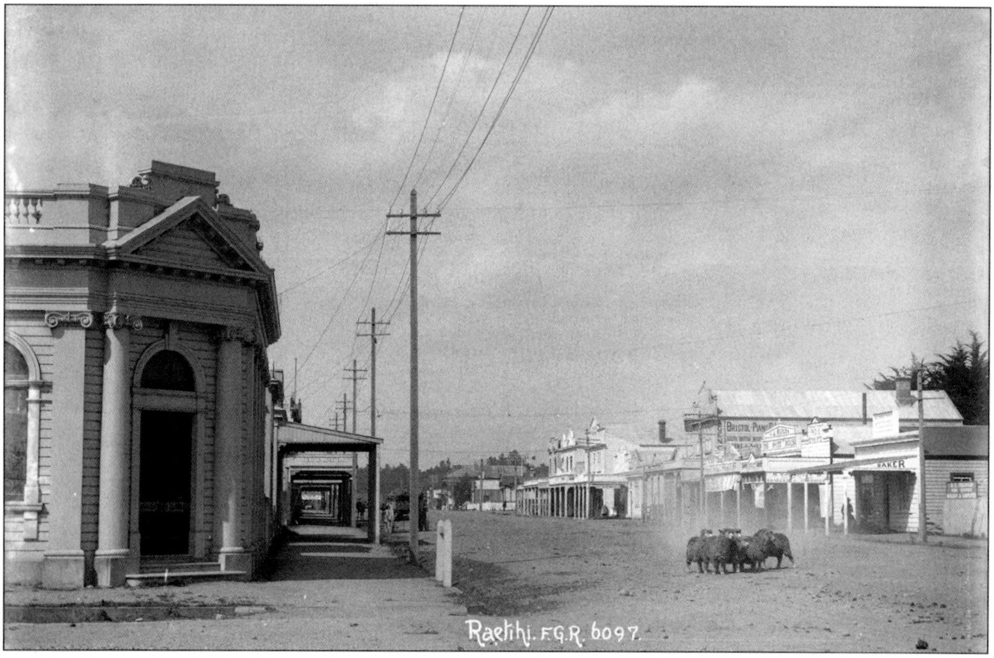

come back. His house was so plain and bare it looked like the set for a Beckett play. Mug. Sink. Table. Chair. Bed. Rug. Outside, his garden, a sunken yard with sheds along the back, was overgrown with a kind of melon, carpeting the concrete, canopied opulently over the sheds, festooning the buildings with innumerable big green hanging fruit as inedible as raw chokos.

Another was in Herne Bay, a big old villa near the top of Ardmore Road, just back from the Jervois Road shops. In 1972, friends of ours were thinking of buying it, which is why we felt able to break in. It had been a family home, then the children moved out, leaving the parents, one of whom, the father, died earlier; now the mother had as well. All red plush and dark wood, with glass fronted cabinets full of china and a line of ivory-tusked ebony elephants on the mantelpiece, it was pristine the way old lady's houses sometimes are. Everything was in place, but dust had begun to fall and was not being swept up any more. We were there at dusk, and didn't dare open the curtains or see if the power was connected; we tiptoed round in the half-dark, disturbing nothing. I felt as if I'd breached my paternal grandparents' suite in Methodist heaven.

Up north, the following year, out the back of Puhoi, I remember walking across flat fields and under pine trees to a grand old farmhouse set back a kilometre from the road, in which there was a collection of austere and majestic kauri furniture too massive to be moved; all the bric-a-brac had already been poozled, but Cameron Thompson, whose gun we used for hunting goats and turkeys to eat, took the stag's head with twelve points on the antlers down from over the mantelpiece and staggered across the rutted ground back to the van with it in his arms.

All of these episodes were exciting in a creepy kind of way. We call this experience gothic, but what do we mean by that word? The Goths were a Christianised Germanic tribe from the banks of the Vistula – the *ostro* from the east and the *visi* from the west – who swept out of the north and sacked Imperial Rome. Gothic cathedrals were built in the Middle Ages with arches soaring skywards, steepling steeples, and a mind-numbing profusion of detail in their ornament, as if grace could be found only through exhaustion.

Gothic no longer meant an irruption of chaos, it now signified an instinct for transcendence; by the eighteenth century, while still linked to a theory of the sublime, it referred to stories, often in a medieval setting, *with supernatural or horrifying events*. What rationalism could not explain or wanted to deny was exiled into the realms of art, where, two centuries later, in our half-ignorant, post-modern way, we continue to 'sample' it.

If one of the post-enlightenment projects is re-colonisation of the unconscious, who are our shock troops? Who will enter the haunted house and bring back news of what is to be found there? And if the instinct for psychic re-colonisation is a gothic impulse, what is its relationship to the historical process? Are fantasies of terror and horror in these obsolete locations an evasion of the real terror and horror abroad in the house on the hill? Or are they an aid to seeing what is going on, not only in the house on the hill, but under our own roof as well? Is it the case that the gothic imagination, suspecting the quest for paradise has led us into hell, wants to know how to live in the hell we have made?

ii

I grew up in a large wooden villa in Burns Street, Ohakune. Burns Street was named after the Scots poet Robert Burns but I didn't know this at the time. I thought the name came from the fact that the old business district of the town had stood in our street until destroyed by a fire in 1917. The original street names in Ohakune, given in 1908, were all Maori, but as early as 1914 the citizenry were advocating that the main ones be changed – *on the grounds that the present … names are meaningless, lacking in euphony and conducive to confusion in pronunciation* – for the names of British poets and rivers: Burns, Moore, Clyde, Shannon, Wye. Burns Street had no name of its own

Goldfinch Street, Ohakune, 1938 (Alexander Turnbull Library)

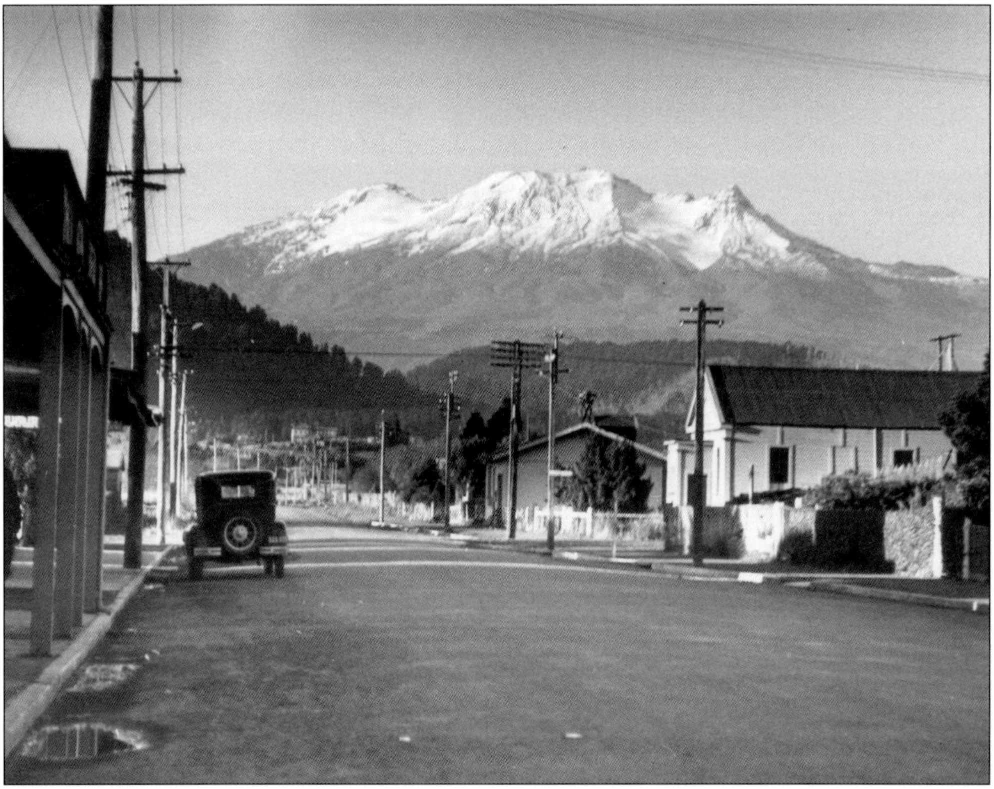

previously; it was simply called Pipiriki Road because that's the way you went then to get to Pipiriki on the Whanganui River.[1]

Our part of the street was over the bridge, and our house amongst a raggle-taggle of about a dozen built on one side of the road only. The house of my eldest sister's friend Thelma. The Reynolds, who had the garage. Another school teacher. The school caretaker who was also a guide on Ruapehu. In the house next door but one to us lived two ancient brothers called Williams who drove an original Model T Ford with the number plate 000 011 and kept a couple of magpies in a cage by their letter box. They would peck you through the wire netting if you got too close.

On the far side was Mrs Aubrey, who had four kids: Tut and Pet, grown-up daughters who were away training to be primary school teachers; Alfie, a cheerful teenage delinquent; and Denise, a quiet girl my younger sister's age. There were rumours that Denise was the child of another older daughter, and thus actually Mrs Aubrey's granddaughter. Mrs Aubrey lived in the grey unpainted falling down whare without electricity or running water along with Charlie Herkt, an old German man who was the college caretaker and a guide on Ruapehu, which he had climbed countless times. They cooked outside and got their water from the river which ran behind us.

Then there were the Jamiesons, unruly, freckled Convent kids who used to tough us up on our way home from school; the stone crusher; the Maori bush; finally the Morrises, another large Catholic family amongst whose sons were Jock, who rode an Indian motorbike, and Johnny, who – I found out later while interviewing a cousin of Philip Clairmont's in Palmerston North – became a country and western guitar player and singer acclaimed throughout Taranaki, Whanganui and the Horowhenua.

On the other side of the road in all that stretch there was just one place, and that was Miss Seth-Smith's. Her house was built up on a hill, with such a thick growth of trees around it you could not see it from the road. You walked up a curving drive lined with massive rhododendron trees which met over your head to make a gloomy tunnel carpeted with fantastic gleams of colour if it was flowering time, then came out on a lawn beneath a ramshackle house with dormer windows and stained glass and finials and wooden lace, literally rotting back into the ground. A classic piece of carpenter's gothic, and a classic haunted house too. Miss Seth-Smith wasn't there much and when she was she just added to the spookiness.

She was the only child of the remittance man who built the crumbling mansion. Who this man was and what happened to him I do not know, but there is a suggestion that his farm, of which the house and the land it stood upon was the sole remnant, was always a folly, and he the most impractical of men. The name Seth-Smith is uncommon, but one H.G.

Seth-Smith was a judge of the Native Land Court in the late nineteenth century, and heard claims in the Horowhenua. Another, Basil, from Surrey in England, farmed and bred livestock in Canterbury in the early twentieth century, but what connection, if any, there was between either of these men and our neighbour is unclear. Remittance men, unless they do something unforgettable, tend not to figure in historical records.

In the 1950s, Miss Seth-Smith was an old woman with white hair, rarely seen, and so absolutely singular you never thought of her as having relatives or friends of any kind. The reason for her absences and the place, or places, she went to were mysterious and fearful. *The madhouse*, people whispered. Later I found out that she did indeed suffer from some kind of mental illness and spent long periods in hospital. How many of the mad are mad from loneliness? When at home, she was a disturbing presence, like a witch up there in the lonely house on the hill. Dogs roamed in numbers unrestrained through her rooms; when they had puppies, she would leave them on other people's doorsteps in the hope they would be looked after. The four she left on ours we took back.

Miss Seth-Smith also kept stock, which she let wander to graze beside the road. One day my mother, about to go with the children to pick up my father from school, found a bull in the vegetable garden, eating cabbages. She rang my father, he called the local cop and the cop came down on a bicycle with a .303 rifle, shot the bull, then rode away again. That night, in the rain, there came a knock on the door. I imagine a flash of lightning and a crack of thunder as my father goes out into the porch to see who it is: Miss Seth-Smith, with bloody knife. She'd come to get some meat for her dogs and was butchering the bull herself, by storm light. The Council dragged the remains away a couple of days later.

My most vivid personal memory of Miss Seth-Smith is the time, on the road outside our place, she gave packets of seeds to us kids. She had a lined face below her white hair, vacant, not unkindly eyes, and was dressed in a faded print frock and worn tennis shoes; she spoke in an educated voice and seemed like someone out of an old tale. My seeds were Coleus, those delicate plants with variegated leaves, often grown indoors. Some varieties are psychedelic, though I have never tried them. I don't remember planting them, and perhaps I wasn't allowed to; my mother wrote later that the seeds had been stolen from a shop in town, so she probably took them back. Miss Seth-Smith sometimes also stole food to eat. The only other thing I know about her is that she was writing a children's opera for the BBC; many years later when I revisited, I found some notes and drawings for a set design among the detritus out the back of the long-demolished house.

Her place was scary but we still used to go up there when she was away. I smoked my first cigarette with my older sister beneath the rhododendrons on the lawn at Seth-Smith's, gagging into the browning blossoms afterwards. I used to play with Robert Chamberlain sometimes, who lived with his mother and sister in a small two-room cottage behind the mansion, hard up against the fence line of the paddock where my sisters kept their horses. Mrs Chamberlain had a pet magpie too; it would *quardle oodle* on command at 4:15 in the afternoon, summoning the children home for tea. Robert would go pale when he heard it, and turn and run: he was beaten if he was late.

Mrs Chamberlain was the local prostitute, hence the need to have her children fed and bedded so early in the evening. She was a buxom, perfumed woman with tall hair, like Elsie Tanner from *Coronation Street*; the men who came to see her either went up the gloomy drive and round the back of the crumbling mansion or, like Robert, climbed the fence and walked up the grass of the steep, terraced, cloddish horse paddock.

The Chamberlains had moved away by the time we broke in to Miss Seth-Smith's place. It was a torpid day as Bobby Hammond, whose family farm started at the back of our horse paddock, and I walked up the drive, across the rank lawn, and climbed the stairs to the veranda. The steps were rotten so we clambered up the banisters, jamming our feet sideways through the rails; then we pushed open the door.

Inside, torn curtains hung crazily in front of the dusty light; there were couches and armchairs with springs and horse hair protruding through great rents in the fabric, stuff all over the floor, and on a dressing table before a mirror, an open casket with jewellery spilling out of it: necklaces, beads, brooches, rings, bracelets. Maybe it was paste, maybe not; to us it was real so we didn't touch it – that would have been thieving. But when we found, amid the debris on the floor, sheets of transfers of characters from Mother Goose, we took them and fled back down the driveway, pursued by phantoms of guilt and excitement.

I have no doubt that a primary source of the affinity I felt for the paintings of Philip Clairmont when I first saw them was that furtive, wondrous glimpse into the ruined world of the remittance man's daughter. The paste jewellery, the rotting gowns, the mouldering furniture of her mansion were a premonition of Clairmont's paintings of doomed, luxe interiors. The two things literally looked alike: the overflowing casque of jewellery before a dusty mirror, in particular, had an uncanny resemblance to the 1974 Clairmont paintings of butterfly mirrors, which were among the first works of his I saw. Even the discovery of the transfers out of Mother Goose has an ironic parallel in those slightly earlier Clairmonts which sample bits of Disney comics. And the theme of the psychopathology of the artist, which the Clairmont oeuvre explores, was also present in the recurrent madness of Miss Seth-Smith.

The remittance man's exile, his impractical dream, his daughter's wreck, were part of the debris of empire, scattered through our lives the way her things were strewn through those rooms. And yet to me, as a kid, the place looked fabulous, something superb belonging not to empire but to someone who lived right opposite where we did. This is a deeper resemblance to Philip Clairmont's work, which comes not so much out of empire as from the experience of being one of the marginal (the word then was *deprived*) people in post-World War II, post-colonial society.

Like many people from the wrong side of the tracks, Clairmont had a special need for the magic that makes each moment supreme. His paintings are rites which transform the painter, his house and family, out of the mundane into resplendence; the audience too, if you want to go along. But for him the way to summon the resplendent turned out to be via an investigation of the occult properties of the mundane. His work constructs a dream house in which an obsessive compulsively rearranges a set of everyday images, looking for that magic combination which will free him from the spell of the past.

An assumption of this method is that a house is a repository for the emotions of those who live there. Objects are stained by residues of human presence even after those people have passed on, perhaps to other houses, perhaps into death. Abandoned houses are primary material for the imagination because there we may restore to existence something which has been lost. Clairmont, by painting the hell the loss of paradise leaves, attempts the resurrection of every dream of paradise ever dreamed.

This strategy is intrinsically gothic, by which I mean its primary mode is an exaggeration of emotional effect for the sake of some kind of release. Frequently the emotions that are dramatised are the complex to which fear, dread, awe and astonishment belong. This complex can be released as much by horror as by beauty and its release leads to a kind of ecstasy.

iii

To get to town from our place, you had to cross a bridge made of roughly trimmed lengths of timber like railway sleepers and with no sides to speak of; it rumbled as the bits of wood moved up and down when you drove over it. On the other side, to the left, across a similar bridge, was what we called *the pa*, actually Maungarongo Marae, very neat and tidy, with its own white-painted school and church, which had been founded by Catholic Maori after a vision in 1925. This was the stretch of road where the old town had been, on river flats at the junction of two streams; after the fire, Ohakune was reconstructed

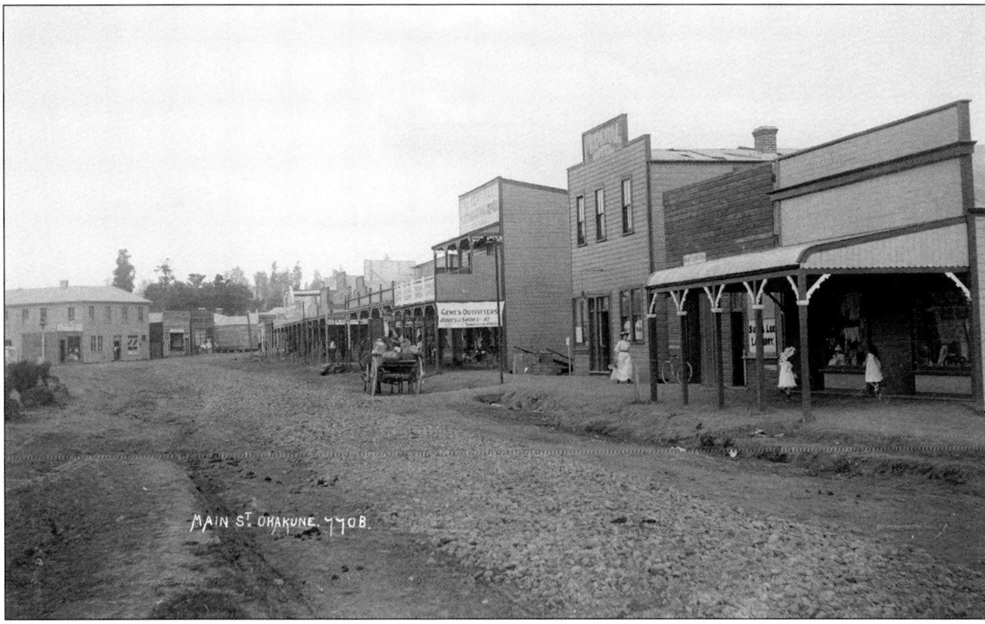

Burns Street before the fire (Alexander Turnbull Library)

further up the hill on slightly raised ground overlooking the former site. In the 1950s, nothing remained of that original town except a sense of desolation amongst the sheds and machinery, and, perhaps, the double-storey, double-fronted wooden building on the corner of Burns Street and the Tohunga Road.

This building had a metal pole-supported, rolled corrugated iron awning beneath which it was always dark, and big plate glass windows painted that opaque, greeny-cream colour shop windows used to be painted so you couldn't see inside. The front doors were flush with the footpath in the old style, but no-one used them any more; to get upstairs, you went down the side of the building, through a gate into a yard and then up some outside stairs. I knew this because a boy in my class lived there and I sometimes walked home from school with him.

Richard Morton was a freckled, plump boy with sandy hair who kept to himself most of the time. The only thing I knew about his family situation was that he lived upstairs in that otherwise empty building just with his father. What did his father do? I don't think I ever knew. A working man of some kind, probably. I can't recall ever seeing him, either, though I sometimes had a sense of a face upstairs in that building, looking out through tightly closed sash windows at the almost complete absence of traffic, vehicular or pedestrian, in that quiet town.

In her autobiography, my mother mentions a building on the outskirts of Ohakune, supposedly a furniture shop, but actually a sly-groggers. In those days the King Country was a dry area, and if you wanted to drink you went either to one of the three licensed clubs – the Sunbeam, the Pioneer or the RSA – or else to a dropper, as they were known. It may be fanciful to suggest that's what really went on after hours at Richard Morton's place, but it would explain the mixture of excitement and foreboding I always felt when I went past there. Or perhaps it was simply the titillation the child of respectable parents experiences in proximity to the marginal.

I never went inside, so I have to imagine what it might have been like: tall gloomy rooms with brown wallpaper sucking in and out in the wind through the scrim, narrow fraying rugs down the middle of creaking wooden floors, dark varnished wardrobes, sagging wirewove beds, bare light bulbs you turned on and off using a hanging cord with a bakelite knob on the end, cracked linoleum on the kitchen floor – did they have a kitchen? What did they eat? Who cooked? Who did the dishes? Richard was always neatly dressed but he wore old-fashioned clothes, sometimes a waistcoat buttoned tightly over his checked shirt, sometimes braces holding up his shorts. It was as if he came to school out of the past and went back there afterwards.

By the time we moved away from Ohakune, Richard Morton and his father had gone already, catching a taxi to the station one day to take the train to parts unknown. Curiously, their sometime dwelling is the last thing I remember seeing when we left town ourselves. We had packed up the house, and the Hillman, and were making that final drive up the dirt road with grass growing along the middle, over the clunking bridge, past the pa, the market gardeners, the truck depots, along that desolate stretch of rusty machinery and decaying sheds where the old town had been.

As we turned right beside that big two-storey building on the corner, I looked out the car window and saw another boy from my class, my namesake, Martin Miller, with his blond hair and big teeth, strolling along in a green striped t-shirt and grey shorts. I watched him walk out of the blinding sun of the summer Saturday morning and disappear into the cool, dark shadow of the empty shop verandas, like my own image passing from the memory of the town. *I'll never be really happy again*, I remember thinking, melodramatically, to myself. I was ten years old.

I have always associated the old shop where Richard Morton lived with Dabney's funeral parlour in Ronald Hugh Morrieson's first book, *The Scarecrow*. This is where Hubert Salter, the Sensational, hides out. I think it was the way the cavernous empty spaces downstairs and in the flat next door to the Morton's seemed inhabited by sorrow and loss. You look at those old buildings in remote places and think: what went wrong? Whose dream died here? This small-town melancholy is a constant presence in Morrieson's work.

Salter the Sensational is a conjurer, an alcoholic, a drug addict and a necrophiliac. Though he appears only rarely in the novel, his nightmarish shadow looms over the action with increasing foreboding until, in the penultimate chapter, he dies from a blow on the temple sustained when he falls against the corner of an empty coffin during a fight over a bottle of brandy in the funeral parlour. By this time he has violated the corpse of the local music teacher, murdered the village idiot and killed and raped a sixteen-year-old girl.

All of Morrieson's books are lurid, and what makes them so is their preoccupation with three crucial areas of human experience: sex, money and death. How much of what he wrote is invention and how much observation? I think his inventions are mostly in his plots; even so, his plots are based on the kind of yarning that goes on in bars and after gigs. With this, and the pulp fiction he read, the movies he went to and the newspapers he read, he made up stories to encompass the characters he met and the language they spoke. *Truth* is a source for Morrieson's fiction, as well as the place where he first showed up in print – as a hit-and-run driver.

Morrieson's sexual imagination is prurient and adolescent and revolves almost exclusively around fantasy, just like the sexual imaginations of almost all the boys I grew up with in small-town New Zealand. Some of them will not have changed as men. And his books are shocking, not least for the way that he is able to make vile crimes and wicked people both everyday and of the essence as well. He writes about blackmail, arson, rape and murder, and his tales are narrated, with a strange mixture of cupidity and alarm, by an innocent stumbling into this nexus of evil and desire. As in Clairmont's work, the emotional complex revealed includes fear, anxiety, astonishment, awe – and the blackest of humour.

One way to look at his work is as spiritual autobiography told as low comedy. It was his honesty about his alter egos that allowed Morrieson to be truthful about his other characters – and also the reason some of the people he wrote about objected to his works. Real individuals were recognised in Morrieson's books – for instance the dipsomaniacal Undertaker, Dabney, in *The Scarecrow*, was a portrait of the Hawera town jeweller. Not all of Morrieson's people appreciated being plucked from obscurity to perform, in gorgeous caricature, on a stage as big as his dreams. Instead, they acknowledged the veracity of his portraiture by trying to destroy his memory after he died. They succeeded in destroying his house.

iv

At some point in my childhood in Ohakune, a friend of my parents tried to give us a farm. The land was around the western side of Ruapehu, but I no longer remember exactly where. We turned left at the end of Burns Street one day and drove out along the Tohunga

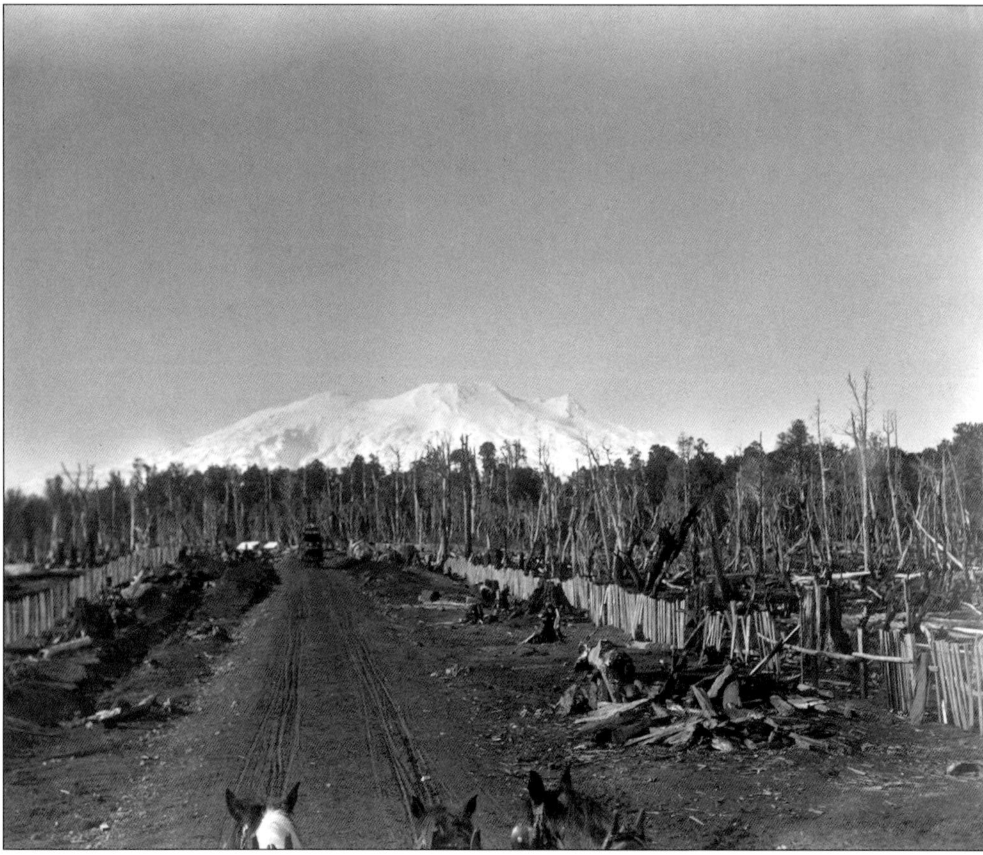

The Tohunga Road c. 1900 (Alexander Turnbull Library)

Road to Tohunga Junction, then through Horopito up Highway 4 towards Taumarunui, to look at it. It was off the main road, in a landscape of sagging fences, weedy paddocks full of burnt or broken stumps, pools of standing water, rusty machinery, bracken and willow, dark hills in the distance … we bumped along the unsealed road, found the place, went through a gate and up a drive full of potholes and puddles to a house on top of a small hill.

It was a weatherboard cottage, painted white, with a flat roof. We parked and got out and walked in the back door to a small kitchen and then through that into a sitting room, the floor of which was covered with half-packed tea chests containing household items; out of these tea chests poured a sleek stream of squeaking rats, so fast and fluid they seemed liquid as they slid down the sides of the tea chests and away – where? I don't know. We didn't stick around. There was nothing to see, unless you wanted to cross the rising paddocks to the dark bush line beyond. Needless to say, we never moved there or took it on in any serious way.

My father sometimes said he wanted to be a farmer, and I think it was from him that I inherited a counter-image to that forsaken place

– a storybook farm, with white picket fences, a red barn, tidy fields of crops and stock, a blue David Brown tractor, beds of English flowers massed around the house and bordering the neatly mowed lawns. To me, this is an image of claustrophobia and silent death, not felicity, while the rat-infested shack full of someone's abandoned gear falling down on its weedy patch of alienated land still has a frisson of excitement about it.

It wasn't just the rats. I was impressed that someone had walked off leaving all their things behind. At the time, and for many years after, I thought the owner had gone, like some kind of anti-remittance man, back to England; recently I learned he actually went to South America. Gilbert imagined himself to be in love with my mother – despite (or perhaps because of) the fact she was married to someone else and with an ever-increasing number of children.

Anyway, in a fit of hopelessness, Gilbert, who had money and was not dependent on the farm for a living, decided to leave the country. The offer of the land was a gesture he made on going, only half serious, an ironic token of his thwarted hopes and, perhaps, his need for some acknowledgment of this from my parents. He turned up again after my mother died, speaking of her as one would a lover of one's youth, even though there had never been anything between them; the intervening years, forty or more, he had spent entirely in South America. He never married.

When I read John Mulgan's *Man Alone*, the King Country farm which the hero, Johnson, lives and works on in the middle part of the book instantly fused in my mind with Gilbert's decaying patch out the back of beyond. I thought the farm's mysterious owner might well have been murdered by someone who then went off, like Johnson, to fight in Spain, even though it was the wrong decade and after the wrong war. In fact, Johnson is one of the Johnsons celebrated by, among others, William Burroughs: stateless working men whose community is global, mobile, without possessions or commitments, except to a shared humanity. He is someone passing through who thought, wrongly, he might be able to make a life for himself here.

Mulgan's book, often praised for its realism, can be seen as closet gothic: while living on Stenning's farm, Johnson has a casual affair with Rua, Stenning's Maori wife, which, in turn, leads to the violent death of Stenning. The sequence following the murder, as Johnson ranges across the country from Waimarino to Rangipo and on through the Kaimanawa, is fantastical in the way of gothic novels; I always see Johnson crouched beneath those enigmatic peaks and dark forests like a figure out of a Tony Fomison painting.

Meanwhile Rua goes home to her people and Stenning's farm, presumably, goes back to bush, rejoining the hills rising to the distant mountains, as the heart of the lost kingdom of the King Country expands in a great gulf of green. This image is make-believe; yet I think we all recognise its pull. It is the other side of Mulgan's disappointed idealism, the atavistic romanticism which makes us long for the country to return to the pristine state we imagine it to have been in before our interventions – a fantasy perilously close to the impulse to total destruction.

Mulgan's book gives a brilliant portrait of the externals of a community which has lost its dream, but his attempt at some kind of interior drama stumbles over his own inhibitions. The repressed matter of *Man Alone* is a love affair, not between Johnson and Rua, but between Johnson and Stenning, and it is this repression which makes the book inadvertently gothic. Yet *Man Alone*'s deconstruction of the putative rural paradise of New Zealand between the wars is definitive.

v

Apart from our old villa in Burns Street, now a backpacker's lodge, none of these houses is there any more. Like the splendidly baroque Ruapehu Hotel which used to stand not far away in Dreadnought Road, Richard Morton's sometime domicile has gone the way of the rest of the old town. Gilbert's house, wherever it was, could not have survived the forty years since I saw it. Miss Seth-Smith's fell

Waiouru, 1908 (Alexander Turnbull Library)

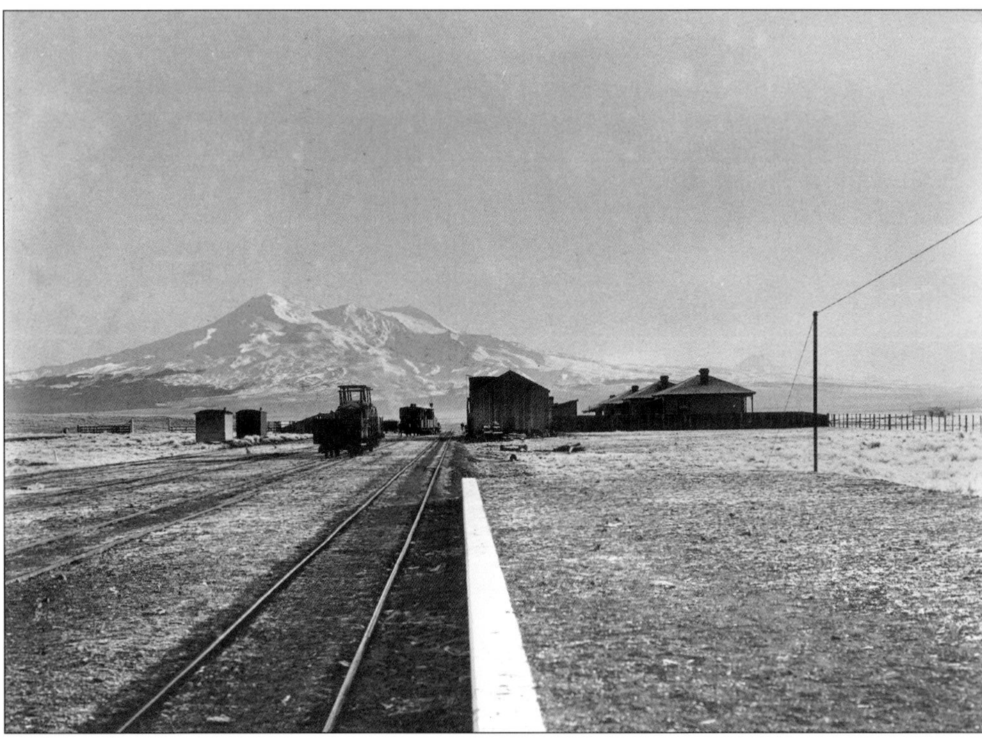

down or was demolished years ago, the land bought by a wealthy businessman from Wellington. The drive and the trees are still there, shrunken with the years, and an army hut now stands, long and low, where the lawn used to be.

The house, built by his Shetland Islander grandfather, in which Ronald Hugh Morrieson lived his entire fifty years, is also gone. Its creepiness was legendary while he was alive. It was dark and gloomy and had a strange musty smell; people shuddered at the thought of eating anything inside. But it was also a house of wonders: one day in the late sixties, while attempting some repairs, Morrieson found dangling from a string in the attic near the chimney one of the bottles of parsnip wine he had made as an eleven-year-old boy back in 1933. This wine was broached and ceremonially drunk with friends, who thought it *better than might be expected.*[2]

The demolition of this house was the revenge of the locals: when the high school art teacher got up a petition advocating it be preserved as a museum, the townsfolk of Hawera, still rankling over Morrieson's portrayal of them in his books, responded with a petition of their own. The figures are instructive: sixty-odd people gave their names to try to save No. 1 Regent Street, while over thirteen hundred signed for its destruction. It was pulled down in 1993 and a Kentucky Fried Chicken restaurant stands there now.

Curiously, most of the houses Philip Clairmont lived and painted in are still standing, including the one he owned and died in, which is also the only one that still looks anything like it did when he was alive. The rest of them are just normal dwellings – or offices – now. In some essential way it is probably true that this return to normality began the moment he moved out: if there is a Clairmont ghost, it is haunting his art, not his houses. And yet, if his art is the house he made for himself, it's a house always in need of renovation and always threatened with demolition.

Whatever the fate of Clairmont's work, his example remains. Like Morrieson's, it suggests that the way to negotiate self and world is not evasion, circumvention or repression. Instead, it is by taking both fallen world and corrupted self as the raw material of what you do. This conviction explains the grunginess of both men's work – the stickiness of real life, its fluid and chaotic tactility, its resistance to imposed order – as well as its fearful fearlessness.

Morrieson was an interior writer the way Clairmont was an interior painter. They were both rigorously mothered boys who grew up fatherless and asthmatic. Both took as their subject the psychic underbelly of the community as a whole, which they represent via their account of what they saw on their own self-abusive, self-destructive ricochet through it. Both rejoice in the revelation of the monstrous masquerading as the norm: creatures of horror are always ourselves in another guise. No couch will ever look the same once you have looked at a Clairmont painting of a couch. None of your neighbours will ever seem normal again after you have read a Ronald Hugh Morrieson book.

If the paradise of the settlers has become the hell we live in, that is because of our exclusions. It is in this context that the gothic imagination attempts its representations of evil abroad in the community and in the psyche. It is immensely difficult to descry, in words or paint, the lineaments of a hell. Then, when you say what you have managed to see, you risk being accused of degeneracy and perversion, as Clairmont and Morrieson each were. They were both also suicides, as was John Mulgan. But the act of descrying hell is not antithetical to paradise; it is preparatory to a view of it. The heresy of the gothic is its suggestion that paradise is to be found only by going through hell.

Demolition of the abandoned house is not the answer; that will only leave our ghosts to wander abroad. What we have to do is re-inhabit it, recollect the lives buried there so that the poor, the lost, the forsaken, the insane come back to join us. When this happens, we find that the ruinous images of the gothic generate, paradoxically, hope: riches born out of squalor, madness which is the other side of sanity, alienated land once again belonging to us all. The gothic, then, is prospective, restorative, a redemption of the botched past.

Gothic Inversions and Displacements: Ruins, Madness and Domesticated Modernism

David Craig

Invention has not been wanting; but the great resources of fancy have been dammed up, by a strict adherence to common life. But if … Nature has cramped imagination, she did but take her revenge.

Horace Walpole, *Castle of Otranto* (1764)

I get unreasonably angry with John sometimes. I'm sure I never used to be so sensitive. I think it is due to this nervous condition … I don't like our room a bit. I wanted one downstairs that opened onto the piazza and had roses all over the window, and such pretty old fashioned chintz hangings! But John would not hear of it. He said there was only one window and not room for two beds, and no near room for him if he took another.

Charlotte Perkins Gilman, *The Yellow Wallpaper* (1892)

Introduction: Cramped domestic imaginations

An 1810 satire by E.J. Pitt offered a recipe for turning a Gothic novel into a nineteenth-century realistic novel:

From any romance to make a novel. Where you find –

A castle, ……………………,	Put a house
A cavern, …………………	A bower
A bloodstained dagger, …..	A fan
A knight, ………………….	A gentleman without whiskers
A lady who is the heroine, ..	Need not be changed, being versatile.
A midnight murder, ……….	A marriage[1]

Pitt's inversion trick is more than hermeneutic acrobatics, at pop fiction's expense: this inversion has the makings of a neat Marxish turning of a grotesque Hegelite idealist phantasmagoria on its head, in order to show up a whole secret material history of gender, family, and public/private culture. Invert it again in the here and now, resubstituting the domestic modern with contemporary NZ provincial gothic sublimes, and what's apparently reasonable, modern, everyday culture can become a dismal but ripe code, readable in terms of regional filmic and representational grotesque perversities: the dark displacements of film work from McGann's *In My Father's Den* (2004) and even Jackson's *Lord of the Rings* (2001–3) to, as in this essay, some recent 'provincial gothic' architectural photography from Ann Shelton, Allan McDonald and Gavin Hipkins.

The conceit that gothic romance, with its 'trappings' of 'ruins, graves, dark enclosures, madness, even the sublime', is the obverse side to domesticated modernity is well established.[2] But it is also a bit more complex – *three*-sided, in fact – in its 'othering' inversions. For example, 'female gothic' is widely regarded as the anti-modernist 'other' of masculinist enlightenment rationality, both in the latter's most instrumental form – industry and the machine – *and* in the Industrial Revolution's more public 'other', the Romantic or liberal revolution.[3] This three-sided 'othering' runs, as above, through most of the common tropes: (1) the (Romantic) exotic ruin as the other of the public fortress of masculine security (empire, the castle) *and* of the domestic commonplace/failed-romance house or closed-in room in, say, Gilman's *Yellow Wallpaper*; (2) the interior of death and confined madness as the other of the public appearance of neatly scaled domestic normality *and* the public, 'out there' rational role of the male breadwinner; and (3) the grotesque as abject, homely/unhomely, *yet still* a sibling of hegemonic (modernist/masculinist) success, and so on.[4]

All of this means that 'gothic modernism' is a long way from oxymoron: 'gothic' and 'modernism' are basically two sides of the same coin. Realising an explicit gothic-modernism, though, would seem a bit more of a challenge. A modernist gothic might be at the very least an exercise in heavy-handed formal discipline (and possibly bondage), if not the engineering of a frank and fraught contradiction brought about by the literal telescoping of antithetical aesthetics under what you'd assume would be very unusual circumstances. Certainly, the most obvious cases of such a miscegenation aren't pretty: a kind of over-scaled modernist industrial sublime, a camped-up masculinism as in *Queen*-style British sci-fi, à la *Blake's 7*, or any late-seventies/early-eighties heavy metal you care to confess. It's brutalised as in notable sixties expressive concrete public architecture, like the ruined Tricorn centre in Portsmouth ('an adventure playground for Daleks', bowled over and finally blown up on 25 October 2004) or its surviving, British film-noir-star counterpart, the Treaty shopping centre and car park in Gateshead, Northumbria (where Michael Caine was killed in *Get Carter*).

But in fact gothic modernism is more common and diverse than you might imagine, especially when you look outside the core modernist canon into its nether regions, where the third domestic element comes more strongly into play. This is particularly the case in work that's about escaping or getting beyond the core orthodoxies and hegemonies of time, public place, scale and aesthetic gender, where less presentable, more grotesque reactions might be hiding. The provincial, then – especially the gendered or sexualised provincial and domestic zones – becomes an immediately plausible repository of gothicised grotesquery, modern or otherwise.

Whatever the scale, Brutalist or domestic, the outcome is commonly a kind of overdressed regional camp or grotesque.[5] Regional camps involve an abject, practised cross-dressing, where provincial artists play with and woefully produce their work in the recognisable codes of aesthetic presentation, while form becomes grotesque through unsuppressible (often local) content rupturing outward. Southern Gothic provides the most ready regional examples: Sherwood Anderson, Grant Wood, Flannery O'Connor. Post-war Antipodean aesthetics, especially male figurative/placed painting, were lousy with this stuff: Gleason, Tucker, Nolan, Drysdale, Dobell, Bullmore, Eric Lee-Johnson, Clairmont, Fomison. It's not always a miserable outcome, as demonstrated by the larrikin camp predilection in Australian film (which is a bit more 'out there', and where gender doesn't seem to be such a domestic trap, even, say, in Oz camp classic *Muriel's Wedding*). But it is often bloody bleak. There was rampant, unsuppressible miscegenation, often across nature/architecture/body boundaries as buildings and natural forms take on grotesque figurative aspect. There was murder and madness, the unhappy progeny/ruin of too much passion in too small a place, where, in Walpole's words, 'the great resources of fancy have been dammed up, by a strict adherence to common life', and where 'if … Nature has cramped imagination, she did but take her revenge'.[6]

Provincial and other grotesquery's most prominent recent outing was in the Sante Fe Biennale exhibition curated by Robert Storr, 'Disparities and Deformations: Our Grotesque' (July 2004–January 2005). As Storr remarks, the grotesque is a plural recuperative strategy, the formal, social and political concept that binds the abject, the uncanny, the gothic, the *informe* together, 'like a vine that weaves in and around weird vegetation and harbours amorphous creatures'.[7] For Storr, grotesques are everywhere and in various periods have even been mainstream. But more commonly they sit abjectly at one duplicitous (inverted?) remove from classical notions of quality and decorum, often within the same artists' oeuvre (Michelangelo's, for example, or Picasso's, or …). More particularly, a modernist gothic has popped up in as unlikely places as regional Catalan art, and in various Latin American magic realisms, and even conceivably in works like Ngugi wa Thiongo's *Devil on the Cross* (Kenyan PoMo Gothic?). Closer to home, it is no surprise to see it turning up in NZ fashion, be it Karen Walker or Taranaki surfy/biker-chick chic (tie-dye, black velvet, foiling the immediate romance of the machine and the smooth glass board).[8]

But most obviously something like it also works in other confined, involuted genres: the telescoped social order of film and lit. *noir*, such as Flannery O'Connor's Southern Gothic, NZ's own provincial gothic film, and the filmic Taranaki Gothic/*noir* writing of Ronald Hugh Morrieson. With film, of course, moving or still, both modernity and arguably modernism are in many ways built in. It's an apparently rational medium, which, as I'll explain, might make it seem ill-suited for registering gothic madness, but as things pan out this makes it deadeye for dealing with ruins (and ruined modernism) in the NZ domestic landscape.

This essay, then, is about rational, largely documentary technique and provincial gothic content running into each other in different ways in three recent architectural photography contexts: Ann Shelton's *Once More from the Street,* which interrogates (and inverts) ruins of NZ mental hospitals; Allan McDonald's *Relocations and Demolitions*, which documents the defaced and displaced dotage of the house that used to be next door but is now ruined; and Gavin Hipkins' earlier *The Habitat*, which shows international brutalism displaced (i.e. built *here*) and brought down to earth both by Hipkins' technique and by getting grungy and overgrown in a range of thinly New Zealand settings.

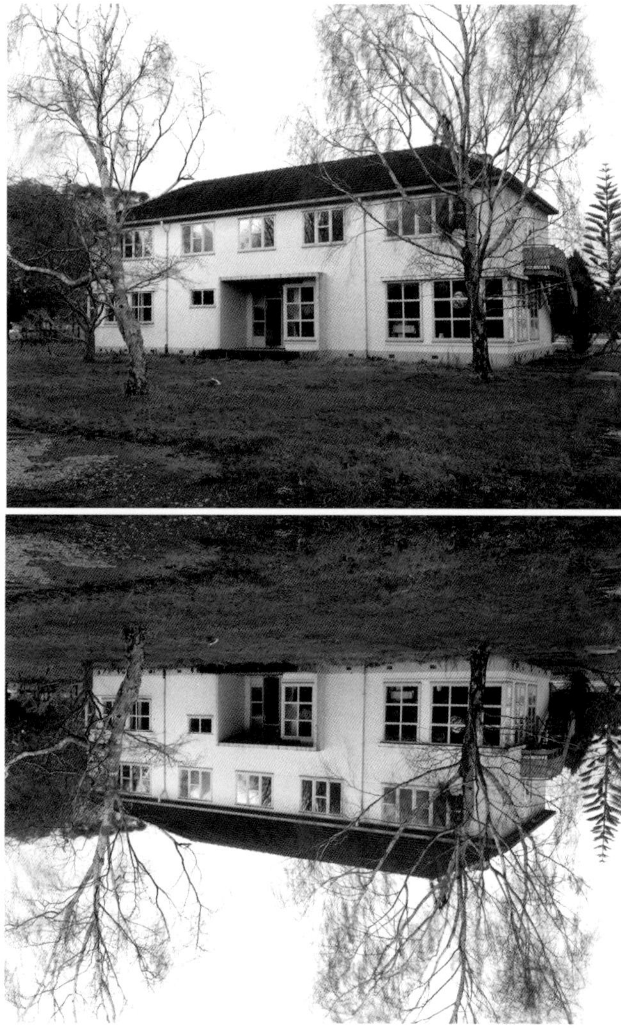

Ann Shelton, 'Villa #8, formerly Lake Alice Hospital, Wanganui', 2004

Photographing ruins: Three (gendered, modern) NZ versions of gothic inversion

Ann Shelton's recent work records dark memorial places, including the ruins of notorious NZ psychiatric hospitals. These latter are gothic relics, bleak in neglected public garden landscapes, just one remove from a *Yellow Wallpaper* sense of a more domestic, placed history. Her recent series on the Lake Alice facility (*Once More from the Street*, Starkwhite Gallery, September 2004) captures abandoned, stand-alone masonry, deco group housing, a provincial version of a Le Corbusier, modernist, public-housing vision of community, now discredited as a kind of architectural institutional abuse and sentenced to erasure from public memory by the demo man. For all their cracked deco modernity, these places still radiate dark public/private questions, which the wider context of Shelton's work genders up nicely.

The sociology of mental illness shows women are over-represented in most mental health numbers but especially in stress-related categories (anxiety, hysteria and obsessive compulsive disorders). Basically, you're much more likely to get *hysteria* if you have a *hyster*, or womb. But when gendered mental illness gets institutionalised (which usually in modernism also means masculinised), the traumatic sequelae are given an even more brutal, re-traumatising address. At play here are both the public-space hegemony of patriarchy and the obverse domesticity of mental illness, in what's ultimately a cruel set of inverted ironies and pathologies. Privately, the family is a first, narrow festering place for just this kind of gothic: guarded family secrets and a fading damsel locked up in a castle with an ogre (husband) and some goblins (kids). But the institutional cultures of modernist mental institutions enable a neat Pitt-esque substitution of family secrets for institutional surveillance records, and of the patriarchy/offspring for the institution and its nursing staff.

Thus psychiatric hospitals in the modern period were characterised by a medicalisation of madness that quarantined it on the public

Allan McDonald, 'Riverhead', 2004

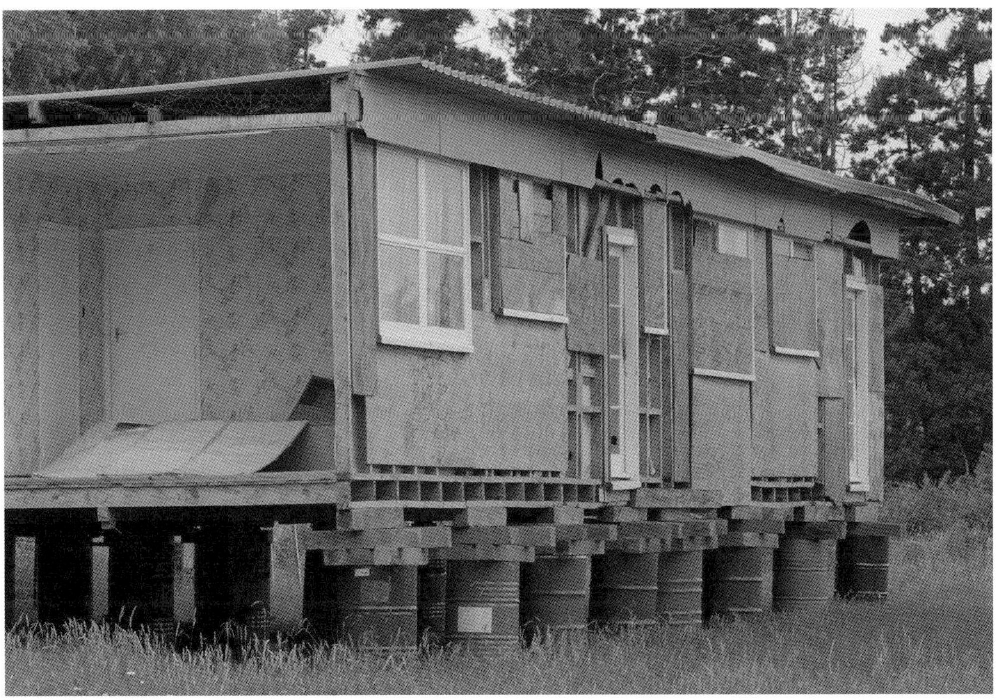

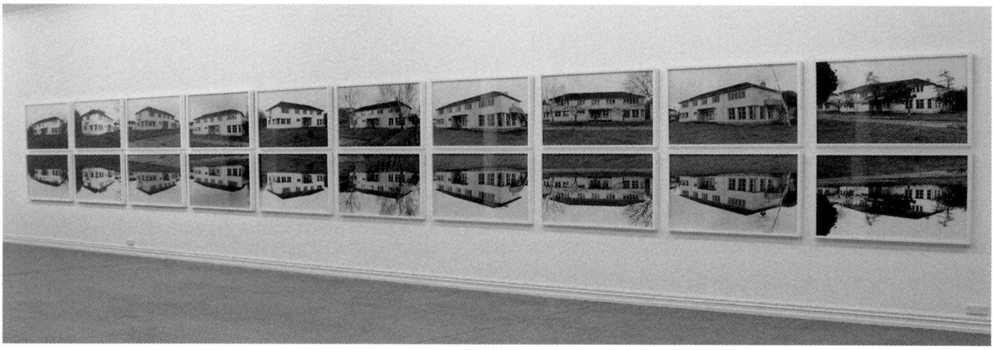

Ann Shelton, Once More from the Street, *installation view*

institutional side of a modernist division of labour between hospital and home. Ironically, when they built hospitals on domestically remote sites, the guardians of this divide felt they needed to produce mis-scaled, über-domestic replacements for more cramped real (and pathological) domesticity: 'stroll around the grounds until you feel at home', Mrs Robinson. Rows of similar grotesque, suburban group houses were built on greenfields sites and housed not just the patients, but also the nursing and medical staff, in separate but often identical quarters themselves remote from urban domestic life (remoteness was why they needed to build quarters at all). But ultimately even these spaces were, in their modernist separation of rational from domestic, deemed too cramped and confining, too prone to the grotesque in-grown behaviours of confined pathology, and these too had to be opened out into a postmodern, plural and apparently communitarian care regimen. Now these empty buildings shout not just their failed modernist clinicism at you; they also function as haunted houses, full of 'if these walls could speak' terrors of pathology and madness.

What gives these images an extra frisson of forensic place is their persistence as mythological places, such as Lake Alice, which also had a secure unit where the worst murdering maniacs were sent, escaped from, and rose to haunt from. The mythology motivates the viewer into their own re-interrogation of the places, and makes the show into a kind of identity parade for a judicial enquiry into past abuses. In this inquisition, as is conventional in architectural photography, the buildings stand in for the absent figures of both the subjects and authors of their rational and aesthetic ambits. Shelton's work, especially at this point of public-domestic mental illness, begs comparison with Ava Seymour's more brutally grotesque photomontages of mentally disabled people in front of state houses. Here, in the territory of apparently similar content, Shelton's work thankfully resists a formal and figurative grotesquery in favour of a more realist/documentary political critique, taking the issue out of the figured/personal and into a more public and principled enquiry.

In McDonald's *Relocations and Demolitions* (Anna Miles Gallery, October 2004), too, there's no one in sight, but we still get to meet something like the institution's inmates. His ruins, mainly family homes now incarcerated in relocation yards around the country, are nearly figurative grotesques: front-on, public façades, they've got the droops, with eyes, brow, mouth sagging. There's a house with its prosthetic nose missing, just a hole there: this naked brick house is stripped bare of cladding, with its gaping vacant front, slight evidence of past elegance in the roman arch of the porchway, and behind it the wind howling through empty rooms. It's vintage grotesque, but McDonald's trick here is to extend the traditional grotesque miscegenation of the figurative, the built and the natural, beyond the nineteenth-century neo-Gothic (an aesthetic which underpinned, for example, the early twentieth-century NZ Kauri villa), beyond the ruined/remote/regional, and into the urban modern.

These places have been torn from modern suburbia's domestic landscape, but they still evoke a whole family's lives flashing before your eyes. Now they're either permanently displaced or well on the way out, committed to low-rent repository institutions where generic violences and griefs of decay get lumped with other cases' personalised grotesques. Most of these houses won't be family homes ever again: they're ruins sinking or growing into a rough-metalled parking lot or peripheral industrial landscape. Scarcely the heavy stone ruins of centuries, these are the wooden houses of our NZ quarry/mill-economy provenance. They are, nonetheless, a kind monument, describable as displaced headstones for departed families. And this adds poignancy to temporality: like our wider history, these ruins haven't been around long. Against longer historical frames, they're more frail, more desperate, more human, more undone; more modern in pretension, they turn out to be more time-prone in the event. McDonald has a fine, portrait eye for dimensions of this proneness and surprising frailty, and for the multi-dimensions of displacement this engenders.

Their modernity is worth unpacking: once, in one way or another, these were modern family habitats, prefabricated/mass-produced villas or bungalows, thin new-world wooden or brick-veneer three-bedroom modern family homes set in modernist utopian suburbanism.[9] They're vernacular, but maybe only in the sense that English is the vernacular in Aotearoa, a borrowed pop diction we have provincially worked up here. Appropriately understated, they refer to aesthetic tradition in a straightforward, inverted-pride way, shorn of surplus decorum, rich in basic pragmatic goodwill. What makes these ruins resonant is the ways they insinuate: it's our own suburban, understated, baby-boom upbringing that's gone to rack and ruin here. So this frailty comes as a bit of a personal, *vanitas* shock: frank suburban modernism was our great Kiwi claim to earthly paradise. Now, it all looks a bit shaky: the fact that they can be ripped up and carried off into dotage so easily means profound provincial unease, displacement, impermanence is registered again.

Shaky impermanence seems antithetical to the kind of brutalism Gavin Hipkins took on in *The Habitat* (Artspace, Adam Art Gallery, 2000), which is perhaps why we've had such an awkward relationship with that architecture here. But Brutalism's intrusive presence in our domestic architectural economy is actually the common, dismal experience of regions everywhere. As Stuart Jeffries wrote in 'The Joy of Concrete',

> Brutalism was something I grew up with (it was big in the West Midlands). It was like having a depressive but not totally unlovable older brother who was always there – inert, sullen, and communicating only a barely scrutable sarcasm.[10]

While skirting depressive illness, *The Habitat* also dealt with hegemonic, travelling masculinist architecture in a faithfully gothic and abject way, using a technique which both plays up the dated, foolish grotesquery of the sublime that travelling Brutalism imposed and shows Brutalism (like McDonald's displaced houses) as becoming barely implicated in our landscape.

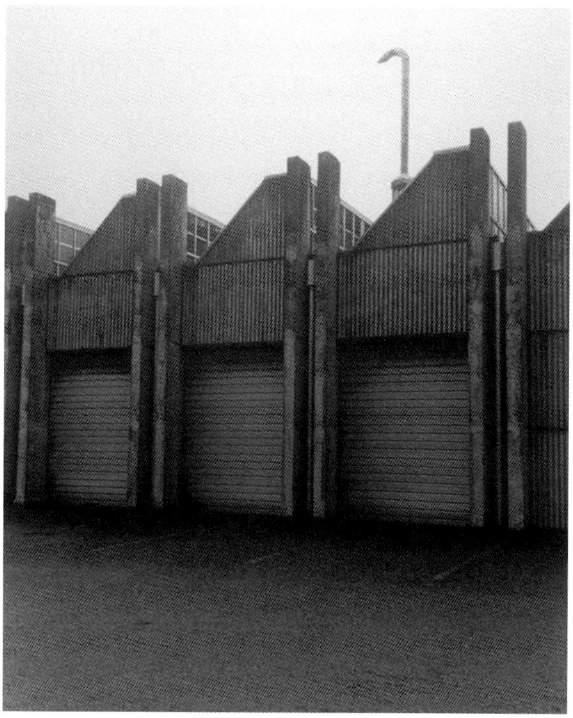

Certainly the placed elements are thin, indeed: an inscription down one side of the photo tells you which NZ university the building stands in. On the other hand, displaced aspects crowd in: both the buildings themselves and the camera technique suggest you could be anywhere on the planet, which, as Anna Miles' *Artforum* review suggests, makes viewers' search for a more particular sense of place in these images a fairly hopeless labour.[11] Here this most brutal public modernist architecture is hardly domesticated, but in Hipkins' presentation it is nonetheless ruined: overgrown with creeping vines and shadowy trees, claustrophobic, and dismembered.

Gavin Hipkins, 'The Habitat, 1999–2000' (detail)

But what's mostly ruined in the process is arguably their grand modernist pretension, which as Miles hints is simply missed by campus students and is certainly not popularly referenced back to any hegemonic, masculinist culture. Something like this mode of provincial ruin is perhaps what Hipkins is trying to achieve: a brutal, uncompromising travelling code is domesticated both by a provincial gothic misreading and by an irreverent, inquisitive snapshot technique (discussed below). The end result is more than a thin re-labelling: it's a sharp rescaling and critical displacement, maybe even an emasculating account of what are usually take-it-or-leave-it Brutalist elements: overweening scale, gross expressiveness, crude detail.

But at the same time Hipkins restates their oddness, turning their grotesqueries of scale and their thoughtless, in-your-face expressive protuberances back on themselves with a pretence of provincial innocence. As a technique for dealing with monsters, it's less than entirely effective. Here, Fay Wray meets King Kong, or young Neddy Poindexter meets the Scarecrow, and emerges less scathed than you'd expect. They, and we, are still overwhelmed by grotesque monstrosities, even if a certain naïve inquiry means the beast does less damage than it might have. So we learn to live with monsters and trauma – which is arguably a basic provincial reality here.[12]

Photography as the new machinery of provincial gothic inversion

Issues of media and technique work oddly to reinforce the overall ambits here. Specifically, the initial surprise that photography ends up being the preferred medium for NZ gothic makes good sense in a bigger context.

Gothic's choked romantic provenance means that it's an *antirealist* genre, which sets its eruptive supernatural engagements and revelations sharply against the capturing ambits of systemic rationalism of all kinds. However, the genre has contradictorily always thrived on scientific investigation (often gone awry) as an organising narrative trope and style: the sceptical journalist, detective or scientist picking over the ruins of a story or house or graveyard, then personally drawn into the increasingly fantastic events. If not that, then innocence (children, beautiful youth) functions as a clean and open template on which to inscribe historically mutilated truths and images. So photography's clean, fresh and modern technical realism now steps forward to fill the place of empirical investigation and impressionable innocence. It naturalises as well as documents; it captures the whole thing and reduces it (like a Pokemon?) to pixels in a box. But as is common in avowedly realist genres, it doesn't ultimately succeed in demystifying. It's this failure that finally cements the uncanny, and leaves the empirical question hanging eerily.

Realism in general functions as a way of capturing, often to political ends: a hard clear representation for a hard clear message. So Mike Stevenson has used photorealism as a provincial weapon against core art canons: in his realist charcoal drawings any *grand seigneur* of art can be brought down to local scale and brought into critical engagement on local terms.[13] Thus capture and parading on local turf is also generic to any process of domestication: get a photo of the celebrity or the horror or the phenomenon, and begin the process of bringing it down to earth.

That, in a number of important ways, has been a crucial role for photography (and wider filmic practice) here in NZ: photos in books and journals have long domesticated and partially demystified genres travelling here (like modernism or someone else's narrative). Photographic images get caught up in this process in a number of overlapping, complicit ways. On one level, it's as straightforward as our reliance on photos of artworks for our provincial reception of them; on another level, as Walter Benjamin was onto, photographic reproduction delivers images to the masses via the media, but in doing so they mess with scale, colour, and numerous other auratic, even sublime, elements.

Here, it may be the political effects (that is, a de- and re-politicising) that matter most. Often what happens here is that the political motivations of an art movement have been evacuated on its journey here. Notably, this has happened with most modernisms, but especially with earth art and other brutal minimalisms. And here, too, the camera has been awfully complicit. Seen mediated through the urbane pages of an art journal, even blistering political statements like Robert Smithson's earth art (the politics of bulldozer drivers in the desert) or Donald Judd's desert survivalism seem domestic, even environmentally grounded.[14] When we reproduced them here afterwards, it was to a different scale and with different political intent. Then, as now, photography was complicit in the re-working.

In these terms the three photographers here all wield the camera to slightly different ends, within an overall gothic inversion/displacement ambit. Ann Shelton is clearly involved with forensic documentation, gathering (public) place-specific evidence for a wider (gendered, public-private) conflict beyond. In terms of gender, these are sites of atrocious/violent struggles, needing to be held up to what ever aesthetic, moral or placed tribunals will consider them. Yet, as the show's title makes clear, it's a revisionist (and thus inverted) view 'once more from the street': there's no desire to revert or go any deeper into cramped internal pathologies, into the imbricated trauma of the yellow wallpaper or the walls that could speak.

Rather, Shelton's wary, gender-sensitised enquiry ranges around these buildings, photographing/interrogating them from a range of eye-level angles. And it does enough: this more plural, inquisitional technique helpfully plays up the monological, modernist seriality of the buildings. But she does more, by a vertical mirror-inversion of the images. It's a gothic inversion which speaks of critical othering, but obviously on a conceptual (gendered, public-domestic, modern-gothic) level rather than that of the formal grotesque (as, for example, in Janet Frame's *Faces in the Water*). It takes you critically inside the *ideas* of the mental hospital, while spatially leaving you outside, on the street, quizzing the formalism for its long-gone content.

There's arguably a different enquiry going on in McDonald, where both a documentary portrait and a local geriatrician's eye seem to inform a photographic registering of mild, placed and figured stories of decline. The result is a certain kind of respectful distance, as well as some representational resistance to interior intimacy of the *Yellow Wallpaper* variety. The grotesque clearly draws and appals, but what you don't get here is a lot of interior prying, not too much of the taxonomic pathologist's ambit. It is, after all, your own domestic/modern ancestry that's being visited here, and so you get that odd old-folk's-home mixture of hushed respect and distance invoking a pop-medicalised picking over of aspects of ruin.

But the way of getting there in McDonald is not as simple as it looks. There's a traditional panoramic technique at work here which involves panning across a subject and results in a series of (in this case analogue, documentary, portrait-oriented) negatives, which are later joined and printed digitally in individual images. The result is mostly front-on, single-house images, presented as individual portraits and underpinned by a forensic veracity of actual film – and, perhaps, by a certain clinical and taxonomic impulse. But it would be wrong to say that *Relocations and Demolitions* ends up as a male perambulator-view from outside the domestic space. McDonald's reasons for keeping his distance are more generically humane, a recognition of a certain frailty in otherwise mundane modern domesticity. The camera does its objectifying, empirical work, but at the same time a different sensibility means there's lots of nicely understated attention to figurative aspects of domestic ruin and to the slim, displaced pickings of provincial scale and minor abjectness. For him to do more might be cruel: these figurative buildings don't need pathological dismembering.

Gavin Hipkins is working with much tougher material, and he does use the camera to dismember, as well as to de- and re-mystify. Here, as elsewhere in his oeuvre, he seeks to capture and wrest away from a modern sublime the imperious aesthetic designs of the last eighty years (modernism and minimalism). Naked, angry modernism (minimalism, Brutalism) up front is pretty scary; all the more need, then, for a machine, Hipkins' camera, that can displace it, pull it all down into a confined, image-containing space, where it can be viewed and manipulated at leisure, and at whatever scale you want. Thus the camera is the perfect weapon for a provincial anti-modernist, capable of turning hegemony inside out and pointing it back where it came from, turned to locally more complicit ends but still globally recognisable.

Hipkins in *The Habitat* is an especially active agent in bringing rampant modernism down to gothic abjection, refusing the heroic monumentalist-masculinist perspective and turning it on its head in favour of odd-angled interrogations of disembodied details of the building. There's exterior and interior detail here, both critically/parodically focussed on the particular overstatements. It's a bit of a snapshot technique (Anna Miles is spot-on to suggest they could have been taken eyes closed[15]), and this rapid and broken seriality is reinforced in the way they're presented, in close sequencing reminiscent of film negatives. The camera thus uses a gothic claustrophobic/*noir* diction, at once simple and close-up, and deliberately defiant of many, even most, of the monstrous claims and fears. Hipkins can't blow these buildings up, like the Tricorn, but he does bring them down to earth in other ways.

Conclusion: A useful forensic obsession?

In drawing the kinds of links it has, this essay is suggesting it's more than an accident that these three photographers have been working over related materials. Rather, it's a fact of both place and a shared aesthetic and cultural problematic, addressed and dealt with in three different ways. All up, gothic inversion and displacement in the hands of these photographers emerges as a kind of reflexive technique, wielded sharply for the effect of framing a forensic field for what's otherwise abject, decomposing subject matter.

Seen together, this work could be seen as a part of a wider cultural forensic and identity-seeking operation, which picks over the remains of hegemonic modernist formalism in this part of the world, and thus is a part of the much bigger and necessary Antipodean project outlined by Bernard Smith in *Modernism's History*.[16] Pragmatically, tactically, it could be seen as a part of a bigger inversion where travelling modernisms get turned on their heads, and as a result we get critically attuned to their travelling hegemonic, masculinist, etc. pretensions. They thus end up rather more domesticated, and we end up less traumatised. More darkly, though, they could be seen as a part of a more chronic and debilitating condition, a long-term, traumatised pathology where we end up forever circling around this uncanny, variously reproducing therapeutic/grotesque forms of travelled and provincial aesthetics, obsessively photographing them for evidence of ongoing crimes, but unable to get to any definitive, post-traumatic kind of closure. Either way, finding different ways to deal with (and get some distance on) obsessive provincial gothic questions about domestic, public and modern culture is a job documentary architecture photographers should keep on helping us with.

Ghost Painting

Poem by
Bill Manhire

Painting by
Saskia Leek

Text by
Justin Paton

Picnic at Woodhaugh

Dunedin: 1863

In the half light of the Early Settlers Museum
there is a world of trees; they rise
on their roots to steal the sun.

But there is no sun.

A small bridge negotiates the stream:
a log and rail, with steps at either end,
a stile across a fence of water.

Men and women
in a Dunedin clearing
detailed off

behind a long white cloth
where four plates and half-a-dozen bottles
represent the feast.

Dark nineteenth-century light
but enough still there to show us
where the light has been …

Each figure has a face, a small one,
and they all face out. They
seem to have finished eating.

Fifty good folk at a picnic –
the men mostly standing, the ladies afloat
on the grass with their children –

plus two who have come to the front:
a woman dressed as a man, black trousers
and, perched on her lap, a fellow in tails.

They are performers, perhaps?
or even the most important guests?

They stare straight out like all the rest.

The exhibition catalogue says
that 'looming verdure threatens
to engulf the group'.

And it is true: they are tiny
and trite among the trees:
safely ashore, yet still at sea.

They know how to stand
on the deck of a ship approaching land …

There are strollers elsewhere in the park,
some lost in a world of shade,
fading or about to fade

two of whom manage to be clear –
latecomers, they cross the bridge
and aim for the middle of the canvas,

pausing only to admire the first recorded
Dunedin dog: a trunk on legs, eyes on a snout,
elephant ears, tail sticking out

though in fact the dog is walking with them

and the man looks faintly embarrassed,
as if stepping across
the surface of a trampoline.

His knees are too near the ground,
and he compensates with a puzzled forward lean:
the incline, perhaps, of thoughtful conversation,

or of someone planning to found a nation

while she …

but really, she can hardly hear …
What was that he said?

And it is so *very* hard to see –
and so she takes his arm and advances

holding aloft her *parasol*

which like her, she thinks, is pretty but unexpected

a fresh flower of the forest,
a wee bit smaller than her head.

Charmed

They've been there all along, flitting through or wafting about the interiors of her small, candy-coloured paintings. Her 'spooky gurls' debuted in 1995, and have since been followed by a wispy procession of spectres, blithe spirits, and little charmers. Haunted stereos, talking tree-stumps, friendly ghosts, invisible friends – these bit-players from the world of childhood imagination are recorded in Saskia Leek's paintings with a smile rather than a snigger. Ghosts are stories that refuse to be left behind, and these paintings ... welcome them into the present. Leek gently shakes the snow-globe of memory, and the ghosts float up into view.

Along the way, she adds a notably nimble and funny chapter to a long and frequently corny history of haunted images. That history runs from Oscar Wilde's *The Picture of Dorian Gray*, through the nineteenth-century vogue of fairy paintings and spirit photographs, and onward to pulp-Gothic novels such as Stephen King's *Rose Madder*. A haunted painting, like a haunted house, is one that has a story to tell. Leek fixes the traces of her stories on eleven placemat-sized wafers of plywood that seem less to hang on the wall than to hover there. Her palette suggests the washed-out light of memory – wan greens, chalky yellows, pinks that are less pink than a memory of red. And the miniaturist intensity of her drawing makes things seem both distant and etched, a world seen through the wrong end of the telescope. To really see them you must get up-close and intimate, as if peering into the rooms of a dollhouse.

They are one-scene short stories, images whose soap-bubble scale is best evoked by Charles Simic's line: 'In the smallest theatre in the world the breadcrumbs speak'. A puffy ghoul dines at a stately table in one painting. In another, a gangly skeleton interrupts a picnic. Santa Claus peers out from a magic mountain, lest we forget that

'Santa's Grotto' occupied the Dunedin Public Art Gallery's basement during its former life as a department store.[1] A little pencil-drawn Kiwi floats like a lamenting angel above Colin McCahon's Otago Peninsula, the landmass recast in ice-cream colours. Leek even makes space for a little bird, dead or resting, on a bed of cotton wool. Such paintings achieve a rare balance of the wry and the heartfelt, as if the artist is smiling at the shop-worn pathos of her subjects while paying unembarrassed homage to the sentiments they provoke – the cute, the sentimental, the nice. Such is the tone of Saskia's World: passionately wistful, wisely innocent, bittersweet.

'Charming' is the obvious word for these paintings, but they are also offered as charms in a deeper sense: as talismans, magical objects, relics of a mysterious past. *Ghost Painting* is itself the product of Leek's responsiveness to strange coincidences and uncanny echoes in the boneyard of Dunedin's past. She has traced those echoes to a source, a kind of epicentre, in the Woodhaugh Gardens, a one-time valley of beech forest now hedged about by North Dunedin suburbs. The Gardens fill the ghostliest of Leek's Ghost Paintings from edge to teeming edge. It is, in fact, Leek's version of an eccentric masterpiece by an unknown artist: 'Picnic at Woodhaugh', from the Otago Settlers Museum. As a connoisseur of 'beautiful paintings by perfect strangers', she was well prepared to savour its strangeness. The painting is based on a photo taken on Christmas Day, 1863, and in it a sober band of settlers puts on a brave face while a wave of 'forest primeval' rears up at their backs. Picnics take the inside outside, thus civilizing the great outdoors. But the poignancy of this picnic flows from the uneasy stand-off between leisure and awe, between finery and forest, between the force of Victorian etiquette and the power of Nature untamed.

Leek redoubles the unease, and heightens the poignancy with it. She painted the 'Picnic' small and then enlarged it photographically, so that her sea of foliage stretches greenly across a surface more than four metres wide. Little figures sail to and from through this

Saskia Leek, untitled work from the exhibition Ghost Painting, *2000 (Dunedin Public Art Gallery)*

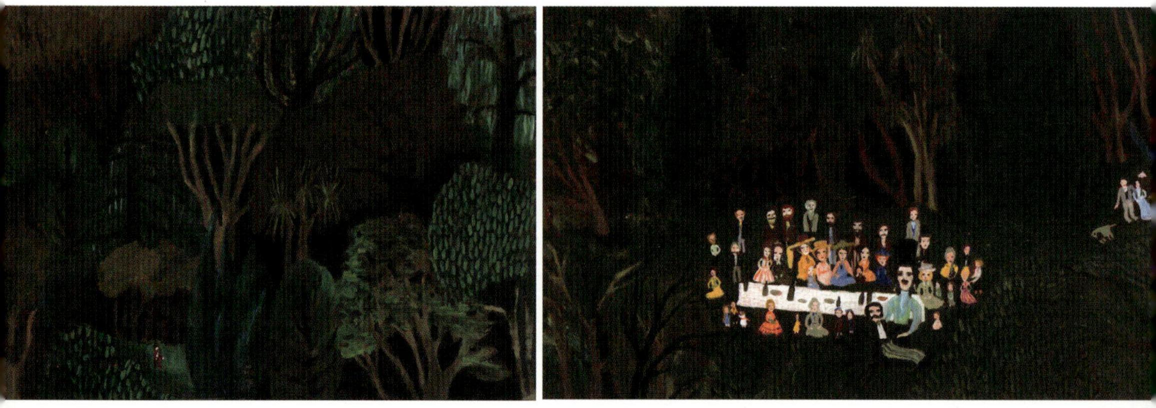

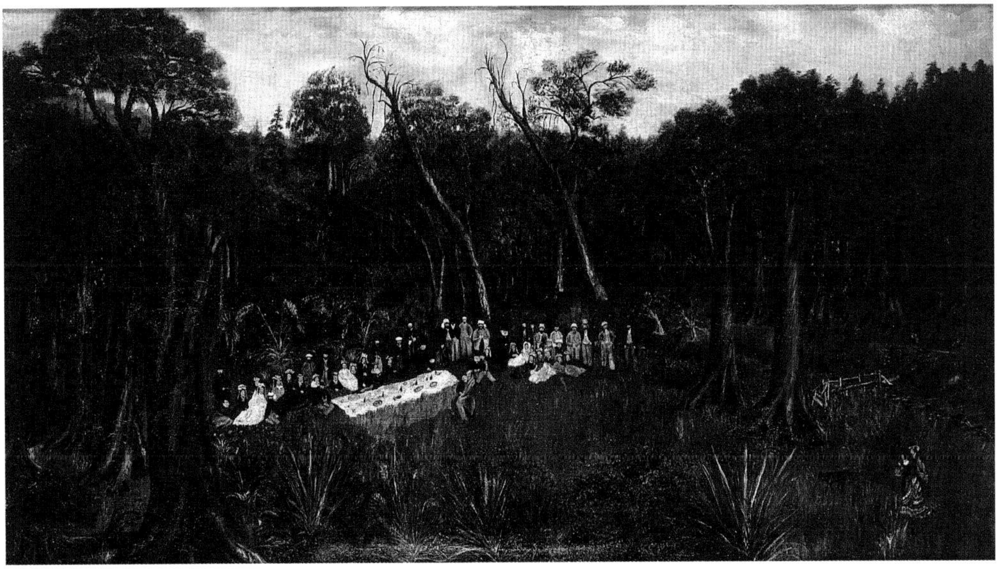

Unknown artist, 'Picnic at Woodhaugh c. 1863', oil on canvas (Collection of the Otago Settlers Museum)

enchanted forest. Stand-ins for the artist and even for us, they lead the way from our present tense into the past that the painting depicts. To follow these little time-travellers is to plot a path through the thick of the forest to the clearing at its centre, where Leek has convened her picnic. The scene is 'precious' in the best sense of the word: crinolined matrons; mustachioed gents in stripey trousers; wee tots with Holly Hobby bonnets. Leek's way with paint – a dib here, a dab there – conveys immense affection and care. Each detail of dress or face is placed, just so, like a petal in a sand saucer. The picnic glows like a flowerbed in the heart of the forest.

Dunedin is a city that wears its history close to its skin; scratch its surface and the past wells up. Fossils of nineteenth-century mercantile ambition, the city's very buildings embody the presence of the past, the grandeur of its ghosts. Leek lived in Dunedin until she was eight, and the paintings she made here two decades later summon up her childhood sense of Dunedin as a ghost-town – a place of creaking mansions with spires and secret passages, of castles on the world's edge, of freshly dewed lawns and forests rustling with mysteries. In revisiting the forest of Woodhaugh, Leek is literally revisiting one of her own old haunts. She attended school near Woodhaugh Gardens, and, yes, even picnicked there as a kid. This back-story helps to explain the lovely ambiguity of her picnic, the sense that it might be a re-enactment of the scene by a party of visitors from the present (the point could be argued, but I think Leek has even secreted a little self-portrait in amongst the crowd). Her forest is at once the Woodhaugh Gardens and the petrified

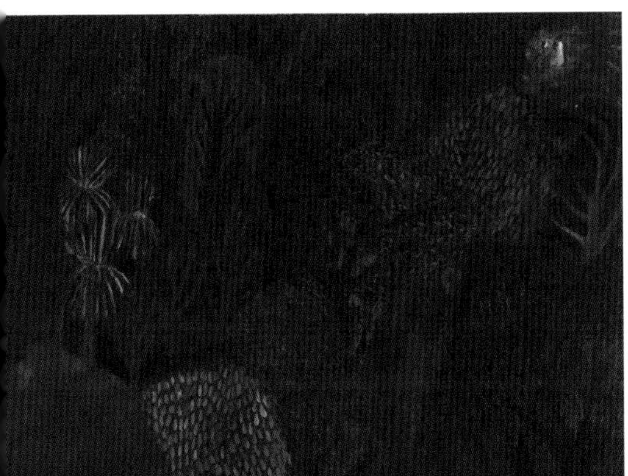

forest of myth, a fusion of all the glades, dells, and darkling woods that rise from fairy tales and picture books. The result is uncannily like the 'original', as though Leek had summoned up the painting's unknown creator – the Master of the Woodhaugh Gardens, let's call him – and channelled his artistic spirit.

Which, in a sense, she has.

Like all good ghost stories, Leek's has a beautiful twist. Leek's first encounter with the 'Picnic' was in a poem by Bill Manhire that she came across early in her Dunedin stay. What makes her version of the painting remarkable is the fact that she made it *before* seeing the original. She painted it 'blind', using Manhire's poem as a script or score. We've heard often enough of artists making copies 'after' the masters, but how do you paint 'after' an unknown master, let alone one whose work you haven't seen? Isn't that a painting 'before'? Who is ghosting whom in this creative séance? Look long enough at the works side by side and it can seem that the copy dreamed the original, that the painting wrote the poem, that fiction has begotten fact. Leek shares with Manhire a miniaturist's light touch, and the loveliest, battiest moments in Leek's picnic are the product of a kind of creative whispering in which Manhire embroiders a detail which Leek embroiders again. None is lovelier, or battier, than the figure at the front of the group – a 'woman dressed as a man' – who in her version becomes a kohl-eyed, top-hatted cross-dresser with a man draped across her legs like a ventriloquist's puppet. *Ghost Painting* itself might be read as a form of ventriloquism, in which Manhire, Leek and the unknown artist each seem to speak through the other …

Here is the promise of *Ghost Painting*: that memory is no less precious for being channelled through borrowed or careworn forms. It finds a home, it has an afterlife, not only in the places we've lived but in the poems read in passing and the pictures glimpsed or salvaged along the way. From the nineteenth century to the early twenty-first, from colonial history to present-day fantasy … Leek spins those afterlives outward in a delicate and beautiful web.

Out of the Kitchen Sink

Misha Kavka

The gothic is a term closely associated with the Old World and the detritus of its decaying aristocracies: mouldy castles on hilltops; gnarled gardens exposed to inclement weather; relatives going mad in attics while undead ones lurk in cellars. The houses of the New World just don't come in such dimensions: most family homes are nice villas on one level, and where would one find – let alone put – the decaying aristocratic relatives? Yet the gothic can be brought home here, too, in any number of Kiwi visual and literary tropes where an undead history meets unsuccessful efforts at its repression. Indeed, however short our past, it seems curiously prone to gothic metaphorisation; however short our history, it seems particularly undead. Here, the anxieties of settling a new country become uneasy stories about adolescence spent in (mis)remembered golden weather, while the past that settlement yearns to forget – the backbreaking efforts to tame the land, not to mention taming its former settlers – intrudes into those nice one-storey houses that can neither invite the outside in nor sufficiently close it out.

The result is a kind of ambivalent, permeable gothic domicile, both in the sense of the haunted house as home (to ghosts) and in the sense of New Zealand as home (to settlers). In this double meaning of gothic domicile, cannot the material history of the land be said to haunt New Zealand stories as Old World spectres haunt a house? If so, it will require looking behind, beneath and beyond – out of the frame, in filmic terms – the utopian stories of settlement.

For a start, the Old World has nothing on our inclement weather, whether we're talking aggressive sun or squalls or sudden, sheep-frozen-to-the-ground frost. In New Zealand, being buffeted, soaked and attacked by weather is just another symptom of the geological threats harboured by this fertile, febrile island afloat on a seemingly endless body of water. Mud, sand and rain seep and leak into houses, demanding remembrance of the civilising tasks of settlement, not just clearing the land but also clearing off the people already on it: this is what really can't be adequately remembered, what Stephen Turner calls the 'long history of place'.[1] In place of long history, the New Zealand gothic is obsessed with short, generational histories; from the discomfiting perspective of children or women, the gothic connects problems of coming of age and coming to terms with a geologically new place – problems of desire and nature.

Jane Campion's film *The Piano* (1994) is exemplary, and not just because of the mud that sucks on shoes and weights the hems of ballooning skirts. The elemental issues of desire and nature are all here: a knowing prepubescent protagonist, her mother a woman of thwarted desire and her would-be father the settler of a new land, starkly imaged as an isolated house in burnt-off bush. This visible sign of settlement, the settler house, becomes shorthand for the problems of newness, generational dysfunction and short history. In much New Zealand film and television, the house in the midst of trees or perched on the beach becomes the site of a piquant form of local gothic, conceived as a triangulation of place/sex/childhood. Think not just of *The Piano* but also of the claustrophobic bach as dark backdrop to a girl's precocious sexual awakening in *Rain* (Jeffs, 2001), or the return of this threatening older man/adolescent girl relation against the backdrop of a decaying family home in *In My Father's Den* (McGann, 2004). In both cases, of course, a child must die as punishment for buried family secrets and dysfunctional dynamics, though it's hard to say that anything or anyone is thus purged. Whether family home, suburban house or bach, the desire for a new life in a new country is troubled by the very processes of settlement which were meant to make paradise inhabitable. The pure place of nature, the pure desire of a child – both of which figure this South Pacific Eden as 'a great place to bring up kids' – are sullied by the short, messy history of the new settlers. The settler wish, proclaimed by an unofficial national anthem that 'nature enter me', is hauntingly fulfilled by walls, floors, even plumbing that let as many scary things into the house as they attempt to close out.

Natural Tenancy

Taking her title from a phrase in Ian Wedde's novel *Symmes Hole*, Linda Hardy uses the idea of 'Natural Occupancy' to demarcate a 'settler poetics of colonisation'.[2] This poetics, she maintains, refers to a set of stories – about shipwrecks and Natives, cook-outs and golden weather, even a piano sinking to the bottom of the 'deep, deep sea' – all of which willingly 'surrender the furnishings of a culture both European and bourgeois [in order] to come into the sensuality of a "natural occupancy" of the new land'.[3] The innocence implicit in a new beginning leaves the indigene of the land's prior history conveniently unmentioned. As Hardy puts it, the fictions of sparkling newness 'allow the heirs of a settler society to imagine our unhistoric origin as the (possibility of the) making of a settlement without a colony'. In such fictions, the workings of colonial power are displaced onto a right of 'natural occupancy'; the prior history of the land, never adequately articulated, is buried alongside the settlers' own European bourgeois history, now seen as deficient because it's unnatural, over-civilised. Once the musical furniture of the bourgeoisie has sunk to the ocean floor, the history of settlement becomes a set of renewable stories about frolicking in the 'golden weather of antipodean boyhood'.

In this paradox of having to create a domicile that will uphold the 'natural' basis of occupancy, what holds these contradictory parts together is not so much a displacement of the past as its burying; the past is pushed beneath the surface, behind the walls, out of the pipes, in order to clear a space of endless golden weather that is the meteorological metaphor for natural occupancy. But even in the new world, to reiterate such mechanisms of the gothic is to invite haunting, for if Freud taught us anything about the uncanny it is that the repressed always returns. We should ask, though, what is repressed in the new country, what can return in a place of short history, and why should a kitchen sink have anything to do with it?

In the first instance the long history of indigenous occupation is pushed aside or away by the imagined newness of an empty country. The very idea of a new country betrays the mechanism of repression and haunting; the settlers repress both the history of indigenous occupation as well as the inevitable history of their own settlement, as if the place they have settled was not just new, but would always continue to be new. Thus the settler house is subject to constant renovation in order to return it to an original state of being new, perched on a new land. Meanwhile, the material properties of the place, including the inclement weather and the creeping back of nature onto cleared land, challenge this cleansing of history that arises from the ongoing makeover of settler property. What comes back, out of the sink, is the residue, the dregs, the mucky remainder of the attempt to maintain the newness of the settlement in a new country. Relentless innovation, making the place anew, is the whole action of the short history of settlers. This will to get out of history free, to have arrived at and to be now living in an untouched country, would appear to bypass the unconscious altogether – not to mention the Viennese-inspired talk of repression – for the sake of a tenancy that is natural. But the settler unconscious is betrayed by the impossibility of an ongoing newness, quite apart from any indigenous reminder that this is actually an old new country.

The settler house does not just stand on indigenous ground; it also contains the short history of its making, and all the elements of place that its construction would build out. To recover this history, and the source of local gothic, we need only look at the construction of the settler house itself, its unnatural tenancy evident in fears of roots undermining foundations, branches scratching at windows, effluents coming back up out of the sink. This new house in the new world invites its own kind of gothic problem. To remain new requires ongoing processes of renovation and modernisation which produce their own inevitable waste and debris, distancing settlers from the nature they embrace as the grounds of their tenancy. Yet to build a domicile consistent with natural occupancy means that the house must remain open to nature, to the onslaught of weather, foliage, and geological strains that characterise the newness of the land yet age houses. The latter seems the preferred path here, but it produces houses whose plumbing, vents, walls and floors only weakly hold the outside out – or keep the repressed down. When nature (re)enters the new-world house, as mud or animals or a sudden chill, then the mundane space of domesticity is haunted by the ghosts of settlement.

This underside of the golden weather is something a woman is perhaps more inclined to notice. I first came to New Zealand in the proverbial golden weather: a month from Christmas to late January, when the lure of the veranda was broken only by the call of the beach. On my return a year and a half later, however, it was July, a month that I spent either huddling under eiderdown, repositioning the few available space heaters, or raging at the architectural stupidity that placed a louvred window right next to the shower head. Nonetheless, my complaints about the lack of proper heating, in effect about the inability to close the inside of the house off from the outside, always met with the same reassurance: 'it doesn't really get that cold here'. This is a statement I consider to be blatantly false, yet I fully believe the speakers' faith in its truth value. 'Golden weather' is not only nostalgia for 'antipodean boyhood' in a new land, but also a means by which the very existence of winter is forgiven and forgotten year in, year out, as though its last appearance were a fluke. For all their supposed natural tenancy, the villas built here by the settlers of the golden weather seem to take little account of the actual weather that so easily breaches their roofs, floors and walls (not to mention louvred windows).

The stories I've heard of boyhood in this new country might well qualify for the 'golden weather' stamp, but the most memorable yet oddly mundane tales seem to focus on events in that indeterminate zone that isn't quite inside or outside the house: the rat caught behind the washing machine, the possum trapped in the roof, even a pregnant cow discovered stuck in the corridor between the laundry and the bath. My favourite 'growing up' story of those I've been told involves not only the requisite fields and bush and small creatures, but also – as is perhaps only natural in a boy's settler story – a .22 calibre rifle. This particular story also involves at least one pukeko in the sights of the rifle (a challenge, apparently, because the shape and shield of the pukeko's feathers make them hard to kill), though the teller remembers having serious misgivings about the punishment that would ensue on killing a native bird. This didn't deter him, of course, but when he did bag a pukeko, he was so horrified that he hid the carcass under his bed – where it stayed, and decayed. Hold on to this image, for this is precisely how antipodean gold turns to antipodean gothic: a ten-year-old boy sleeping with a rotting pukeko under his bed.

Suburban Gothic

How about antipodean girlhood? What lies under the bed of settler domicile for girls? Jane Campion has more than once offered an answer to this question. Prior to suspending a shoe and its inhabitant from a sinking piano, Campion made *Sweetie* (1989), a film that opens with a female voice-over explaining the protagonist's fear of trees:

> There was a tree in our yard with a palace in the branches. It was built for my sister and it had fairy lights that went on and off in a sequence. She was the princess – it was her tree; she wouldn't let me up it. At night their darkness frightens me. Someone could be watching from behind them, someone who wishes you harm. I used to imagine the roots of that tree, crawling, crawling right under the house, right under my bed. Maybe that's why trees scare me; it's like they have hidden powers.

The tree feared by Kay stands in for her sister and possible alter-ego, Sweetie, visualised in the film as the abject, sexualised body of the feminine grotesque. The uneasy bond between prim Kay and appetite-driven Sweetie will function in the film as an allegory of feminine subjectivity, constricted and distorted like the undernourished tree planted by Kay's boyfriend in the tiny concrete backyard of their rented, suburban house. At the beginning, however, what is emphasised is a fear of roots – of something crawling under the floorboards, 'right under [her] bed'. Like the flowered carpet in the opening sequence, whose colours are so unnaturally bright that the petals seem three-dimensional, as though they were growing right up from under the floor, this gothic house is a manifestation of the homely/*heimlich* made unfamiliar/*unheimlich*. The floors and walls that should keep the interior separate from the exterior invite incursion, and nature is represented as a creeping, crawling, over-reaching menace – the ghost, perhaps, of the golden weather. When her boyfriend Lew attempts to plant an 'anniversary tree' to celebrate their first year together, Kay rips it out in the dark of night and throws it in her closet (then later, yes, under her bed). For what can she do with such a symbolically weighted gift? Either the undernourished sapling will die, and betoken the death of the relationship, or it will thrive, its roots pushing under the house and threatening to strangle or suffocate the woman within. The suburban gothic house, open as it is to the organic, writhing, decaying material beneath its floorboards, is nonetheless a paradoxically claustrophobic place, at least for a woman.

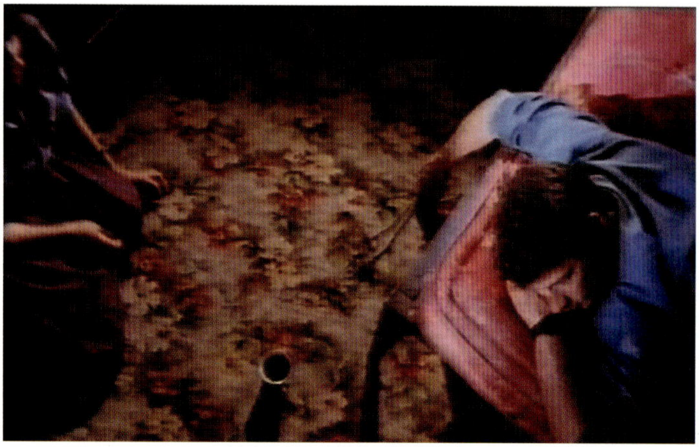

Still from Sweetie *(Jane Campion, 1989)*

If *Sweetie* works as a parable for the difficulty of female sexual maturation in antipodean suburbia, then it shares both this theme and its creepy-crawly mechanics with Alison Maclean's short film *Kitchen Sink* (1989). In this film about what comes up out of the pipes, a kitchen plughole doubles as a gothic birthing canal, divulging a dirt-covered foetus which – just add (bath)water – then transmutes into a silent, Neanderthal hunk who proves uncomfortably attractive to the female protagonist. The opening close-up of water swirling down the kitchen plughole introduces plumbing as the immediate site of concern. In good folksong fashion, the hair the woman pulls from the plughole is attached to a rope, the rope to a root, the root to an umbilical cord, and presto – a perfectly formed face covered in mud emerges from the entrails of the innocent-seeming plughole. The connection made between femininity, roots and the spaces of suburban gothic has definite resonance with *Sweetie*, but here the gothic trope of roots pressing up from below is not just metaphorical; it is firmly located in the domestic architecture as the trouble with settler plumbing.

By definition plugholes serve as passageways between the interior and exterior of a house, between habitation and nature, but of course the movement is meant to go only one way, expelling internal waste to the outside. As I've argued, though, the problem with the settler/suburban home's position in a new land is the detritus that settlement produces, a material history which may very well come charging back up the pipes. In the maw of the plughole, then, the horror visualised in *Kitchen Sink* is the possibility of a hidden 'return' from below, where the twists and turns of piping under the sink take the place of the dark corridors and stairwells of the gothic house itself (for another such vision, see Yvonne Todd's 'Clammy Pipes' in this volume). If New Zealand as a colony lacks the history to produce a properly haunted house, then it can certainly compensate by producing haunted plumbing, the slim opening of the plughole acting as a doorway for the intrusion of overly fecund nature into the settler domicile.

Renovating the New

The striking thing about *Sweetie* and *Kitchen Sink*, both released in 1989, is that with a more modern eye we would judge these houses to be 'unrenovated'. That modern eye is not encouraged by the films themselves, which take the houses to be standard for antipodean suburbia, yet our very notion of suburban architecture in the last few years has come under onslaught from a different visual medium – television, specifically in its 'makeover' form. Initially derived from British shows like *Changing Rooms* and *Ground Force*, the property makeover genre of reality television has swelled the ranks of local production in this country, ranging from several series of *Mitre 10 Dream Home* to *DIY Rescue* and *The Ultimate Do-Up*. The connection between birthing plugholes and shiny steel-and-granite kitchens may seem tenuous at first, but I suspect that we're simply looking at contrary manifestations of the same obsessive concerns with settler domicile.

Indeed, from a different perspective, *In My Father's Den* rehearses these concerns as part of its own gothic mode. The knotted tensions between past and present, between procreation and death, between the prodigal son with blind claims on the secrets of the father's den and his mummy's-boy, stay-at-home brother – all are compressed from the start into the difference between two houses: the cluttered, sagging, unrenovated family home to which the prodigal son obsessively returns, and the modern, concrete house of clean lines and open spaces in which the younger brother seeks to exact his freedom from the past. Though this younger brother may valiantly clutch at the curative power of the new, the film's own gothic sensibility knows better; in an ironic twist befitting of dark humour, it turns out that the missing adolescent victim, Celia, has been killed not by the sins of the past but rather by the dangers concealed in the architecture of the new. What kills her, after all, aren't the hands of the brother's neurotic wife who has attacked her in a jealous rage, but rather the atrium space of this light and airy modern home into which Celia drops like a stone. While the idea of 'natural occupancy', as reiterated in stories of the golden weather, finds its gothic underside in the nature that comes up through floorboards and plugholes, *Father's Den* envisions a body falling from a mod-home mezzanine as the appropriate gothic outcome of attempts to paper over the detritus of settlement.

Still from Kitchen Sink *(Alison Maclean, 1989)*

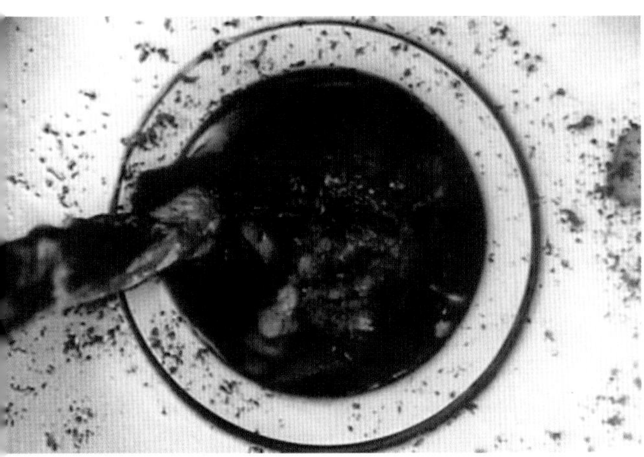

There is thus more than a tenuous link between the suburban gothic and property makeover programmes. In *Hot Property* (TV3), for instance, presenter Petra Bagust teams up with designer Peter and builder Wayne to 'do up' a house for auction – in a limited time and with an eye to budget, of course. The half-hour format is always the same: the team shows up at a house much in need of cosmetic repair; designer Peter points out the aesthetic and pragmatic infelicities, and comes up with quick solutions; builder Wayne puts his muscle to the 'big jobs'; Petra devotes herself to an artwork; and the house then sells (or doesn't) for a higher price at auction. What is gothic in this is the crucial initial phase; the horror is not outside the house, but rather what the design team finds *in* the house: the decayed state of the house itself. DIY renovation, in other words, is an anti-gothic cleansing agent, a way of clearing away the traces of (architectural and personal) history that is not unlike the earlier settler project of clearing, and claiming, land. *Hot Property* itself, in fact, has moved more toward this model since the first series, when the team really did work to a tight budget of paint buckets and hired furniture; in later series, in keeping not only with the extreme-makeover trend but also with a more convincing project of natural tenancy, all traces of earlier design 'flaws' are removed – walls torn down, staircases built in, windows enlarged, decks attached. The result, not surprisingly, is a uni-design, with the stamp of the show affixed to the basic unit no matter what the neighbourhood or who the owners are. (This leads at times to attempts at aesthetic resistance by hapless house owners, such as the mother-son duo from Auckland's North Shore, who – themselves curiously gothic-looking – yelped in dismay at their newly fluorescent green walls, bright blue house, and whitewashed floorboards.)

Viewing *Hot Property* alongside *Sweetie* or *Kitchen Sink* (or even the rotting pukeko) might suggest that property renovation in this place ought to take a particular form, that of fervently sealing the inside of the house off from the outside, stopping the cracks in floors and walls, and literally plugging the holes to prevent Nature from invading the bounds of domicile. But, I must admit, this may be a European perspective. For despite the incursions of Nature that I have been describing as the gothic underside of 'natural occupancy', the renovators of property makeover shows exhibit little interest in sealing a house off from the external elements. Rather, the push is toward erasing the horror within by cleansing, remodelling, radically modernising. Across the genre of property renovation programmes so beloved of the local viewing public, historical traces are repeatedly painted over, knocked out or scrubbed away, in a project of ghost-busting which aims to increase the stakes of settlement through a process of making-new. Like the renewable stories of golden weather, doing up your house is a utopian project, a sign of your proper tenancy.

Don't get me wrong – I am not making a plea for more appropriate renovation strategies, which would 'return' a house to its original form. The point is rather that the houses now being torn into with such gusto, on- and off-screen, were themselves 'modern' when they were built, were themselves a way of stamping the 'new' on a prior place as a mark of natural occupancy. Whether Nanna's house or the father's den or a concrete-and-glass structure that challenges you to unearth a single family secret, renovation creates the very residue it seeks to escape: what really lies beneath the bedding-down of settlement is neither a sinking piano nor a rotting pukeko, but some kind of trouble with plumbing.

Christopher Braddock,
'Repository 1', 2001 (detail),
flocking on foam, mirror, light
& chromed steel
500 x 500 x 400 mm
(Collection of the Museum
of New Zealand Te Papa
Tongarewa)

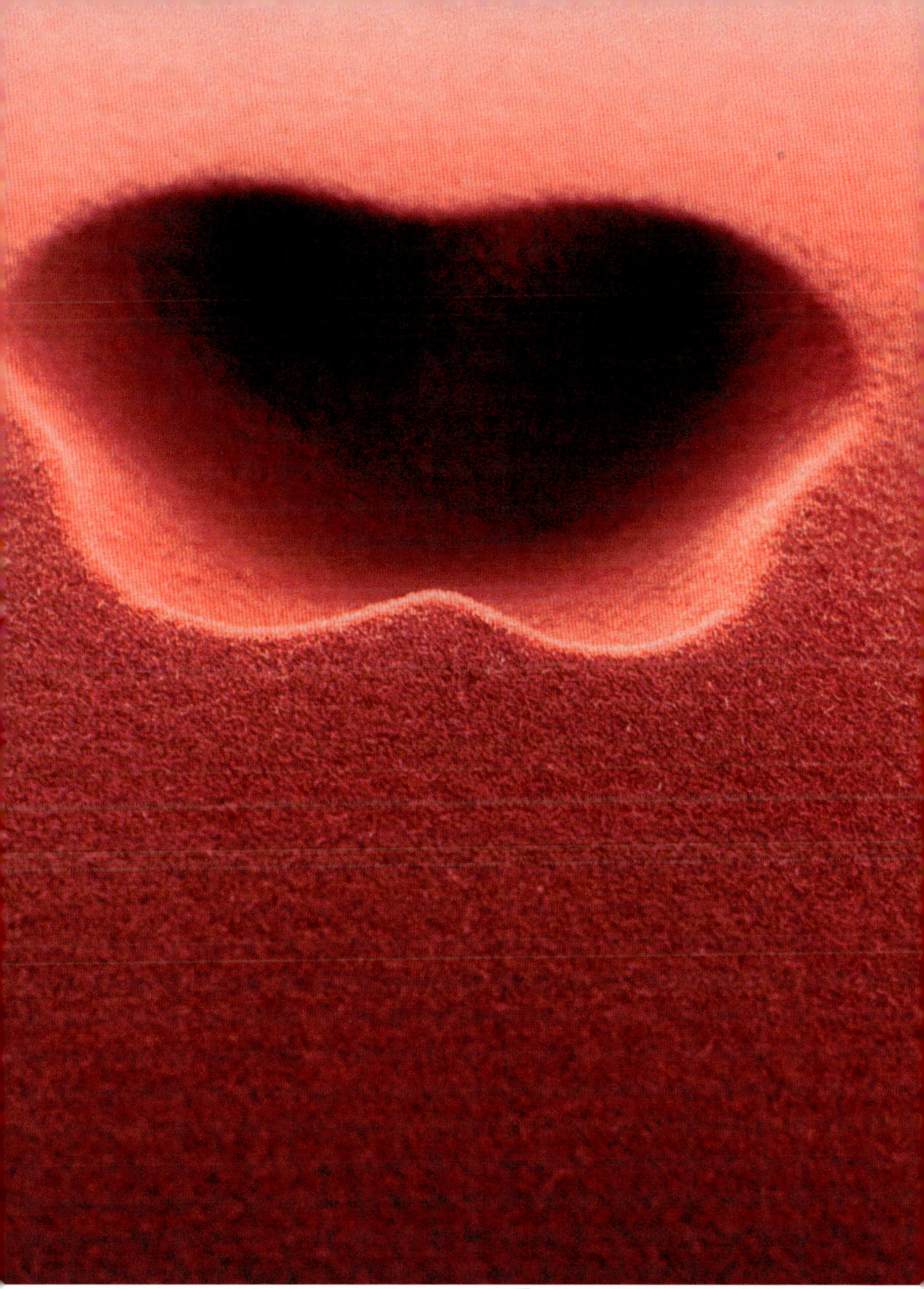

from Tiger Country

Jack Ross

The title 'Tiger Country' was suggested by the Joel Schumacher film *Tigerland* (2000), set in an American military training camp which is designed to be an exact copy – in terrain, climate, danger – of the Vietnam Colin Farrell and his buddies will soon be shipped off to. Madness and mayhem are (predictably) the result. Portions of the film's dialogue survive in part two of the poem 'Tiger Country'.

When I first saw the film I'd just undergone a messy breakup, and was working at a Language School in central Auckland. As I walked every morning though the small park in Eden Crescent, at the top of Shortland Street, it seemed to me as if the city itself was standing in for something more real, as if the cracks in its façade were becoming ever more apparent.

I was also trying, at the time, to write a story inspired by the Mesopotamian myth of Ishtar and her descent to the underworld. There are two principal versions of the myth, one Akkadian, featuring Ishtar, and an older Sumerian version, featuring Inanna. In the overlaps I felt I could see the shape of a poem, a poem I tried to compose in the voice of one of my characters, a tormented adolescent girl. When it was finished, I realised it was less about her, and more about my own situation.

In general, the poems seem designed less to paper over the cracks than to display them for our mortification.

I wish I could feel they'd been contradicted by subsequent events.

Jack Ross, 'Disorder and Early Sorrow'

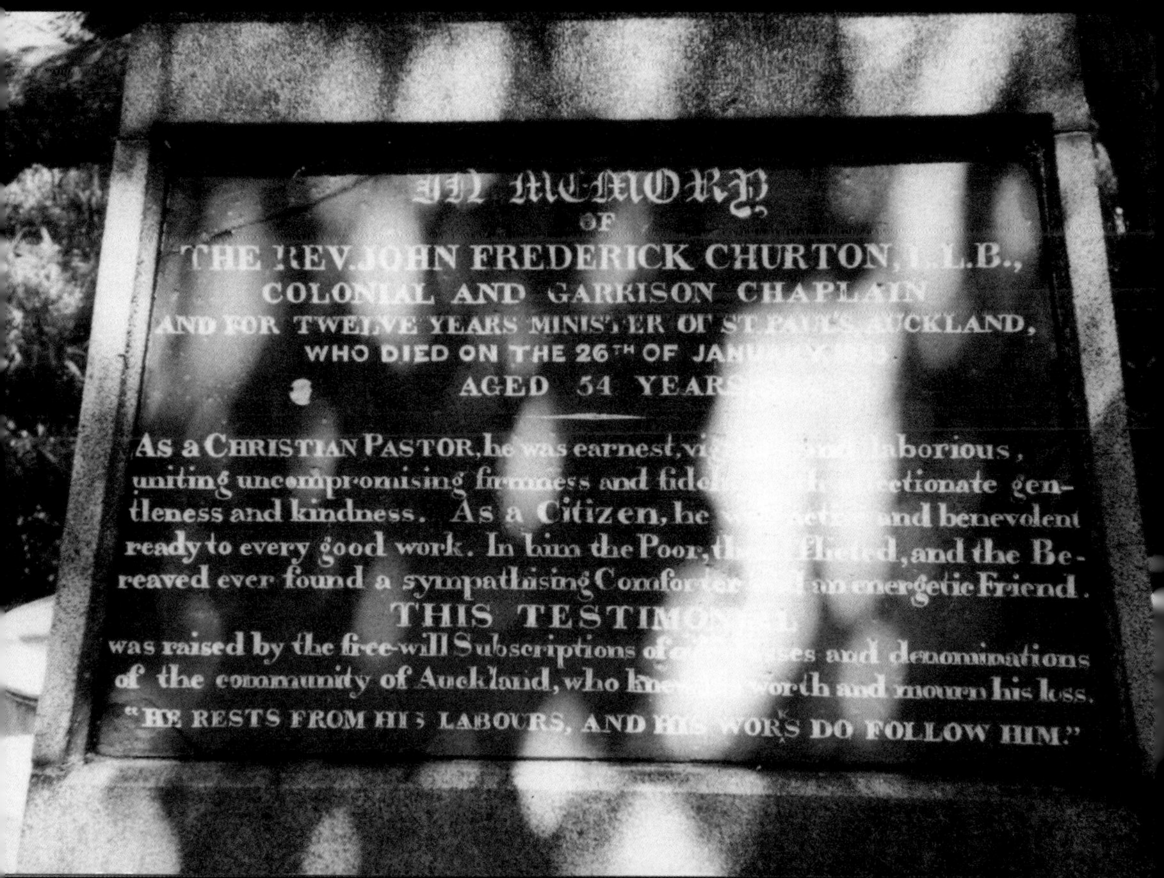

i

Goodbye Love

Ishtar
          daughter of Sin
          where are you going?

To the Land of no Return
          Ereshkigal's country
to the house none leaves who enters it
the road where there is no way back
the room whose tenants have no light
where dust is drink and clay is food
where darkness has replaced the day
where rust eats into door and bolt
to sit like a bird
          with wings for clothes

She took the seven signs
put on her sandals
donned the Shugurra
the great crown
arranged the wig across her forehead
took the yardstick in her hands
hung lapis lazuli around her neck
clasped golden bracelets on both wrists
masked her eyes with inky kohl
cupped her breasts with oval gems
drew on the Pala
robe of sovereignty

Time for the cutting
to start he muttered
staring at the sky

One horn of plenty's
never enough she chuckled
tugging at his dong

Later pizza-face
said Sunny Jim
the loner as he torched the school

When Inanna reached the Land of no Return
the gatekeeper came to let her in
as he made her enter the first gate
he stripped the crown from her head **Walkman**
Why do you take the crown from my head?
These are the orders of the Queen of the Dead
as he made her enter the second gate
he stripped the pendants from her ears **Dark glasses**
Why do you take the pendants from my ears?
These are the orders of the Queen of the Dead
as he made her enter the third gate
he stripped the chain from around her neck **Gold cross**
Why do you take the chain from around my neck?
These are the orders of the Queen of the Dead
as he made her enter the fourth gate
he stripped the ornaments from her breast **Tank-Top**
Why do you take the ornaments from my breast?
These are the orders of the Queen of the Dead
as he made her enter the fifth gate
he stripped the girdle from her hips **Black Jeans**
Why do you take the girdle from my hips?
These are the orders of the Queen of the Dead
as he made her enter the sixth gate
he stripped the clasps from her hands and feet **Watch-strap**
Why do you take the clasps from my hands and feet?
These are the orders of the Queen of the Dead
as he made her enter the seventh gate
he stripped the loincloth from her body **G-string**
Why do you take the loincloth from my body?
These are the orders of the Queen of the Dead

Naked Inanna dropped to her knees
as Ereshkigal mounted the throne
the Seven Judges discussed her case
they turned their eyes towards her
eyes of death
they passed sentence
on the accused

Release against Ishtar
the sixty miseries
misery of the eyes against her *eyes*
misery of the sides against her *sides*
misery of the heart against her *heart*
misery of the feet against her *feet*
misery of the head against her *head*
against her whole body
every part of her

They all cried out
She is accursed!
Inanna immediately slumped
down dead
her body was hung
on a spike

Since Ishtar went to hell
the bull won't mount the cow
the ass won't service the jenny
the man won't love the virgin
the man lies in his own room
the virgin on her side

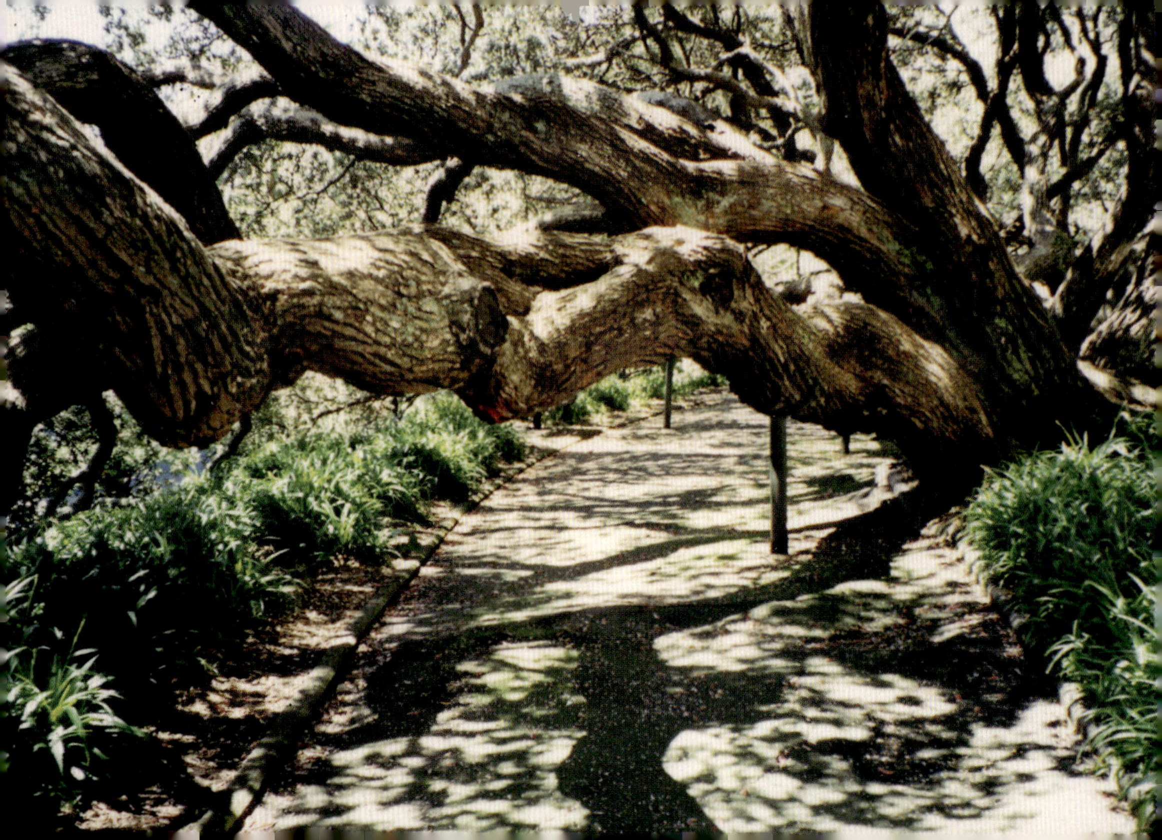

Tiger Country

Before I left for India, I was in a strange mood. Working at the Language School – talk, talk, what do *you* think, Myung-Sook, Min-Hee, Charles? What's your sign? What jobs would *you* be willing to do (nude model, race-car driver, surrogate mother/father, soldier?). Exchange ideas.

Sometimes I'd wander round the streets photographing things, trying to trace patterns in the gaps.

I'd forgotten how to write poems (if I ever knew; I can see some of you are in *considerable* doubt about that). What I produced aspired more and more to the condition of gibberish.

I couldn't read – *The Hero with a Thousand Faces*, *Mary Chesnut's Civil War*, *Brief Lives*, *Le Rouge et le Noir* – all of them sat by the bed untouched.

I just need to get away, I told myself. I just need to lie there, somewhere else, in a hotel room, where I know nobody, and *twitch*.

In tiger country, it's always raining
Ladies and gentlemen, welcome to the war
Here you will learn to hunt and kill
        search and destroy
You will sleep one hour a night
        I know how you feel
I know what you're thinking
        This is where it starts

Japan was too cold for me
        in Harbin
I lay in bed for a month
        watching the wall
Good job, you move
        like soldiers, Tracy
like the day

Disorder and Early Sorrow

Please help yourself to the buffet and enjoy all the fresh meat & vegetables available for your good health. But please, a special request from management, do not waste the food, think of all the hungry children in our world – we are sad for the starving children.

– Jin Joo Meat Buffet Restaurant

His wors do follow him
Last line of the inscription
in
him
His works *do follow him*

wars? worse?
squeeze it
His wor^s do follow
words? whores?

iii

Breast Cancer Doesn't Just Affect Women

Eye counter eye the fulcrum of two faces
on a poster
rain-pocked screen ahead
or screen of trees dark pine trees

Were not, as 'twere, the merest mask of gloom,
But stretched away unto the edge of doom

Not *that* no pointing out the moral
archaising like a stepladder

eye
eye
nose nose
mouth
chin

Father and child both in denim
blue equals *sincere*
or else that ritual dance
Is there something on my heel?
curvet your body

Or greeting friend
knees crooked into the hollow
overbalance
the balance
of their lives has been disturbed

Last Night at the Party

The voice that unsettles me today must be prophetic. I can be nothing but a writer
– Mikhail Bulgakov (6 November, 1923)

Dionysos – the desire to be possessed

Constant, repetitive motion can (we know) put one into a trance,
ready to be seized
by the voodoo gods: *candomblé*

A looseness takes the limbs
we shuffle backwards
Lord, these sweating bodies!   *Elliott*
open to the sky   outside the window / rain-dark
crescent moon   the rainy street
black at its centre – Patrick, Idy, Wolf,
the Russian girl
in red/ hoisted to shoulders.
Spin until you fall

MANU SAMOA
They're back, right here, the Baron …
They're here, right back
Baron Samedi, lord of the cemetery

Would you like to get a coffee? Maybe
it's too late …

the bull-ring – the canaries – mutiny
music as tinnitus

Each of us is made in turn to strut: St Vitus' Dance –
a constant quiver

Are you all right? Want beer? Nah, water. My heart is weighed
against a feather – *ma'at*
Let me inside your kingdom, children, let me die inside

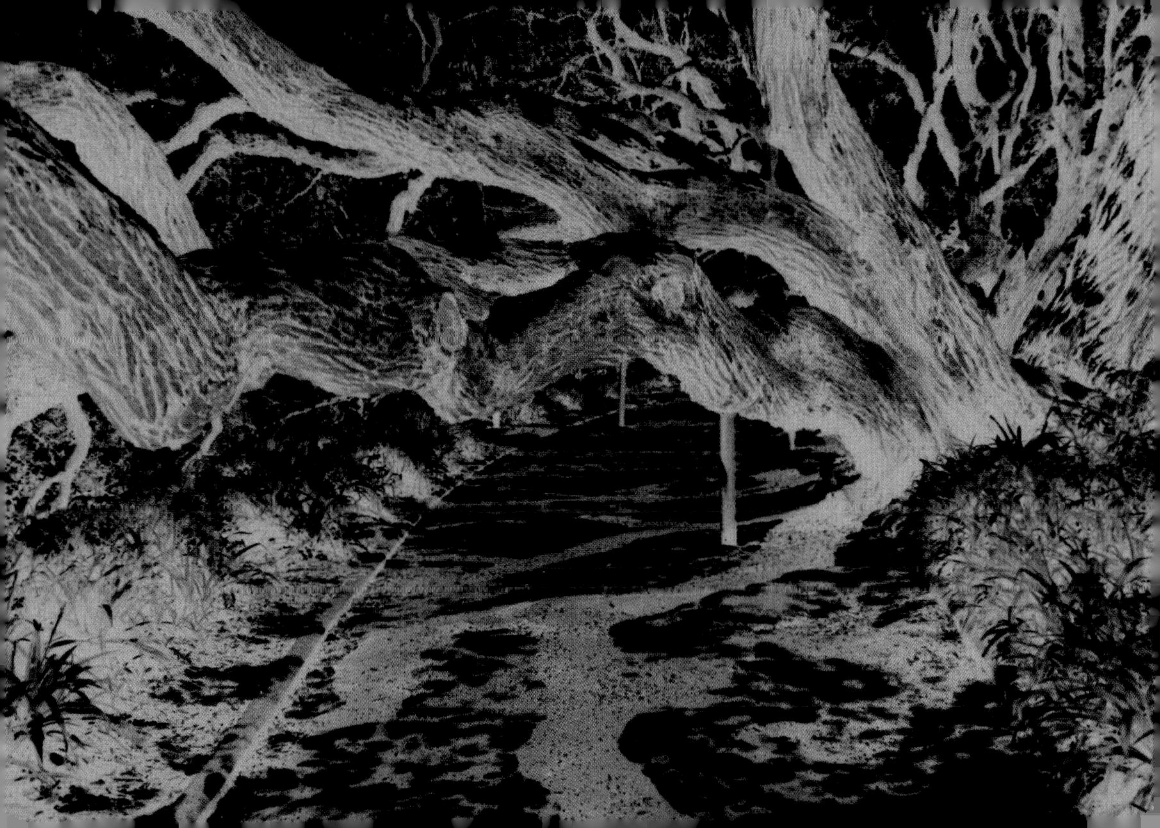

Corrugated Iron Gothic

Ian Lochhead

Introduction

The term gothic was first used to describe the architecture of the Middle Ages in the mid-seventeenth century at a time when the architecture of the period was little understood or appreciated. What had begun as a term of opprobrium gradually took on more positive connotations during the course of the eighteenth century. Beginning with garden pavilions and subsequently extending to private houses – Horace Walpole's Strawberry Hill being the best known example – gothic architecture was slowly revived. In the first decades of the nineteenth century gothic was again employed as the style for churches, but it wasn't until the 1830s that the Gothic Revival began to challenge the dominance of classical architecture.[1]

The movement's most influential polemicist was Augustus Welby Northmore Pugin, whose book *Contrasts* (1836) compared the Christian architecture and society of an idealised, late-medieval world with the debased, pagan architecture and godless society of contemporary Britain. As a designer, Pugin is best known for his contribution to the Houses of Parliament in Westminster (1837–67). By the 1850s and 60s the Gothic Revival had become the dominant architectural movement in Britain, influencing the design of buildings of every type and size. The adaptability of gothic to meet the needs of the modern world, including the challenge presented by the new materials of the industrial age, was one of the principal reasons for its success. This same adaptability also played a crucial role in the international dissemination of gothic in the middle decades of the century. From the 1840s the Gothic Revival spread globally in the wake of British colonial expansion. In New Zealand its impact was especially marked, since the colonisation of the country coincided with the movement's rise to lead architectural taste in Britain.[2]

The colonial building world was very different from that in Victorian Britain, with timber buildings greatly outnumbering those in brick and stone. Both Pugin and the equally influential Ecclesiological Society argued that irrespective of what material was used it was essential to build according to the principles embodied in the architecture of the medieval world.[3] The Ecclesiologists believed, for instance, that if log construction was used to build churches, it was essential that the logs were fixed in an upright position, in order to achieve the verticality they considered an essential characteristic of ecclesiastical architecture.[4] Medieval timber buildings, both secular and ecclesiastical, provided valuable models for architects working in New Zealand. In 1852 Sir George Gilbert Scott designed a timber church based on medieval prototypes for the newly-founded Canterbury settlement, but the most important contributions to timber gothic church architecture in New Zealand were made by Frederick Thatcher (1814–90) and Benjamin Mountfort (1825–98). Thatcher's Old St Paul's in Wellington and Mountfort's St Mary's pro-cathedral in Parnell are the culmination of this New Zealand timber gothic tradition.[5]

The Gothic Revival in Britain may have looked to the past for inspiration, but it was also a product of the industrial revolution. The Victorian fascination with the medieval past was a reaction to the often brutal reality of the modern world but architects were nevertheless quick to exploit the new materials of iron and glass that the industrial revolution had made available as never before.[6] The Crystal Palace of 1851 demonstrated the potential of iron and glass in building, although doubts were expressed as to whether it could be considered architecture. Pugin despairingly described it as 'a glass monster' but the art critic John Ruskin had already conceded that 'the time is probably near when a new system of architectural laws will be developed, adapted entirely to metallic construction'.[7] These new architectural laws were investigated by Benjamin Woodward in his design for the Oxford Natural History Museum (1855–60), a building described as bringing together the architecture of the Middle Ages and the materials of the railway age.[8] Although conventionally gothic in style on the exterior, the central court was a forest of iron gothic columns and arches supporting a canopy of glass tiles. Francis Skidmore, the Coventry ironmaster responsible for this structural skeleton, argued that it was essential in building with iron to follow the example of medieval architects: 'it would be unlike their actions, and unworthy of ourselves, to use [iron] only as a cheap expedient, instead of giving to it that development in Christian art of which it was capable'.[9] According to Skidmore, iron construction could be made fitting and beautiful only if modern architects applied the same principles to its use as had guided their medieval forebears.

Inspired by the designs for the Oxford Museum and the rapid erection of the Crystal

William Slater, Design for an Iron Church from Instrumenta Ecclesiastica, *Second Series, 1856 (University of Canterbury Library)*

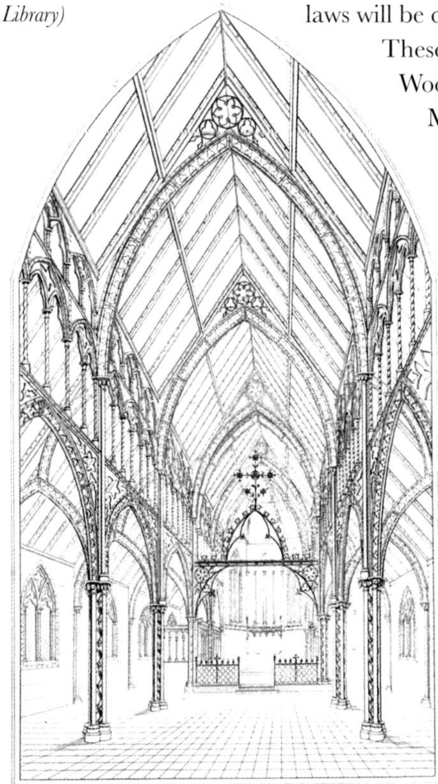

Palace, the Ecclesiological Society recognised the potential of iron for providing inexpensive, pre-fabricated churches for colonial parishes. It commissioned William Slater to produce a model design for an iron church, which was published in a collection of designs for colonial churches in 1856. Skidmore provided costings and advice on its execution, but there is no evidence that this design was ever built. In 1858 an iron church designed by Matthew Digby Wyatt was erected in Rangoon,[10] while James Edward Fitzgerald offered to supply an iron cathedral for Christchurch in 1859:

> If wood be objected to … then I should go for iron. I am going this week to Coventry to see Skidmore's works in iron; he has built the new Museum at Oxford which throws a new light on iron architecture and tells me the difference between iron & stone is as *hundreds* to *thousands* in price. He is building some very ornamental iron churches with *slate* roofs for £2 a sitting.[11]

Benjamin Mountfort, Victoria Street Clock Tower, Christchurch, c. 1859 (School of Fine Arts, University of Canterbury)

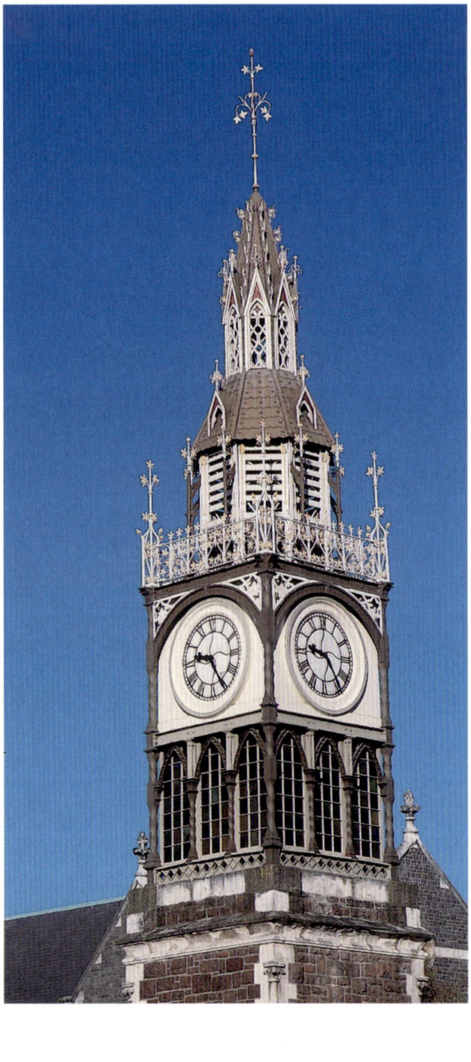

The claim that iron construction was inexpensive compared to traditional materials had much to recommend it in cash-starved colonial settlements, although the aesthetic dimension of the new material challenged conservative tastes.

Christchurch's iron cathedral never eventuated, but an iron clock tower, fabricated at Skidmore's celebrated Coventry ironworks and designed by Benjamin Mountfort, was built in the city.[12] Originally intended as part of the Canterbury Provincial Council Buildings, it proved too heavy for the timber base constructed to support it, and was erected in the adjacent courtyard where it can be glimpsed in early photographs of the buildings. Subsequent efforts to incorporate it into both the Provincial Buildings and the Canterbury Museum failed, but it was eventually erected at the intersection of Lichfield and High Streets to commemorate Queen Victoria's golden jubilee. It was removed to its present position in Victoria Street in 1930.[13] Mountfort's Clock Tower shares features in common with both Slater's iron church and the Oxford Museum, indicating that in 1860 Christchurch was no colonial architectural backwater. The Clock Tower stands as an incongruous monument to the Victorian world's contradictory preoccupations with medievalism and industrial progress, but it also exemplifies colonial Canterbury's identification with the Gothic Revival as well as the willingness to embrace new materials and technology that has characterised New Zealand society ever since.

Corrugated Iron

If cast iron provided one means of reconciling the materials of the railway age and the architecture of the gothic era, corrugated iron was to prove a more flexible and useful material for colonial builders. A product of the industrial revolution, it was durable, light, inexpensive and almost infinitely adaptable – and, perhaps just as important, there were no precedents for its use. It was the colonial building material *par excellence.*[14] By the mid-1840s it was widely available in both New Zealand and Australia. Some of the earliest surviving corrugated iron roofing, dating from around 1843, can be found on the farm of the pioneer whaler Johnny Jones at Matanaka, near Waikouaiti.[15] The ubiquitous use of corrugated iron as a roofing material in colonial New Zealand is less interesting, however, than the ways in which it was pressed into service as a wall cladding, partly in response to the need for economy and durability, but also with the intention of creating specific architectural effects. Although builders were ready to use corrugated iron in a pragmatic and utilitarian manner, just as Skidmore feared, some architects realised that it had much greater potential. It soon became apparent that corrugated iron could be readily adapted to the gothic style.

No architect working in colonial New Zealand was more

Benjamin Mountfort, Christchurch Hospital, Administraion Building and Surgeon's Premises, 1875 (Cotter Medical History Trust)

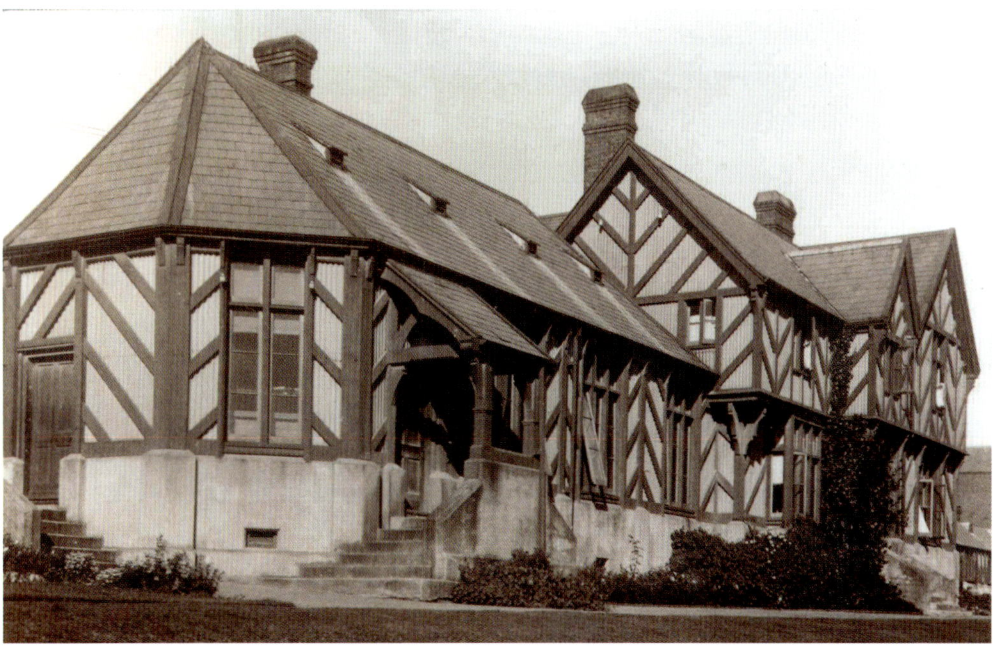

adventurous in his use of corrugated iron than Benjamin Mountfort.[16] Strongly influenced by the ideas of Pugin and the Ecclesiological Society, Mountfort sought ways in which to use corrugated iron that were consistent with Gothic Revival principles, although the buildings in which he used the material were primarily utilitarian. One such building was Christchurch Hospital.[17]

The system of construction used for Christchurch Hospital's buildings between 1860 and 1878 was described by Mountfort in a letter to the Bishop of Nelson in 1884, suggesting that the system may also have been under consideration for building churches:

> The hospital walls are carried up about 10 feet [3 m] from the ground to the window sills in concrete, and above that consist of a light timber framing covered with corrugated iron and filled with concrete, outside of which a constructional framework is carried in the half timbered style.[18]

The cheapness and availability of corrugated iron, along with its weather- and fire-resistant qualities made it a particularly serviceable cladding for such buildings. Gothic was seen as an appropriate style for hospitals because of its association with the medieval church's role in providing medical aid. Thatcher's Colonial Hospital in New Plymouth (1846–8) was built in a similar, half-timbered style utilising a single skin of vertical boards and battens,[19] and Mountfort had used this form of construction at the Canterbury Provincial Council Buildings in 1857. Christchurch Hospital adapts the system to the modern materials of iron and concrete. Mountfort's unprecedented combination of an expressed 'constructional framework' of timber, in conjunction with vertical corrugated iron sidings and concrete infill, can be seen as a direct product of colonial circumstances.

Mountfort treated the inherent qualities of this new industrial product with the same respect and skill he applied to any traditional material. Pugin's 1843 advice that 'we should neither cling pertinaciously to ancient methods of building, solely on the score of antiquity, nor reject inventions because of their novelty, but try both by sound and consistent principles and act accordingly' precisely describes Mountfort's approach.[20]

By asking himself how medieval architects might have employed these materials, Mountfort was able to use concrete and corrugated iron without fear of compromising architectural principles. The result was a building that Mountfort's contemporaries would have considered both 'truthful' and 'real' in its use of materials and method of construction, meaning that materials were employed in ways that respected their inherent characteristics and were not made to look like something else. At the same time as he satisfied purely architectural concerns, Mountfort produced a building that served the needs of modern medical science at a reasonable cost. It also proved to be remarkably durable, the last sections surviving until 1979.

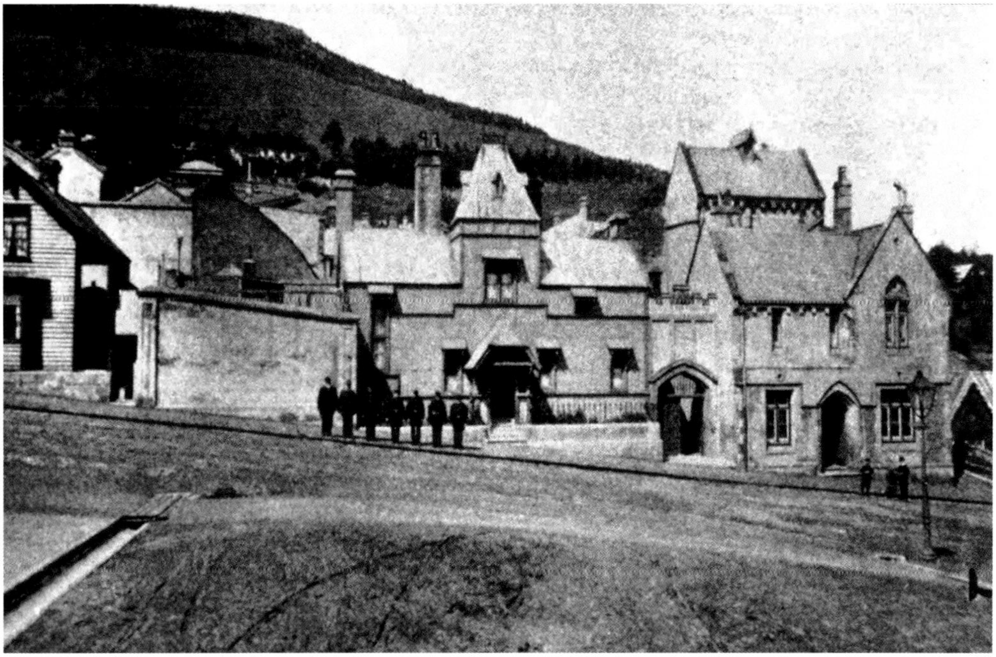

Benjamin Mountfort, Lyttelton Gaol, 1870–5 (Cyclopedia of New Zealand, *Vol. 3 1903. University of Canterbury Library)*

Colonial gaols were hardly noted for architectural innovation and, although castellated gaols were commonplace, a gothic gaol was certainly inconsistent with the Victorian medieval ideal of a society pervaded by Christian charity and bound together by ties of deference and interdependence. The earliest buildings of the notorious Lyttelton Gaol were replaced in a major rebuilding programme between 1870 and 1875 under Mountfort's direction in his role as Provincial Architect.[21] The new buildings were gothic in style, with most of the complex being constructed in concrete, a material that was used with increasing frequency from 1870 onwards.[22] The entrance block on Oxford Street consisted of the Gaoler's and Chief Warder's houses arranged on either side of a central tower with the main entrance below. Mountfort designed a timber-framed structure with an outer shell of vertical galvanised corrugated iron, the wall cavity filled with concrete. Although the materials used were entirely different, the gaol's main façade resembled, in general form, the earliest sections of the Canterbury Provincial Council Buildings, continuing the consistent gothic theme of the province's governmental buildings. The vertical lines of the corrugated iron created a clear visual parallel with the vertical board and batten construction of both the Provincial Buildings and Mountfort's timber gothic churches. Indeed, the gaol was described at the time as being 'somewhat of the ecclesiastical style of architecture'.[23] At Lyttelton Gaol, as at Christchurch Hospital, Mountfort exploited both the utilitarian as well as the aesthetic qualities of corrugated iron, long before these were appreciated by the architectural profession as a whole.

Dr A.C. Barker, Synod Hall and Library, Christ's College, Christchurch 1873 (Christ's College Archives)

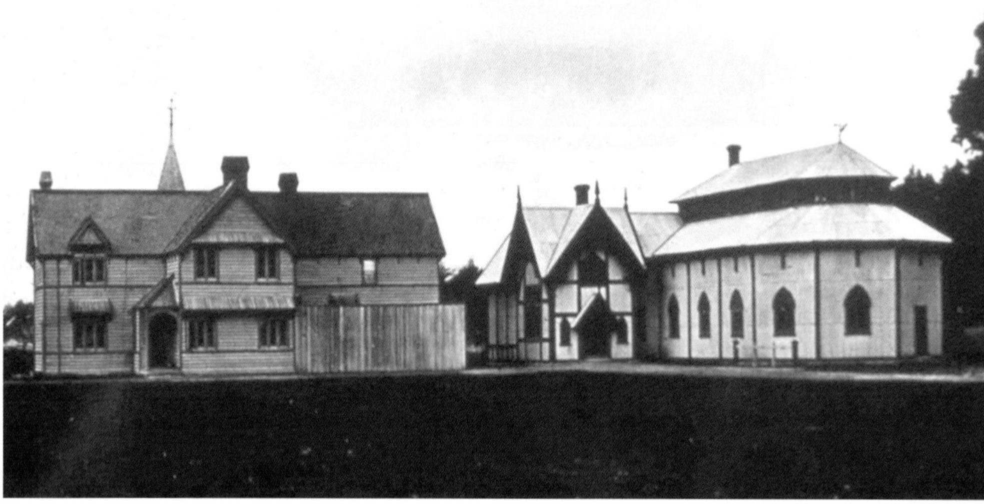

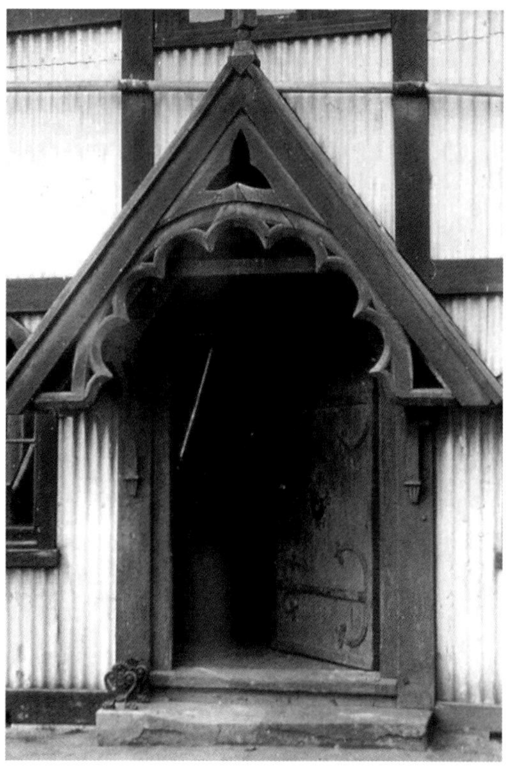

As an experienced professional architect, familiar with contemporary architectural debates, Mountfort's ability to exploit the visual qualities of corrugated iron is understandable. For an amateur designer to achieve comparable results suggests a more widespread appreciation of the architectural potential of corrugated iron. The Synod Hall and Library, built for the Diocese of Christchurch on the grounds of Christ's College in 1873, was a more prestigious and prominent building than either Christchurch Hospital or the Lyttelton Gaol. The use of corrugated iron to house criminals and the sick suggests that corrugated iron was a marginal material; a building to house the deliberations of Canterbury's Anglican hierarchy gave it unprecedented respectability. Its architect was Dr A.C. Barker, the physician best known as a photographer in early Christchurch.[24] Barker and Mountfort were friends and must have discussed the possibilities of the new material.

The Synod Hall was a curious structure

with an apsidal west end and a raised clerestory, a gabled entrance lobby and windows with pointed gothic heads. The walls were of corrugated iron, laid vertically over an exposed internal frame of timber, with facings of timber, including elaborately carved barge-boards over the entrance. In a manner that would have pleased those wits who claimed that things were done in a contrary manner in the Antipodes, the traditional material is hidden on the interior while the unconventional, modern material is boldly stated on the exterior, the reverse of the situation at the Oxford Museum. Sadly, this strikingly idiosyncratic building was demolished in 1919 to make way for Cecil Wood's Memorial Dining Hall.[25]

St Alban the Martyr, St Bathans, 1873 [top] and the Naseby Athenaeum, 1865 [bottom] (School of Fine Arts, University of Canterbury [top] and Maniototo Early Settlers' Museum [bottom])

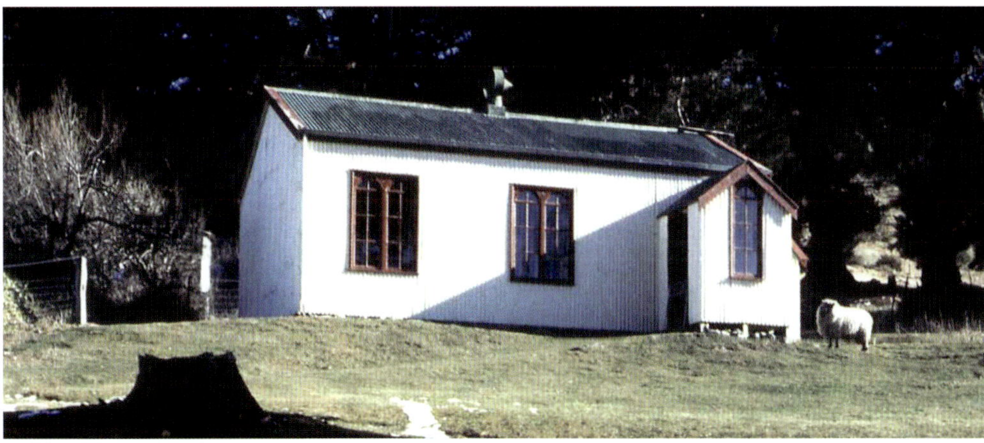

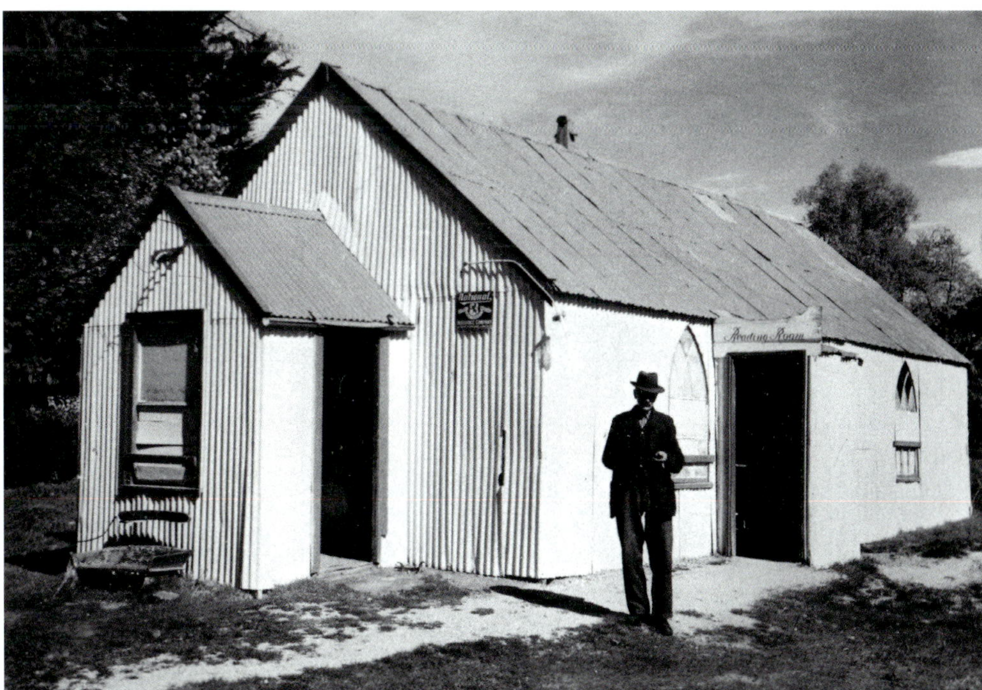

The use of corrugated iron as a roofing material on the many timber gothic country churches that are scattered across the country from Northland to the deep south is a familiar feature of the New Zealand landscape, the building type being given iconic status in W.A. Sutton's 1950 painting, *Nor'wester in the Cemetery* (Auckland City Art Gallery). Comparatively rare are gothic churches both roofed and clad in corrugated iron. Such buildings appeared in areas such as the Otago goldfields, where speed and economy of construction were paramount.

Naseby's modest corrugated iron gothic Union Church was built in 1865, although it was converted into the town's Athenaeum in 1873 after denominational churches began to be erected. It retains its pointed windows and vertical iron sidings although its proportions are more shed- than church-like.[26] The nearby Anglican Church of St Alban the Martyr in St Bathans was prefabricated in Britain and erected in 1883, replacing a Union Church similar to that in Naseby.[27] Like the Naseby Athenaeum, St Alban's could easily be mistaken for a humble 'tin' shed, but its rudimentary gothic character is conveyed by the pointed window heads, the steeper pitch of the porch roof and the vertical lines of its corrugated iron walls. St Alban's illustrates how a few architectural signs can transform our perceptions of a utilitarian structure in the twilight zone between self-conscious architectural design and vernacular building traditions.[28]

Peter Beaven, Farmhouse, Marlborough, 1990 (Peter Beaven)

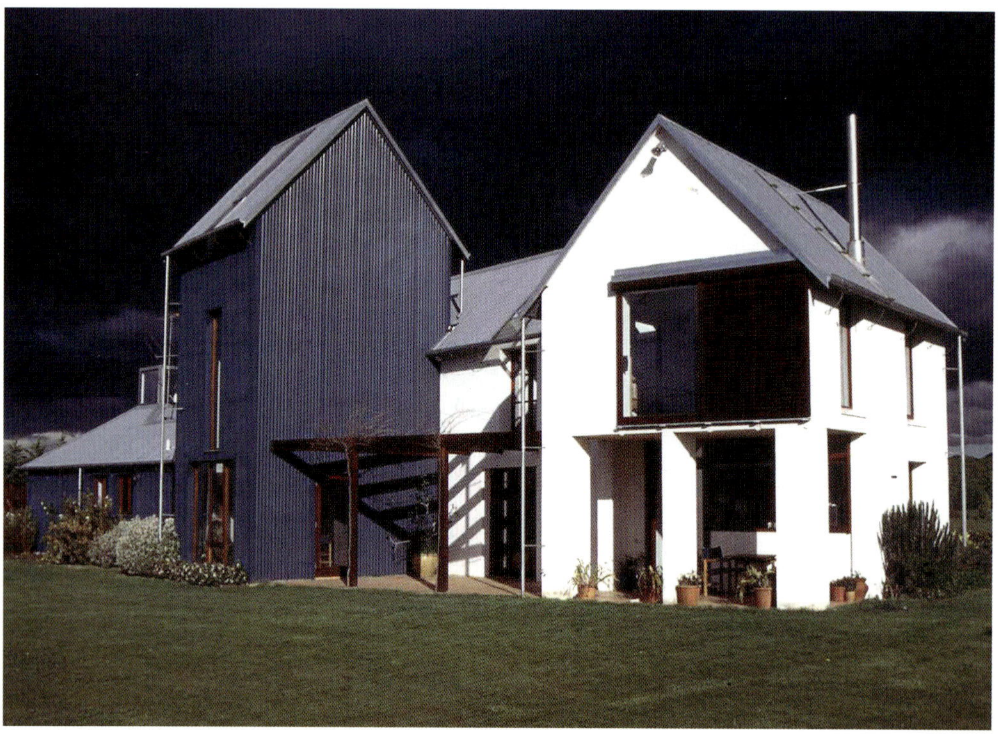

The story of corrugated iron gothic is primarily a nineteenth-century one, but its influence continued into the twentieth century. The recent popularity of corrugated iron as an architectural material, as opposed to its continuing use for utilitarian and vernacular purposes, owes much to the work of the contemporary Australian architect Glenn Murcutt.[29] Australia has its own tradition of vernacular corrugated iron buildings, and in New Zealand architects such as David Mitchell began exploiting the vernacular resonances of corrugated iron in the 1980s.[30] Peter Beaven, an architect who has consistently drawn inspiration from New Zealand's colonial gothic architecture and the works of Mountfort in particular, has also in recent years explored the vernacular tradition of corrugated iron construction. In a farmhouse near Blenheim dating from 1990 Beaven has combined those influences in a bold new expression of corrugated iron gothic.[31] The house's emphatic verticality, steeply pitched roofs and saddle-back tower are enhanced by walls of vertically-fixed corrugated iron, while a sense of the material's lightness is emphasised by the contrast provided by an adjacent wing of concrete block. In continuing to find ways of incorporating vertical corrugated iron into buildings in the expansive Canterbury landscape, Beaven suggests that corrugated iron gothic has a future as well as a past.[32]

Conclusion

Writing of the Oxford Museum, Ruskin extolled the capacity of gothic architecture to adapt itself to the requirements of new building types and the new materials made possible by the smelting of iron on an industrial scale. The 'fixed arrangement' and 'accepted proportions' of classical architecture offered no such flexibility. In colonial New Zealand the infinite adaptability of the gothic style also allowed architects like Mountfort to incorporate corrugated iron into buildings in innovative and unexpected ways. While the majority of colonial builders used corrugated iron as a cheap, utilitarian cladding to be hidden on side elevations behind pretentious classical façades, men like Mountfort and Barker gave it a status it has regained only in recent years.[33] Although corrugated iron has become a universally available industrial material, it is now paradoxically recognised as an essential part of New Zealand's vernacular building tradition. For an artist like Jeff Thomson corrugated iron is the quintessential New Zealand material, as much part of the culture as the iconic images he sculpts from its seemingly intractable flat sheets.[34] Yet more than a century before Thomson began to use it as a material for art, corrugated iron had been transformed, through the alchemy of gothic, into a material of unexpected expressive possibilities.

Incised Skin and Other Spurs

Ye shall not round the corners of your head, neither shall thou mar the corners of thy beard. Ye shall not make any cuttings in your flesh for the dead, nor print any marks upon you …

Leviticus 19: 27–8

Images by Christopher Braddock

Text by Mark Jackson

Loss of Faith

How might we understand the drift of this word 'gothic' as it migrates across continents, across centuries and across cultures such that it might find a destination in New Zealand of the twenty-first century and in particular have some relevance to the singularity of the art practice of Christopher Braddock? Would New Zealand 'gothic' bear any of the traces of a medieval thinking of this word as it became applied to architecture in the twelfth century, or would it still trace a nineteenth-century British revival of 'gothic' as it became the connotation of 'Catholic' moral values expressed in architecture? And would it extend to another coinage of this word 'gothic' with respect to nineteenth-century literature that we especially associate with Edgar Allan Poe and the American Gothic horror genre, not to mention Poe's equally celebrated French translator, Charles Baudelaire, and his enigmatic overture to modernity in the literary masterpiece *Les fleurs du mal*?

It is perhaps the gothic novel that has most significantly carried through to the twentieth century, as resurrected, translated and reframed in the broad genre of horror cinema. A touchstone here would be Ken Russell's *Gothic*, which famously celebrates the sixteenth of June as the date Mary Shelley conceived her 'gothic' hero Dr. Frankenstein and the animation of the machinic. (This date is coincidently, within another literary genre, Bloomsday, another day of fecund re-Joycing). Would it now make any sense to take the genre of 'gothic' as more than the kitsch of popular culture? Would one want to seriously engage in the gothic, or has it levelled out to a suburban subdivision of schlock Elm streets? How would one even account for that drift from medieval architecture to a horror literary genre in such a way that something essential and serious is maintained and is still at stake in a contemporary art practice in New Zealand that would willingly appropriate the modality 'gothic'? Our aim here, in addressing these questions, is to briefly trace a lineage or legacy of the gothic from medieval thinking to the nineteenth century, so that we might get a sense of some continuity that we can see being maintained and activated in the art works of Christopher Braddock.

Let us start in our explanation with the notion, from Saint Augustine, of

'Mary', *2001, 600 x 600 mm, cibachrome*

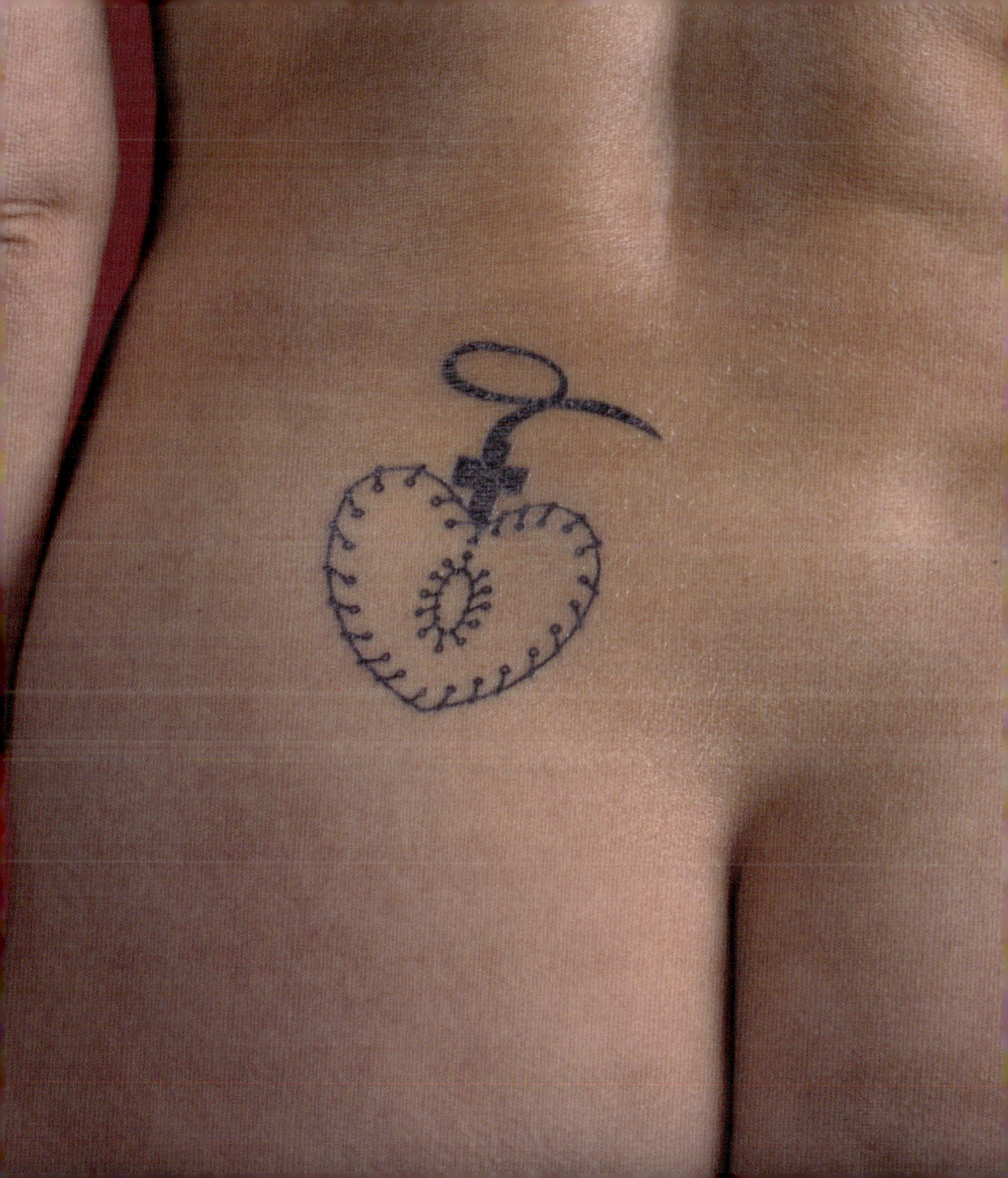

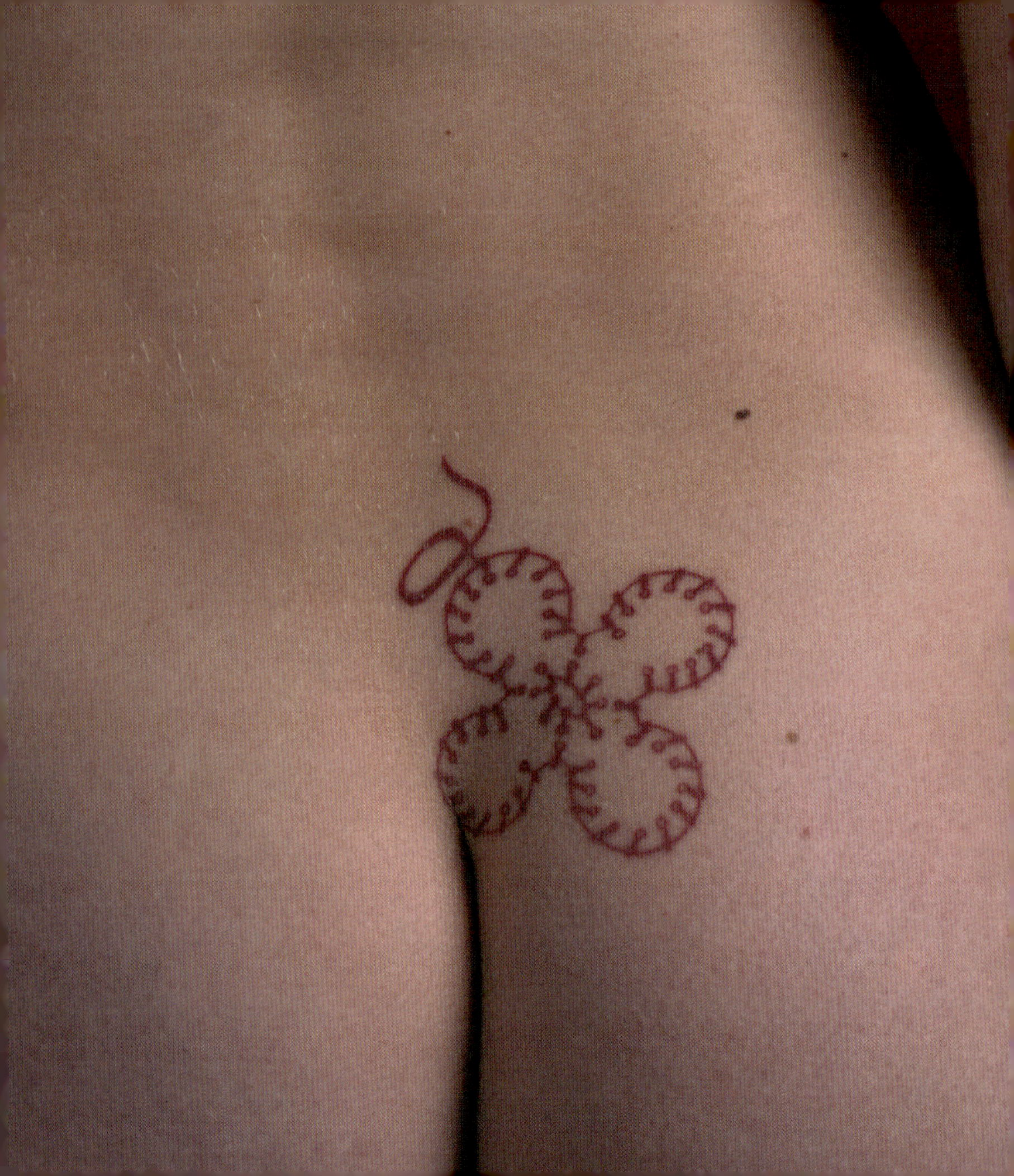

the 'breath of life' and the 'dust of the ground'. The human soul, though recognised as immortal, was held to be the organising and unifying principle of the body itself, rather than a substance independent of it. A plant was thought to exist as a plant and not as a copy of the idea of a plant. The existence of God was believed to be demonstrable from his creation rather than as an ideal that comes before all creation. This notion of demonstration is crucial. The medieval world, with its monotheistic God, saw in everything the work of God's creation. The word 'demonstration' and the word 'monster' come from the same root, the Latin *monstrare*, to show.

At the heart of Medieval Scholastic thinking at the time gothic architecture emerged (around 1140 AD) was the task of writing a permanent peace treaty between faith and reason. To reconcile faith and reason meant to use reason not to prove faith, but to make clear (*manifestare*) the doctrines of faith. This making clear by human reason is a demonstration of the revelation of God in things in this world, the soul inhabiting the body of things. Making clear, manifestation, is the first controlling principle of Scholasticism. To manifest faith by reason first required that reason – as a system of thought – had its completeness and limits. That is to say, reason itself had to be made clear so that reason could then clarify faith. But reason was made clear by appeal to imagination, as in the formal schema of works of art, architecture and literary presentation. Imagination in turn was made clear by appeal to the senses. The senses themselves were considered to have a kind of intelligence. It was in architecture that this principle of making clear achieved its greatest triumph. As High Scholasticism was governed by the principle of *manifestato*, so High Gothic architecture was dominated by the principle of transparency.

So, while we now look at gothic architecture as a fascinating architectural style of a past culture, we need also to recognise how it embodies or expresses in a complex way the fragility of faith in the face of reason, or the massive danger that knowing this earthly world could sever us from God, producing the entire surrender of the sacred to the profane. If transparency was paramount it is because of the dangers of darkness in the risk of a loss of faith. The disintegration of late medieval thinking led in two directions, one on the side of faith and mysticism and the other on the side of reason, in the emergence of humanism and empirical science. Indeed, human reason and science will come with modernity to constitute a new enlightenment, tantamount to the death of God, or the sacred only becoming recognisable in its representations, which is to say in the profane world of things.

We might begin to think of the nineteenth-century gothic literary genre as a literary production that takes up Scholasticism's sacred and profane but from something like an inverted trajectory. It concerns itself intimately with the breath of life and dust of the earth, with faith and

'Bathsheba', *2001, 600 x 600 mm, cibachrome*

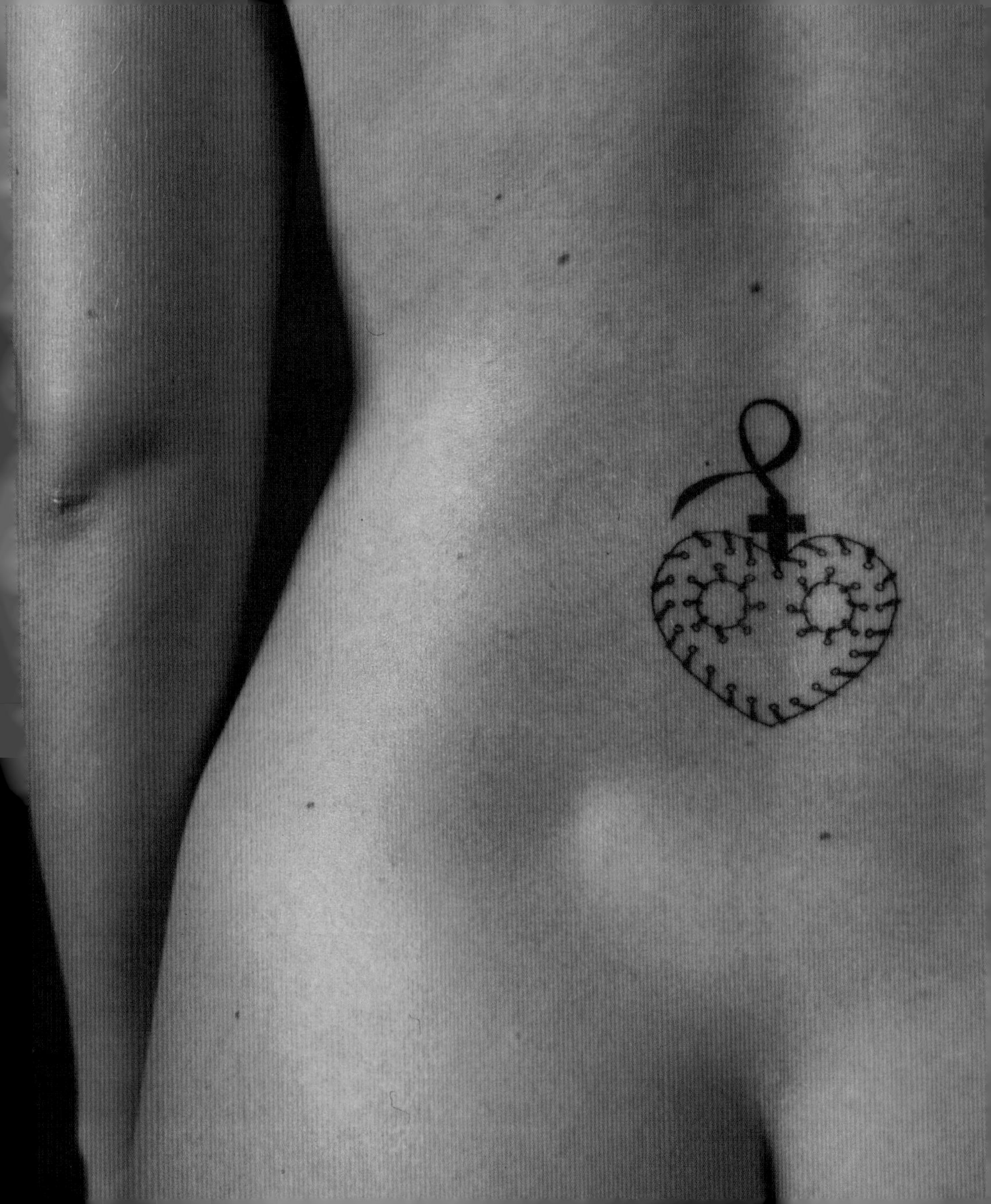

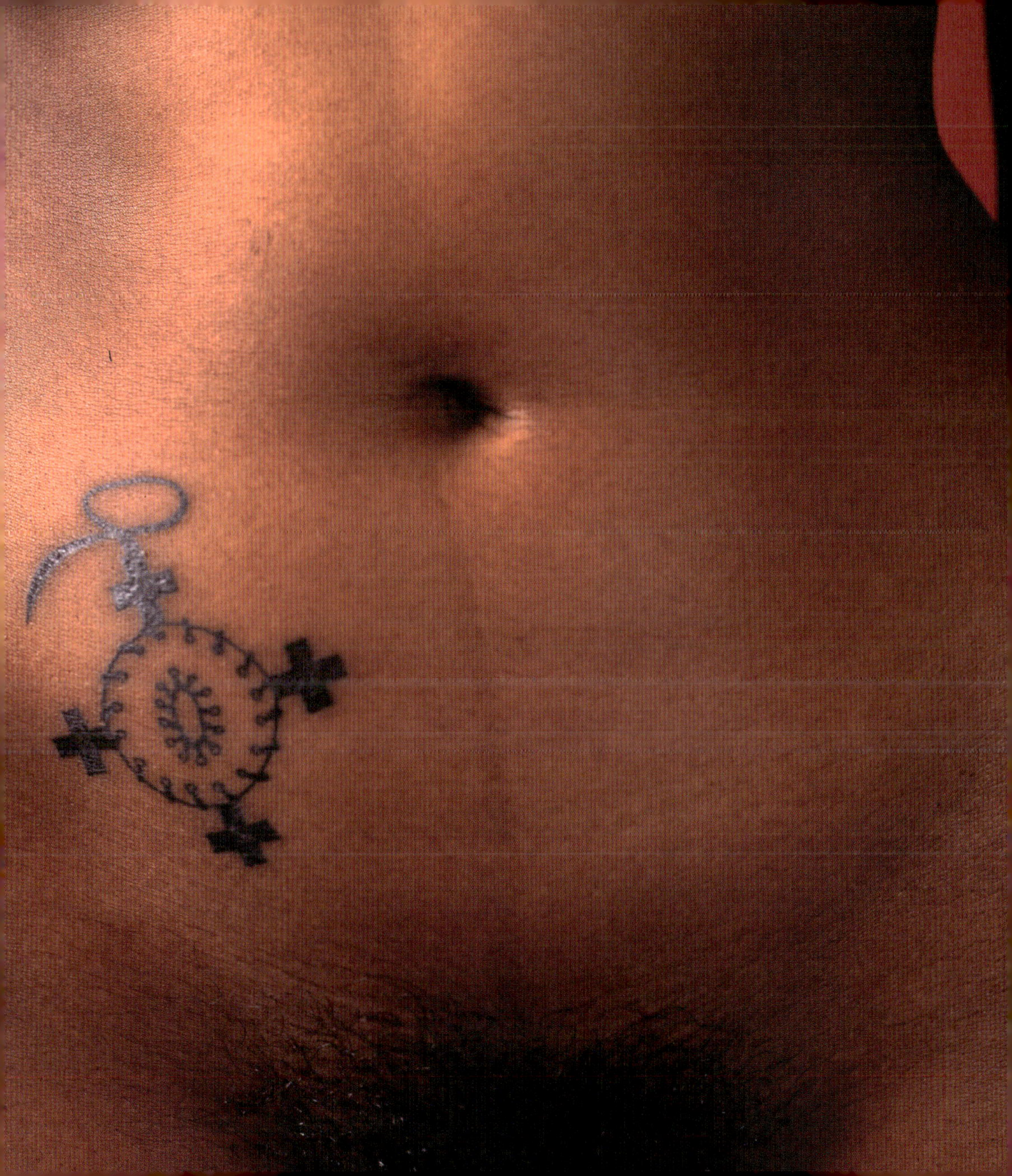

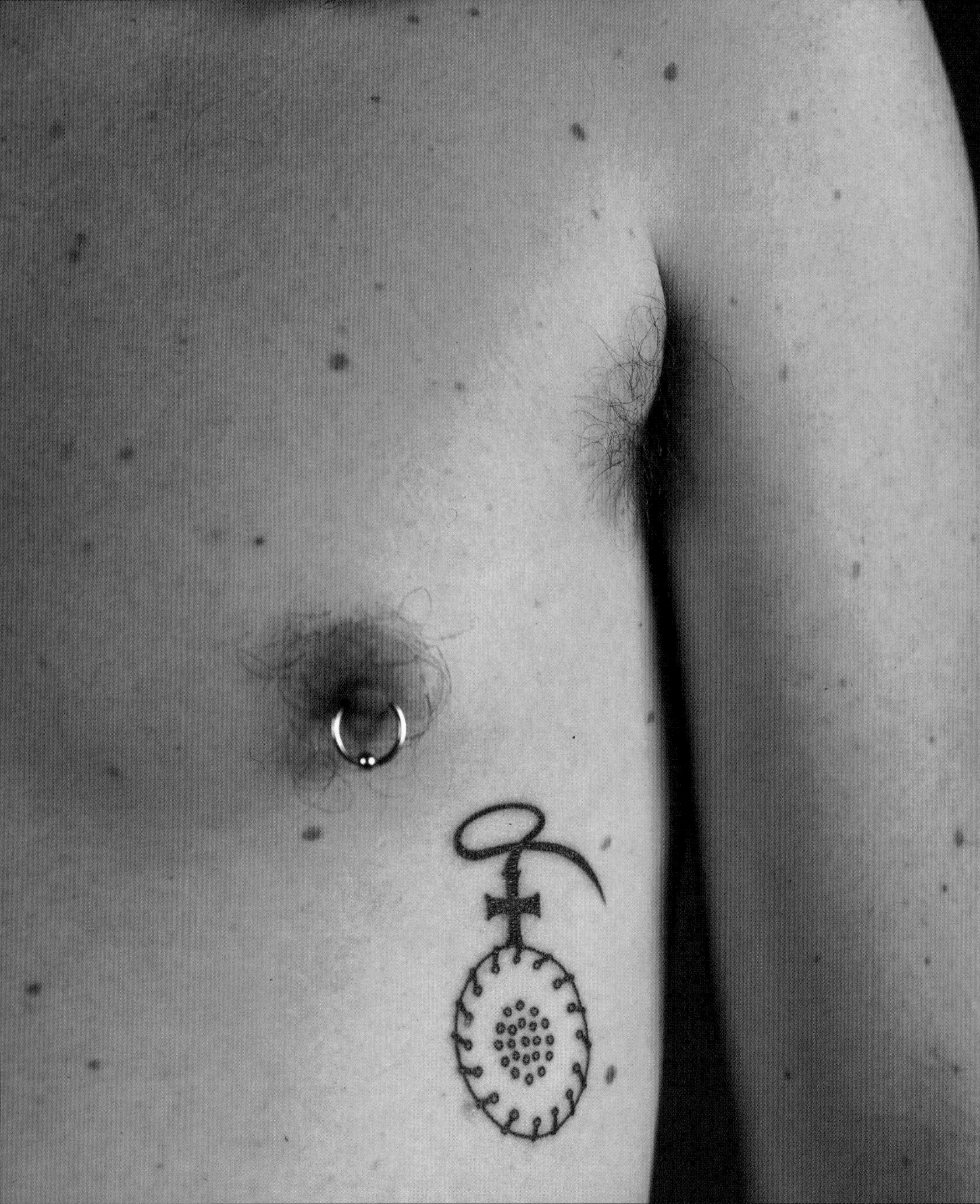

Poe introduces detection as a key, which suggests that it is this world of things that is a mystery to solve. Equally, it is the dark interior of a human soul, its force or spirit that is in need of explanation. And it is the harnessing of the profane world of science that unleashes human invention as the animation of the world – scientific reason giving birth to strange forces of unreason that will inevitably wreak havoc on this world. The early twentieth century will find a name and site for these forces deep in the interiority of reasonable humanity. It will name that site the 'unconscious' and the catalyst 'perverse desire'. The sexualised body will come to present the great enigma to reason, and this body of drives and passions will become the location of a new pact with reason. The gothic will come in the twentieth century to inhabit the polymorphous interiority of the human as its double but also as reason's very reason, faith in a reason that limits the perversity of the human. The sacred becomes the manifestation in ritual performance of a double sacrifice of the human: the divine is to be found neither by reason nor by the senses. We are fallen humanity. The gothic is our profane recourse to the utter profanity of sacred ritual. And it is death, the spaces of death, that figure the meeting of the finitude of the human and the infinity of the sacred or divine. Death and the rituals of death, forces of darkness and the negation of the divine, figure large in the modern gothic as a profane sublimation of the name of God. This profanity of the sublime marks the enigmatic impossibility of the finite reasoning the infinite.

The Tattooed Body

The early twentieth-century Austrian architect Adolf Loos is notable for the significant innovation he presented in the formalism of modern architecture. In a celebrated essay, 'Ornament and Crime', Loos associates ornamentation with degeneracy, evil and the primitive. Loos also provides an account of the origins of architecture in the simple grave, in the site or space of the dead. His scenario is gothic in its import. One is walking through a forest and stumbles upon a mound in the earth of the forest floor. This encounter is an interruption to one's path and causes one to halt and recognise that a body lies buried here. It is an unmarked site, free of the rituals of building, the additions or ornaments of building. It shows human finitude. For Loos it shows the essential in architecture. We would want to find an intimacy between these two scenes of architecture for Loos, an essential concern with death and a degeneracy that marks the ornamental. They are both expressed in a concern with bodies, those living and those dead, and in this they return us to that essential realm of

'Aaron', *2001, 600 x 600 mm, cibachrome*

the gothic, in its negotiation between the breath of life and the dust of the ground. While we easily recognise Loos's architectural formalism to be far removed from the ornamental detailing of gothic architecture, what essentially concerns him coincides absolutely with relations of the sacred to the profane. The ornamental in its degeneracy, its profanity and degradation, will be defined by reference to the tattooing of bodily flesh.

Hence, Loos famously associates the tattoo with ornamental degeneracy: 'The Papuan covers with tattoo his skin, his boat, his oar, in short anything in reach'. The tattoo may be thought of as a symbolic scar, ambivalently a mark of social identity and a mark of difference. It is physical harm directed at oneself, thereby conferring invulnerability, a protective wrapping. The tattoo is not a covering but an incision. It cuts open the skin to create another skin under the skin, confusing the difference between surface and interior, especially so with Polynesian tattoos where the pattern is the unpigmented skin. This dislocation of interior and exterior was significant for Loos, whereby the tattoo was read as an opening to the interior, with its disgust. Also exposed is the possibility that there is no interior, only the scar of social existence, a social inscription. We might think of this as an exterior with no interior, coming from another, for another's gaze. Often tattoos are invisible to the one who wears them. This would imply there is no expression of the inner self. One is here totally and socially excribed: no soul, a savage. For Loos, the modern self who tattoos herself is a delinquent or a degenerate.

Looking Away

To view a tattoo is already to be in a position of seduction, a body looking at a body intrinsically sexualised, where the tattoo's locale reflects on the erotic possibilities of the body. Voyeuristic looking requires and promotes distance between selves, while narcissistic identification promotes at least the illusion that the image is a mirror. It is the ambivalence of this near and far, voyeurism and narcissism, the seeable and the unseeable, that establishes the economy for Christopher Braddock's series of tattoo images. This economy also establishes a resonance between tattoo and taboo, between the doubling of a skin incision and a realm of prohibitions, profanities and the sacred.

These works insist most intensely on censorship and obscenity as well as establish the closest proximity between the possibility of prohibition and the creation of work in general. This would be the possibility for transgression: that there is law, and that it constitutes prohibition. We might associate this law within a legacy of the gothic, a law ambivalently sacred and profane. Without the possibility of transgression, there never would be law. And the inscription of law guarantees the possibility of transgression. Braddock never ceases to work on and within this paradox, which is the condition in general for an ethics of labour, of work. Fallen humanity is destined to labour, to make works whose ordering principles attempt to regain paradise, paradise of this world and not that of a life after life. In the profanity of work we attempt to approach the infinite, the sacred, and the divine; the greatest profanities will be those that invert the rituals and objects, the spaces and materials of the sacred, as a turning away from God in a detour through gothic darkness. In the feign of a turning to God, the mere quotation of the sacred, we cannot escape the significance of the ecclesiastical within Braddock's work, an alert to concerns with religion, belief, spirituality, ritual and the realm of the sacred, which yet open a space of their inversion or subversion. This realm is established through ritualised repetitions, marking out a space of difference, invoking the domain of otherness to profanity within the profanity of bodily labour. Braddock goes to the heart of this divide, folding a certain iconography of religion onto the profane body of Loos's degenerates: the tattoo.

The tattoo motifs are designs derived from Braddock's long-standing encounter with sacred heart imagery, the Christian mystery of the infinite becoming finite, God becoming human, the sacred becoming profane and thereby redeeming fallen humanity. These images of the sacred heart present, in one sense, merely a display of earlier themes. On the other hand, though, this display is doubled. The designs are inscribed onto flesh in a manner that makes them a permanent trace, a body surface that is also the bearer of the artwork. These tattooed designs, as if to amplify that uncertain distance separating the sacred and the ecstasy of sensualised or passionate bodies, inscribe the skin of the breast or the buttocks or the lower stomach. But what is actually being exhibited here? Are we engaging with the photographic, or are these photographs merely the medium for exposing the bodies that are the work? Or are the bodies merely the medium for exposing the tattoo motifs? Or does Braddock fold three moments of exposition or manifestation? And what of the relay between image, body and motif? If these questions arise, it is because this work insists so crucially on the very conditions of the work's appearances, on the manifestation or revelation of appearances, on the manifestation of the sacred heightened in the sensualised or sensationalised image of the ecclesial motif incised, spurred into flesh. Braddock here brings to such proximity the sacred and bodily flesh, a turning to a contemplation of the darkening opacities at work in this artwork, some thing made radically and impossibly absent by the labour of incision on living bodies which will never make their presence visible within the space of exhibition.

This infinite deferral of the appearance of the work coincides with the exorbitant presence of what is there to make up for that loss. And this would be the work's most profound resonance with the sacred: a compensatory labour for an infinite loss. This labour, like the gothic's profane sacred, would be a useless expenditure, a labour that produces nothing, that does not ground itself or a thinking of the body on the basis of utility and reason. With this sacred, there is nothing inside, no soul, no divine centre that shores up our humanness. Rather, it is perhaps the tattoo motif, as surface scarification, as a kind of writing of oneself, a kind of excription that so poignantly alerts us to a profane reverie constituting the sacred self. And the oscillation between photographic surface, scarified skin and inked motif is not a movement to any sense of interior. Rather, each is the bearer of the simple notion that to be touched at all, by anything, only happens with the intensities of affective surfaces.

The Horror of Power

'The horror, the horror': we may recollect Joseph Conrad's gothic geography of Africa and Kurtz's heart of darkness. If Conrad yet made something sacred of this heart of black Africa, in another scene Francis Ford Coppola, in *Apocalypse Now*, tattoos this heart onto the fleshy bulk of American culture. What is that economy that seems to operate between power and horror, between the power of horror and the horror that is harboured in the coalescing and excising of power? We may consider in this vein, for example, W.J.T. Mitchell's *Landscape and Power* and his account of a nineteenth-century recourse to the sublime in the depiction of colonial New Zealand, as if to undo the picturesque tradition's taming or domesticating of the land. The sublime shows a savage nature that overwhelms its human presence, a force that we humans cannot match. Geographies of the gothic, their colonial geographies, move along these fault lines of nature's abyss that seem to swallow the best of human endeavours; these faults rip the earth to release chthonic forces, underworld forces, dark and subterranean forces. Gothic hearts of darkness construe the sacred, the heart of the sacred, rising from these earthly vents, as a nature to be subdued, equal to the dark interiors of civilizing or savage peoples. And in New Zealand nothing could reckon with the missionary zeal of a sacral civility, a burning Sacred Heart of Christo[1] logical purity, a scorched-earth policy of clearing and cleansing, an admonition to the savagery of the tattoo. The horror of power does not operate on the drawing of territorial maps. It happens on the brutalising of bodies; on wounds, scars, maiming and killing; on the decimation of peoples; on the rights of victors to write their history. No irony is lost here in the coincidence of body scarification, religious iconography, tattooing practice and the ultimate opacity of the body in its imaged representing. Braddock enacts all of the horror of the rituals of power and conquest that come to bear on colonial takings, and on the gothic geographies of power that have figured the taking place of New Zealand.

Tattoo designs and photographs by Christopher Braddock. Thanks to the models, Otis Frizzell for tattooing, and Carolyn Kingscott for photographic assistance.

Underworlds Down Under: Under the Mountain and The Navigator

Elizabeth Hale

They reckon there's a hole up there so deep that if you dropped a stone in it, it would come out on the other side of the world.

The Navigator: A Mediaeval Odyssey

Vincent Ward's 1988 fantasy epic *The Navigator: A Mediaeval Odyssey* envisions New Zealand as a place where the sins of the world can be expiated and evil can be purged. A group of medieval pilgrims tunnel to the other side of the world from their remote mining village in Cumbria, in the far north of England. They believe that they are travelling to 'God's City', which one of them has seen in a dream vision; their task is to place a cross, forged from Cumbrian copper, on the steeple of the great church. They make this sacrificial offering in order to cleanse their village of the plague, the Black Death that has laid waste to Europe. As they tunnel through the earth, they also tunnel through time, to modern-day Auckland. When they reach Auckland they find that, despite the bright lights of its buildings, God's City is an underworld down under: its people are isolated from one another, loomed over by soulless buildings and machines, and lacking in community and faith. Unlike the upper world, where a literal plague encroaches upon the survival of a tight-knit village community, Auckland is under threat from diseases of the soul and of society. The pilgrims are successful in raising the cross; in so doing, they purify their own village of the plague, and restore faith and communal values to Auckland.

Maurice Gee's 1979 children's novel *Under the Mountain* explores similar themes of sin, expiation, and purgation by fire. It depicts a world in imminent threat of destruction by a group of plundering aliens, giant super-intelligent worms with shape-shifting abilities called *The People of the Mud Who Conquer and Multiply*. These worms masquerade as a human family called Wilberforce, living in the Auckland suburb of Takapuna. Their headquarters extend underneath the harbour, reached by a network of slimy tunnels which link to the various volcanic outpoints in the city. There, they wait and plan for the day when they will have the strength to change the Earth to their preferred habitat, a sea of cold mud. Meanwhile, Mr Jones, a representative from the worms' ancient enemy, a good race of aliens called *The People Who Understand*, is gathering strength to battle them. He selects a pair of New Zealand children, twins from a farming community who have telepathic abilities, and hence have the power to use weapons developed by his race. When the twins come to Auckland to visit their uncle and aunt, Mr Jones begins training them to use their weapons and to fight the Wilberforce worms. The novel culminates in a final battle that leads to a cataclysmic eruption which destroys much of the city, but the Wilberforces are vanquished, and the globe is saved.

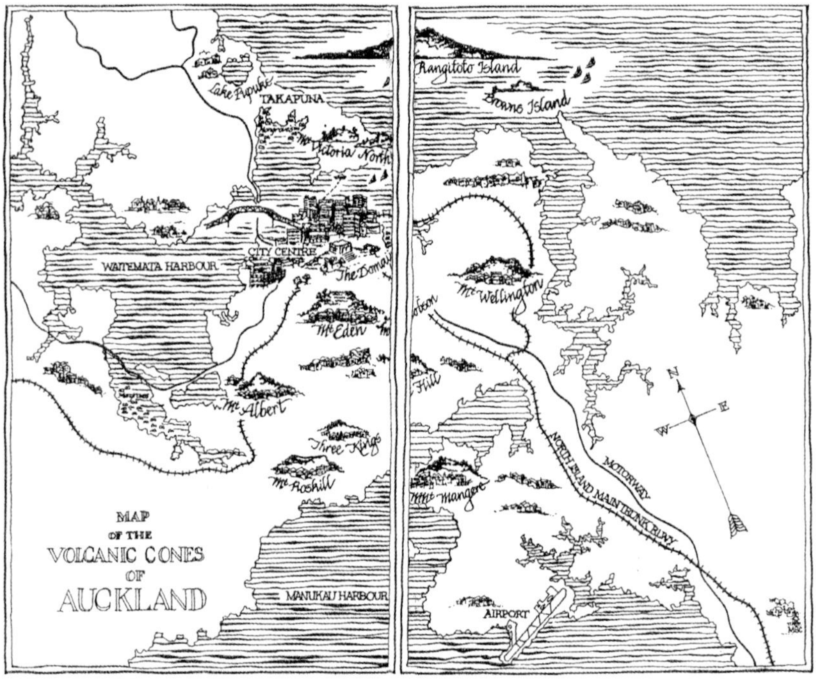

Underground map of Auckland, frontispiece from Under the Mountain, *1982. Wellington: Oxford University Press*

Under the Mountain and *The Navigator* depart from the image of rural isolation so common in gothic New Zealand film and literature.[1] Instead of emphasizing the loneliness of New Zealand's geographical isolation, they reconnect the country to the rest of the world by exploiting the idea of the antipodes as a kind of underworld, an infernal realm existing close to, but separate from and literally below the northern hemisphere. They suggest that the skin between upper and lower worlds is particularly thin in New Zealand, whose volcanic geography and seismic upheaval make it particularly appropriate to act as an infernal realm. This gothic vision, then, incorporates concepts of urban and suburban gothic, science fiction and the natural world, as well as Christian and classical ideas of Hell and the underworld.

Urban Gothic: The Vulnerable City

The city came down to the sea, the wharves jutted out, ships lay in the harbour – and out beyond the North Shore, Rangitoto turned dark as the sun went down behind the western ranges. Rachel stared at the island. 'It's a volcano,' she said. 'Or was. I read about it. Rangitoto means bleeding skies.'[2]

From the beginning, *Under the Mountain* sets up a tension between human endeavour and the raw and destructive power of nature. We see this most clearly in the way that the city is blanketing itself over the land, in a suburban sprawl that contrasts with the idealised 'white cottage with flowers growing wild over its lawns' that belongs to Mr Jones, the representative of the good aliens.[3] To make these identikit streets of concrete, manufactured suburban houses, nature is paved over, represented grotesquely by 'plaster seals with bird-baths on their noses'.[4] A further defiance of the natural order can be seen in the mansion of the twins' Uncle Clarry, which is 'made of glass with only ribs of concrete holding it together'; it juts out over the water, resembling 'a flying saucer ready to take off'.[5] Touches like these indicate a collective turning away from the natural environment, and from one another. The twins thus feel both an urban alienation, where they are shut out from the warmth of human contact, and an alienation from the landscape, which can become menacing without warning. To extend his analysis of the city's alienation from nature, Gee draws a parallel between the Wilberforces' brutality and what humans themselves have done to the earth. Mr Jones explicitly compares the Wilberforces to human political leaders: 'They're creatures of tremendous will – no imagination, no feeling, no conscience. They remind me of some of the leaders of your race'.[6] The twins' battle with the Wilberforce aliens thus symbolises the need for contemporary society to cleanse itself, to eliminate its polluting forces; the cataclysmic ending to the novel shows that the effort required is huge, and that such a battle is won only with great difficulty.

Similar themes of pollution, and human responsibility for that pollution, run through *The Navigator*. They are accompanied by a sense of the role that the metropolis has played in alienation from nature, and an alienation from human contact. The medieval miners, who, like Rachel and Theo, are rural visitors to the city, make an implicit commentary on the city's problems simply by wandering through it. Startled by the fast-moving vehicles, terrifying machinery, and bright lights of the skyscrapers, they provide a central image of the contrast between humanity and the city, between antiquity and modernity, and between old and new models of community. In particular, *The Navigator* takes swipes at the emptiness of corporate culture (by showing the shells of skyscrapers, aglow at night but devoid of life), at the human cost of redundancies (in the group of laid-off foundry workers who help the pilgrims forge their cross and place it on the spire), and at the threat that nuclear power and weaponry offer to our security (in the magnificent set piece, where a submarine surfaces underneath the pilgrims as they cross the harbour in a rowboat).

In exposing contemporary social problems, *The Navigator* brings the gothic to Auckland, literally and symbolically. The shaft the miners dig comes out in a sewer beneath the city; indeed, sewers are a common motif in urban gothic, representing the dark underbelly of society, a place for refuse and the rejected. (As one of the pilgrim miners observes, 'Only great cities have them. Underground sewers where every household can empty its bucket'.) As they come from a gothic age (the Middle Ages), their understanding of the metropolis is essentially gothic. Thus, frightening beasts seem to them to roam the city in the form of giant machines, such as rubbish-dump graders, night-trains, and even a nuclear-powered submarine, each with a counterpart in the medieval bestiary. One pilgrim, Connor, is taken for a terrifying ride when he is trapped at the front of a night-train resembling the medieval 'wyrm', a serpent-like beast known for devastating fields and farms. And the nuclear submarine that rises up from beneath the pilgrims as they row across the harbour in a small boat is the Leviathan, the sea beast that lures unwary sailors onto its back by pretending to be an island, then drowns them by plunging abruptly beneath the surface.

This concept of an isolated, small nation fighting a large battle holds as true for medieval Cumbria as for present-day Auckland. The mining village's fight against the Black Death mirrors New Zealand's defiant anti-nuclear policy, as Vincent Ward explains:

> So you have two isolated pockets fending off a threat that has the potential for annihilation, in one case it's the Black Death which wiped out almost two-thirds of Europe, in the other case it's the nuclear threat which has the same potential. It's a clear analogy. They both take measures, entailing giant acts of faith – in the Mediaevals' case it's religious faith because it's in the context of their culture – to try and avert that threat.[68]

Both of these stories, then, link New Zealand firmly to the rest of the world through this sense of urgency: what happens here is globally significant.

Redemption and Sacrifice in Purgatory Down Under

Martin: God's Goodness! It makes sense. Anything flat's got two sides and if evil was our side then surely God's goodness would be on this one! Oh, it's God's city all right. Can you see his great church?

Griffin: No …

Searle:	But nothing's higher than a church spire!
Martin:	It must be God's City. There's so much light. (*The Navigator*)

When Vincent Ward talks about how the medieval concept of the antipodes influenced his construction of *The Navigator*, he touches on the notion of the antipodes as an underworld, an infernal realm:

> [This] is the idea of the antipodes, literally the opposite foot. The belief, which I think was Greek and inherited by the Mediaevals, was that there was a continent at the bottom of the world which matched the continent at the top of the world, an exact mirror image. And the Mediaevals believed that here were people who walked on their heads, had one eye in the centre of their forehead, and used one big foot as an umbrella against the boiling sun. We were in a place beyond heaven and hell, beyond redemption, beyond the boiling sea.[8]

It is a Eurocentric idea that the northern hemisphere is at the 'top' of the world and the southern hemisphere is at the 'bottom'. The

Gustave Doré, 'The Destruction of Leviathan' (1865)

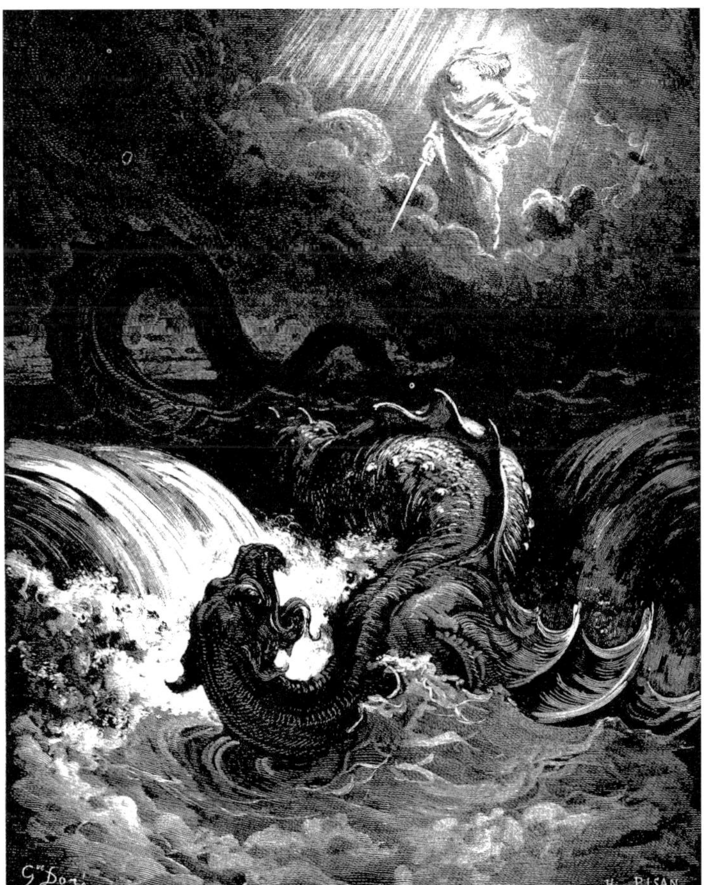

medieval pilgrims of Ward's story assume that when they tunnel through the earth they are tunnelling downwards: if they think about it much, they might fear that by tunnelling thus they will encounter a netherworld, akin to Hell or Hades. Certainly, they are taking part in a long literary tradition of associating Down Under with infernal realms, as well as a long tradition in literature of heroic quests to the underworld. The Greek literary hero Odysseus talks in Hades with the ghost of Hector in the *Iliad*; there, too, the Roman hero Aeneas encounters the ghosts of Dido and his father in the *Aeneid,* while, in British literature, Alice's journey to Wonderland takes her down to what she thinks might be the 'Antipathies'.

The term 'infernal' comes from the Latin 'infernus', meaning 'below' or 'underground'; it is associated with the classical idea of the 'shades', an underworld where the souls of the dead reside, or with the Christian connotation of Hell, where the souls of the damned are eternally tortured after death. Ward's medieval pilgrims certainly are confronted with the hellish aspects of night-time Auckland life, especially as represented by the mechanical bestiary discussed earlier. But because they have tunnelled through the earth to escape the 'evil' rampant on their own side of the world, they are less willing to consign Auckland to the forces of Darkness than perhaps their modern viewers are. They are confused by the lack of religion in the city ('but nothing's higher than a church spire!'), but glad to make their offering, and in fact to restore religious faith to this godless God's city. So, although the Auckland that the film represents may seem infernal – populated as it is with savage beasts in the form of mindless machines, devoted to Mammon in the form of big business, and under constant threat of fiery annihilation as represented by the nuclear submarine – it is not precisely an urban, modern hell that they travel to.

Similarly, the Auckland of *Under the Mountain* is not precisely hell, either. Certainly it is located at the bottom of the globe; certainly the skin between upper and lower worlds is thinner here than anywhere else. Certainly it, too, is under threat from fiery annihilation, a threat that is in fact partly carried out when Rangitoto erupts. But it is also a profoundly human place. Rachel, the humanist, reminds us constantly that the city is populated not with beasts, but with people, who build sports grounds and hospitals, borrow books from libraries and walk on the beach with their children. The Auckland of *Under the Mountain* is caught between the Wilberforces' sinister tunnellings below the city and the menacing volcano of the title. The Wilberforces, should they get their way, will reduce the earth to a kind of Hades, the cold, limbo-like underworld of classical mythology, rather than to a fiery Hell. But what lies in store for the city is in fact the inferno.

Ultimately, the Auckland (and the world) of both stories is saved, which offers another possibility in the imaginative representation of the antipodes. Perhaps Auckland is a place where sin can be expiated, where redemption is actually possible. Not a Hieronymus Bosch painting of Hell, but one of Purgatory, a place where through great suffering, sinners can redeem themselves and ascend to Heaven.

The concept of Purgatory gained currency in medieval times, Dante Alighieri's *Purgatorio* being the most fully-fledged imagining of Mount Purgatory, where sinners would expiate their sins and ascend to heaven. According to medieval map-makers, and Dante himself, Mount Purgatory was located on our earth, exactly antipodal to Jerusalem (the centre of the Christian world). Based on this, we might find Mt Purgatory to be an unexplained outcrop (perhaps invisible to the eyes of the living) at a point equidistant between Fiji, Sydney and Auckland. Accepting such a notion might mean that instead of being a hellish outpost to which upper-world sinners must repair eternally to pay for their sins, Down Under becomes a place from which they can ascend to heaven, once they have expiated their sins.

It also becomes a place in which the world itself can be cleansed. This, I think, accounts for the fiery ending of *Under the Mountain*, in which the twins hurl their magic stones into the craters of Rangitoto and Mount Eden. A weakness in Theo's stone means that the Wilberforce worms do not simply vanish, as intended, but explode, triggering the eruption of Rangitoto:

> The mountain trembled, trembled. It gave a groaning sigh. Then everything was still … Then it came. The sky was filled with concussions, with cracking, with the scream of air torn apart. The sea buckled like tin. Over Rangitoto, over the lake, towers of fire and ash reared up like monsters in a dream. The sky turned to blood.[9]

Though Theo blames himself for the cataclysm, the city, or rather the volcanic landscape over which the city is spread, has long allowed for the possibility of this battle. It has sheltered the Wilberforces for centuries, 'under North Head and Mount Victoria, under One Tree Hill, Mount Wellington, Mount Eden, under Rangitoto, under Lake Pupuke'.[10] The porousness of the rock, the underground caverns, the volcanic outpoints into the city have all contributed to the Wilberforces' ability to survive and plan. And despite the threat that the Wilberforces represent to the Earth, it seems to me that the landscape is equally menacing. Everything in the book has been leading up to this moment, promising that Rangitoto will deliver the skies of blood of its name and that the Wilberforces will be purged by fire.

The twins themselves are depicted as agents of fire: their red heads are symbolic beacons of fire and light, as their uncle jokingly tells them. When they explore the Wilberforces' house and the tunnel beneath it, they find that the worms are wounded by light and use their torches as weapons when they are detected. Mr Jones, too, the last of *The People Who Understand*, is allied with fire, warmth and light, which he uses to different degrees to protect the twins. At the end of the novel, he exhausts himself by drawing on his natural shape – 'a huge golden-red flame that burned and flickered' – to help them out of a tunnel where they have been trapped by the worms.[11] Once he has lifted the twins out of danger, Mr Jones collapses, exhausted, and they must go on alone.

> 'My children, it is safe,' whispered Mr Jones. 'But you do right to grieve. That was the way it happened.'
> ... They raised their heads and saw a pale flame floating over the crater. It turned into a mist. The wind broke it and flung it away.
> In a little while they stood up. Under the fierce red sky they climbed down from the mountain and walked hand in hand through the streets. They found a knot of people and asked for shelter from the wind and ash.[12]

The quasi-religious tone of this ending is striking, as is its imagery of fire and light, of sacrifice and redemption, and its facing of tragedy square on. Mr Jones' sacrifice, the death of the twins' cousin Ricky, and the sacrificial role the city plays (though without being consulted) reinforce the cosmic significance and seriousness of the fight against the Wilberforces.

This imagery of light and fire, purgation and redemption, is more overtly religious still in *The Navigator*, given that it is a story about Catholic pilgrims on a quest to bring a cross to God's city. The volcanic nature of Auckland does not make itself felt in the film. But the city alternates between being the kind of underworld I have described, full of hellish beasts, and being an earthly city, though one that seems to strive towards the sky, if the Babel towers of big business that dominate the cityscape are any indication. Light and fire can be seen in two ways: in the lights of the city and in the light brought by the pilgrims. The street lights and the lights of office buildings confirm to the pilgrims that they must indeed be in God's city. But the pilgrims themselves bring light to the city in the form of the flaming torches they carry. A resonant repeating image in the film is of a torch tossed down the mine shaft, to test for depth and for quality of air. It becomes a symbol of the religious light they are bringing to God's city; it also emphasises the enormity of their journey to the underworld. Fire can be seen most significantly in the sequence at the foundry, where the image of blazing copper reinforces the idea of religious light; it also reinforces the idea of purification, of purgation by fire. Significantly, this purification cannot be carried out at home, in the miners' village. They must carry their copper ore to God's city and forge it there. So the joint effort made by Auckland foundry workers and Cumbrian miners is responsible for the purification of North and South.

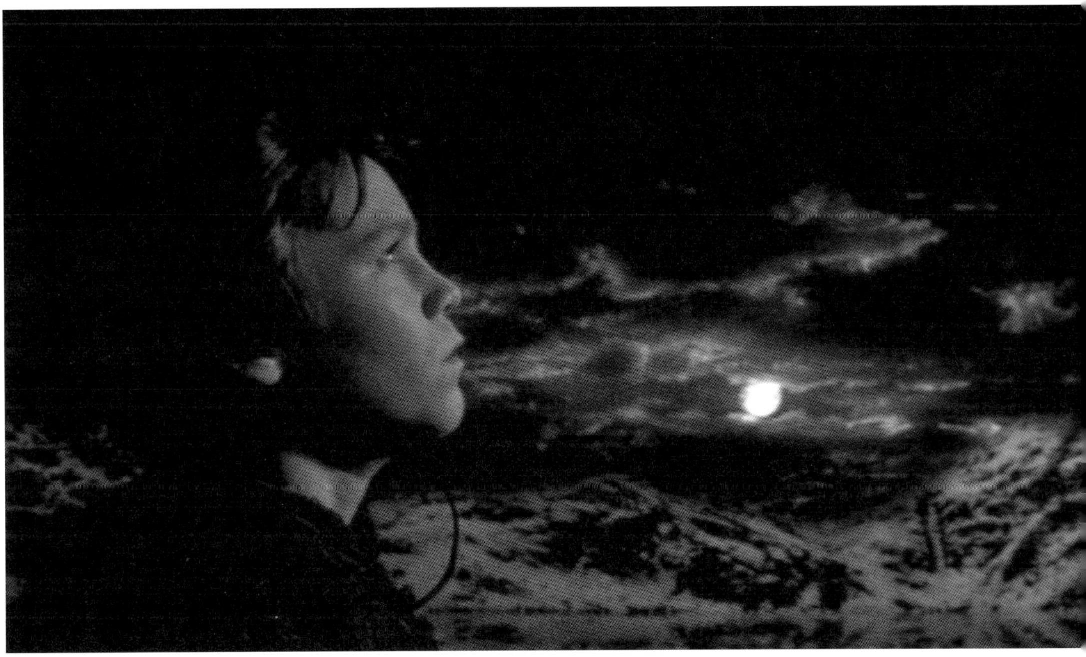

Still from The Navigator *(Vincent Ward, 1988)*

The ultimate redemptive sacrifice, of course, is the death of Griffin, the boy visionary who has dreamed the journey to God's city and who leads the miners there. He has nightmare visions of his brother, Connor, falling to his death from the spire of the cathedral, but it is he who, as the smallest and nimblest, climbs the spire to guide the cross into position. And on his return to the village, it is he who suffers the last deadly case of the plague. He is the scapegoat: the plague concentrates on him, and leaves the village alone. His death, then, purifies the village.

Griffin's is the perfect purgatorial journey, for he expiates the sins of others by suffering himself. He is not infected with the plague when he leaves the village (though Connor is); he is infected when he returns and soon dies. He is the last of the village to die from the plague; he takes the plague away with him in death. For him, the journey is like the *pharmakon*, the cure that kills. He initiates the journey downwards, the tunnel through to the other side of the earth; it is he who climbs the spire. His journey then mimicks the descent into Hell, and the ascent to Heaven, and he does it to save his brother, in which aim he is successful. And by his actions he has also purified Auckland, restoring faith and community (through gothic, or medieval, virtues) to the city.

In these stories, then, Auckland is God's city, but it is alienated from itself. It is under threat from outside forces, but it is also a threat to its own existence. It is in need of purification, but it also purifies those who visit it. Neither story resolves all these paradoxes, and indeed each ends on a tragic note. Nevertheless, Auckland is an underworld down under that is worth tunnelling to.

Well-laundered Elves: Purity and Degeneration in The Lord of the Rings

Sarah Shieff

As a viewer, I came to Peter Jackson's *The Lord of the Rings* film trilogy relatively cold – or as cold as anyone living in New Zealand could be, after exposure to several years of pre-release hype: I had avoided reading Tolkien's books as an adolescent, so had little sense of the world in which their narrative unfolds. Not many minutes into the first film, however, the archaic moral underpinnings of that world became abundantly clear: the primal conflict between the forces of good and evil which drives the story is also a racial conflict, in which the goodies are members of 'white' races, and the baddies are largely dark or misshapen. While hardly surprising in itself – Tolkien's narrative did take shape in the 1930s, after all – the films' apparently uncritical adoption of this creaky morality introduced a gnawing worm of disquiet that all the whiz-bang special effects, dishy actors and stunning New Zealand locations could not quite silence.

Races, writes Kwame Anthony Appiah, are like witches: 'however unreal witches are, *belief* in witches, like belief in races, has had – and in many communities continues to have – profound consequences for human social life'.[1] Appiah, an historian of the idea of race, makes a vital distinction between racialism and racism: both derive from the discredited but still influential belief that the world's peoples can be divided into discrete racial groups and both are at work in Tolkien's narrative. Racialism was part of educated common sense from the middle of the nineteenth century to the middle of the twentieth; it simply explained differences between people in terms of the various inherited physical characteristics and mental qualities that combine to form races. This belief can be seen in Tolkien's representation of the peoples of Middle Earth. Dwarves are short, strong and hairy, and their guttural language is the natural sign of a people who understand iron, rock and commerce. The language and bearing of the Elves mark them as an ancient and noble race. Hobbits, famously, have hairy feet and pointy ears and like nothing better than a party. Racism, racialism's close affiliate, is a mindset which arranges hierarchies of value on the same basis. Although Tolkien's apologists have gone to some length to defend him against charges of racism, his representation of evil is marked almost exclusively by race.[2] Gollum is a 'little thin black fellow'[3] and the Uruk-hai warriors also tend to be black.[4] The evil servants of Saruman who enslave the Shire while the Hobbits are on their quest are ill-favoured half-breed men, with squint eyes and sallow faces.[5] The traitorous but 'wise-faced' Gríma Wormtongue, with his fawning ways, wizened body and heavy-lidded eyes, is a caricature Jew.[6] In fact, the entire movement of Tolkien's plot is predicated on the racialist assumption that the 'white' – i.e. 'Western' – races of Middle Earth are able to form an effective fellowship because they share certain positive, fundamentally spiritual values: loyalty to friends, family, community and the environment. Of course the dark races of the East and South also form an alliance of sorts, but they are inclined to turn on each other when the going gets tough. These races do not have a future in the narrative, because their values are material and self-serving.

Needless to say, these tropes – dark/light, homely/unhomely, pure/corrupt, self/other – characterise gothic thinking in its most familiar forms and give the film version of *The Lord of the Rings* its most obviously gothic moments. I would argue, however, that the films' repressed awareness of its racist antecedents – Tolkien's apparently unacknowledged debt to Wagner's vast, notoriously anti-Semitic *Ring* cycle springs to mind here – produce rather more subtle gothic effects: no matter how insistently members of the films' creative team refer to the various *cultures* of Middle Earth,[7] they cannot efface the spectre of racism that haunts virtually every frame.

How much of this un-PC baggage could Jackson's film jettison, given that without it the conflicts which drive the narrative would evaporate like morning mists over Lothlórien? And what happens to that ambient racialism when the narrative is translated for a contemporary audience? Finally, what bearing, if any, might the films' New Zealand locations – an ongoing source of pride for New Zealand audiences, and of fascination for *Lord of the Rings* tourists – have on the saga, as it moves through its tropes of purity, degeneracy and race?

Questions like these are perhaps too easily assimilated within – or dismissed as – fairly predictable forms of 'political correctness'. I would instead like to find a way of reading the films which considers their too-easily moralisable oppositions between good and evil, pure and impure, white and dark much as an anthropologist might: as terms in a structural rather than a moral code. To do this it will help to think about dirt. While this may seem a trivial suggestion, a consideration of the relationship between dirt and cleanliness provides a key not only to the mechanics of the films' structuring binaries, their wider cultural associations and the hierarchy of values they imply, but to the relationship between the narrative's racialism and its environmentalism, and how these involve its New Zealand setting.

Of all the races of Middle Earth represented in the films, the Elves are the cleanest. From that point of purity, everything dirty can be measured: at the opposite pole we find the foul pits of Isengard, the slag-heaps of Mordor, and their filthy denizens. Dwarves aren't overly fastidious in their habits, but their dirt is honest working-man's dirt. Men and the Riders of Rohan are also likely to become a bit grimy in the course of their day's activities. Hobbits are basically clean creatures, although some agricultural matter may cling to their feet. Tropes of cleanliness and dirt also apply to food preferences: Orcs will eat anything, and the fouler the better; Gollum, Shelob and the Uruk-hai warriors will happily eat Orc if nothing tastier comes to hand. Hobbits like fruit: apples figure largely in their on-screen diet. Elves appear not to eat anything, but Elven lembas bread – food reduced to its ideal, sublimated form – sustains the Fellowship for much of its journey. Neither do Elves smoke or drink, and their language is the 'purest' of Middle Earth, spoken at moments of heightened emotional connection. Aragorn and Arwen speak Elvish together at Rivendell; Legolas welcomes Aragorn – presumed dead – to Helm's Deep in Elvish; Aragorn calms his horse in Elvish. From these simple positions, the film elaborates its structural vocabulary for moral degeneracy. The very clean but very corrupt Saruman is a whited sepulchre: his obvious counterparts are, on the one hand, the slightly travel-soiled (but very good) Gandalf and, on the other, the morally repugnant and physically slimy Wormtongue. Gollum was once a hobbit, but his love for the Ring has turned him into a crawling, creeping creature who eats worms and who burns at the touch of an Elven rope, which is endowed with all the virtues of the race that made it. The semiotics of cleanliness and dirt also underpin the spiritual geography of the quest. Mordor is the foulest place in Middle Earth and it besmirches all those who approach it: the more heavily the burden of Sauron's ring weighs upon Frodo, the dirtier he becomes. At the opposite pole lie the 'undying lands' Gandalf describes to Pippin during the siege of Gondor: their 'white shores', and the far green country beyond them, await those who die a hero's death.

These observations about the structural significance of dirt derive in good part from *Purity and Danger: An Analysis of Concepts of Pollution and Taboo*, Mary Douglas's influential study of pollution beliefs, symbolic behavior and social order. Dirt, Douglas argues, is no more or less than matter out of place: 'dirt is essentially disorder'.[8] Its presence tells us nothing about hygiene and everything about social pattern. A conception of dirt is vital for a conception of order, and ideas about separating, purifying, demarcating, and punishing transgressions all take shape around culturally-specific definitions of dirt: 'it is only by exaggerating the difference between within and without, above and below, male and female, with and against, that a semblance of order is created'.[9] Carefully-policed differences between cleanliness and dirt delimit and underscore these pairings, marking out relationships between the sacred and the profane; contamination beliefs and behaviours carry symbolic freight, which express social symmetries, values and hierarchies. Definitions of dirt may be arbitrary, but agreement about those definitions and their implementation is necessary for social cohesion.

Early on, however, Douglas notes that the rules of dirt-avoidance can be set aside for the sake of friendship. To illustrate her point, she quotes a passage from Thomas Hardy's *Far From The Madding Crowd* in which a group of farm labourers commend the shepherd who refuses a clean mug for his cider as 'a nice unparticular man':

> 'A clane cup for the shepherd', said the maltster commandingly.
> 'No – not at all,' said Gabriel, in a reproving tone of considerateness. 'I never fuss about dirt in its pure state, and when I know what sort it is ... I wouldn't think of giving such trouble to neighbours in washing up when there's so much work to be done in the world already'.[10]

This homely moment, in which agreement about the difference between 'clean' (harmless) dirt and real pollution immediately produces fellow-feeling, proves surprisingly suggestive for a reading of tropes of cleanliness and dirt in *The Lord of the Rings*. What could be termed its three-world structure devolves largely around patterns of dirt. Mordor is wholly filthy; the Elven kingdoms are wholly pure. The Fellowship, charged with saving Middle Earth, occupies the middle ground and is mixed: the very clean Legolas and rather grubby Gimli inherit a race-based enmity and are initially suspicious of one another, but they soon come to share an understanding of what constitutes *real* filth. By the conclusion of the films their racial differences have been set aside entirely:

> Gimli: I never thought I'd die fighting side by side with an Elf.
> Legolas: What about side by side with a friend?
> Gimli: Aye, I can do that.

If the fallible, the mortal and the wholesomely grubby are to inherit the earth, however, the two opposing zones of dirt and purity must be emptied out: it is as necessary for the Elves to fade as it is for Frodo to bring down Barad-dûr.

Patterns of dirt and cleanliness also emblematise the moralised environmentalism that the films foreground. Much of their key 'dirt' imagery derives directly from Tolkien, and is closely associated with industry and evil: in both narratives, the slag-heaps of Mordor, the technology that emanates from Isengard, and the destruction of

Fangorn Forest are symptoms of moral degeneracy. But from these points of reference the film extrapolates its own visual vocabulary of environmental irresponsibility, taking its cue from Tolkien's racialist suspicion of supposedly defiling hybrid forms, but turning this suspicion to environmental rather than racial ends.[11] The Balrog, unleashed when the Dwarves delved 'too greedily and too deep' in the Mines of Moria, is imagined as a cross between a bull, a lizard and a dog.[12] Tolkien has surprisingly little to say about the genetic make-up or birth of the Uruk-hai warriors; Jackson's Uruk-hai are a cross between Orcs and 'goblin men' and the film imagines them writhing out of the ground at Isengard like monstrous test-tube babies.[13] Neither does Tolkien have much to say about the physiognomy of Orcs. Jackson's creatures, however, display all the deformities popularly imagined to be the result of Frankenstinian medical experimentation. 'The age of Men is over', their leader proclaims. 'The time of the Orc has come'.

Mary Douglas is again helpful on the subject of pollution anxiety in relation to hybrid forms. She suggests that ambiguity and anomaly – and, by extension, hybrids – all occupy a similar structural position. That position is similar to the position of dirt, in that they all tend to induce culturally specific pollution-reactions, but whereas dirt tends to be a 'closed' or stable category which includes all the rejected elements of an ordered system, ambiguities and anomalies occupy no precise category of their own; they are, therefore, even more difficult to deal with and hence likely to provide the most suggestive moments for a consideration of pollution behaviour. Further, any given system of classification must give rise to anomalies, or events which seem to defy its assumptions. In turn, the anomaly clarifies the outlines of the set of which it is not a member: the 'fixed' categories of solid and liquid, for example, produce the anomalous, and – significantly – repellent category of the sticky.[14] Similarly, the abominations listed in Leviticus, which prescribe the Jewish dietary laws, prohibit the consumption of creatures which are anomalous in that they are not appropriately fitted for life in any of the three discrete realms of creation. These creatures are literally matter out of place: animals which live on the land must go on four legs or two; creatures which creep or go on their bellies are therefore an abomination and must not be touched or eaten. Birds live in the air, so ospreys and other birds which dive into the sea are an abomination. Likewise, sea creatures which do not have fins or scales are an abomination.[15] Douglas argues that reflecting on such anomalies tends to confirm our confidence in the main structural classifications; hence, agreement about what constitutes an anomaly, and the correct response to the anomalous – like the shared knowledge of what constitutes dirt – affirms social coherence.

Anomalies, then, are inevitable in any complex system and are as necessary for the maintenance of social stability as more clear-cut cases of dirt and cleanliness.

What bearing might these observations have on the representation of hybrids and anomalies in *The Lord of the Rings*? Remembering Douglas's point that anomalies are inevitable, necessary and likely to be repellant, I would now like to turn to the figure of Gollum.

Tolkien explains Gollum's history in his various books, including *The Hobbit*, and the creature's back-story is made quite explicit in the films: we are to know that Gollum was once a hobbit named Sméagol, a peace-loving, pure-blooded and therefore legitimate occupant of a racialised – and racially territorialised – Middle Earth. One day, while out fishing, he and a friend discover Sauron's Ring of Power and Sméagol murders his friend to obtain it. But the Ring betrays him. While it endows him with virtually eternal life, it reduces him to a creeping, abject creature of no clear racial status. It robs him of normal speech and forces him into exile: the name Gollum derives from the strange guttural sounds he makes in his throat, and his physical home is now wherever the Ring happens to be. Neither is he able to eat the food proper to his kind: his inability to stomach the good, wholesome fish and chips so beloved of Samwise Gamgee marks exactly the depths to which his love of the Ring has brought him:

> 'Sméagol won't grub for roots and carrotses and – taters. What's taters, precious, eh, what's taters?'
> 'Po-ta-toes', said Sam … 'Rare good ballast for an empty belly … If you turn over a new leaf, and keep it turned, I'll cook you some taters one of these days, I will: fried fish and chips served by S. Gamgee. You couldn't say no to that'.
> 'Yes, yes we could. Spoiling nice fish, scorching it. Give me fish *now*, and keep nassty chips!'
> 'Oh you're hopeless', said Sam. 'Go to sleep!'[16]

Gollum's love of raw fish also provides one of the films' more disgusting moments: Sméagol's final transition into Gollum is signalled by an extreme close-up of discoloured teeth sinking into wriggling flesh.

Over and above his physical abjection – he is unclean partly because he occupies no clear racial niche – Gollum is anomalous in other ways: in a world of races with national territories, he is stateless and wandering. He is untrustworthy: although he will serve anyone who holds the Ring, he wants it for himself and is loyal only to himself. Unlike decent creatures who go on two legs or four, Gollum swarms:

> Down the face of a precipice, sheer and almost smooth it seemed in the pale moonlight, a small black shape was moving with its thin limbs splayed out. Maybe its soft clinging hands and toes were finding crevices and holds that no hobbit could ever have seen or used, but it looked as if it was just creeping down on sticky pads, like some large prowling thing of insect-kind. And it was coming down head first, as if it was smelling its way.[17]

In his uncanny ability to descend sheer rock faces head-first, he resembles no creature more than Dracula, as Jonathan Harker observes him leaving his castle:

> I saw … the Count's head coming out from the window … I was at first interested and somewhat amused … but my very feelings changed to repulsion and terror when I saw the whole man slowly emerge from the window and begin to crawl down the castle wall over the dreadful abyss, face down with his cloak spreading out around him like great wings … I saw the fingers and toes grasp the corners of the stones, worn clear of the mortar by the stress of years, and by thus using every projection and inequality move downwards with considerable speed, just as a lizard moves along a wall.[18]

I'm not necessarily suggesting a specific literary borrowing here, but rather a structural homology, in the biological sense of characteristics shared by creatures who trace their descent from a common ancestor. The common ancestor, in both cases, is the pervasive nineteenth-century stereotype of the Jew. Dracula and Gollum are racial outsiders who insinuate themselves into civil society for self-serving ends; both are graspingly material; neither have any loyalty to the nation state, but may display some residual loyalty to their own kind; both are associated with the East. Both are ancient beyond measure, and work by stealth and covert means. Both are repellent, alien creatures which must be brushed off the sleeve of the narrative in order that homely values may reassert themselves. I don't intend to push this analogy too far, however: Dracula is noble and powerful, and a worthy adversary of the 'Crew of Light' which finally masters him. Gollum is entirely abject. Indeed, if Sam – the text's most explicit embodiment of the homely values of loyalty and friendship – had another vocabulary at his finger-tips, he might be tempted to describe the hateful creature not as Slinker and Stinker, but as *Kreatur*, *Stück* ('piece'), or *Schmätter* (literally, 'rags') – the euphemising language of eugenicism which enabled the Nazis to consign Jews to the category of the non-human.

But, like the dirt which is structurally essential for the functioning of any social system and like the Jews he so closely resembles, Gollum has a role to play in the working-through of Tolkien's redemptive

– and wartime – theology. This theology requires the suffering of a representative, elect individual: Frodo Baggins is charged with the task of ridding the world of evil. The task falls to him simply because hobbits are small and good, and if the small and the good do nothing, evil will triumph. But Frodo is not just a doughty British army officer aided by his trusty batman. He must complete his terrible task alone. He is wounded. He is tempted, and he nearly falls. Having achieved his mission, he is endowed with eternal life. But where does Gollum fit into this familiar allegory? Gollum desires the Ring, and dogs every step of Frodo's journey. Several times Frodo is in a position to be able to kill him, but pity stays his hand: he recognises that they are both fallen creatures, bound to each other and to the Ring.[19] Neither can the poor forked animal bring himself to kill Frodo: he abandons Frodo and Sam to their fate in Shelob's lair. The standoff is resolved when Gollum and Frodo fight on the edge of the Cracks of Doom. Gollum bites off Frodo's finger, and at last he has his 'precious'. He stumbles backwards, falls into the abyss, and the towers of the enemy crumble.[20] Gollum – the enemy within, the Jew – is at once the depraved inner self who must be eliminated in order to achieve salvation, and the necessary catalyst for the new world order.

This deeply conservative allegorical material was bound to pose a problem for Jackson and his screenwriters: they had to make it relevant for a contemporary audience without alienating a fan-club of Tolkien traditionalists. The filmmakers' most significant revision was to link Gollum more strongly to the environmental themes that now function to partially mask Tolkien's unfashionably racialised theology. In the novel, racial, environmental and moral degradation are essentially like each other. Each is a disease-symptom of the will-to-power which is at the root of the world's ills. In the films, however, racial degeneration is not simply another sign of evil in a world badly in need of saving; it is the explicit outcome of the environmental degradation which is made to carry the trilogy's most significant moralising baggage. In all versions of the narrative, dirt, in the form of racial and environmental impurity, is associated with evil. But in the films, Gollum, the polluting anomaly, must be driven out if the cherished classifications of cleanliness and dirt are to be maintained: the wretched gangrel creature, who yet is close enough to the ordinary inhabitants of Middle Earth to stand as a terrible warning, must die before environmental order can be restored.[21]

If the filmmakers employ these environmental connotations as a form of ideological reinvestment in another currency, as it were, then the rate of exchange is not in their favour. The semiotic relationship between dirt and cleanliness also happens to fit Tolkien's racialism to a tee; indeed, the films can do little to disavow the baggage that accompanies those tropes. This has important implications for the last of my original questions, which concerned the potential difference a New Zealand setting might make in resolving these issues.[22] Locations which viewers would identify as New Zealand play a restricted but important role in the films. Many scenes take place indoors or in built – and largely computer-generated – environments: the inn of the Prancing Pony; Weathertop; the Mines of Moria and the pits of Isengard; the cities of Minas Tirith and Osgiliath; the towers of Orthanc, Minas Morgul and Cirith Ungol; Shelob's lair. Exteriors, on the other hand, fall into three general categories, which broadly correspond to the films' three-world structure: volcanic landscapes (fittingly diabolical settings for Sauron's evil empire, which will in the end be lanced like a boil); populated environments such as Edoras and Hobbiton; and empty spaces, which are almost always 'travel-through' wilderness zones. The green paddocks of Hobbiton and, most especially, those vast pristine wilderness zones draw on images which are regarded as quintessentially New Zealand, images which also drive the bulk of our tourism advertising. The return to Hobbiton is ostensibly the films' end-point; Hobbiton's location near Matamata was chosen because it suggested fertility and long habitation. The set design emphasised those homely virtues: the design philosophy for Hobbiton was meant to convey a simple rural life-style, where people were 'very much in touch with nature'. Andrew Lesnie, the films' director of photography, intended that Hobbiton should 'make everyone feel like it was a holiday destination. People would love to want to go there'.[23]

But what other regions of Middle Earth would those virtual visitors travel through to reach Hobbiton, that tourists'-eye version of safe little New Zealand, cosily nestled at the bottom of the world? If they were tourists following an itinerary through the films' three-world structure, they might do imaginary battle with the forces of Mordor on the slopes of Mt Ruapehu, but would spend most of their time, as the characters themselves do, in the great outdoors of our national parks. The films draw positive environmental value from those very clean, very empty landscapes – those travel-through spaces in which we have previously encountered representatives of the good, the evil and the mixed. By the trilogy's conclusion, however, those landscapes have been purged of all but pure-breeds and the occasional traveller. They are empty lands fit for the right people. No longer a source of threat, they simply separate the peoples who have more in common with each other than they do with the banished forces of evil. They are the peoples who understand the true meaning of dirt. The security of Hobbiton has been bought at the exact cost of an emptied landscape: purged of its contaminating hybrids, that pristine New Zealand landscape now looks like nothing less than *Lebensraum*.

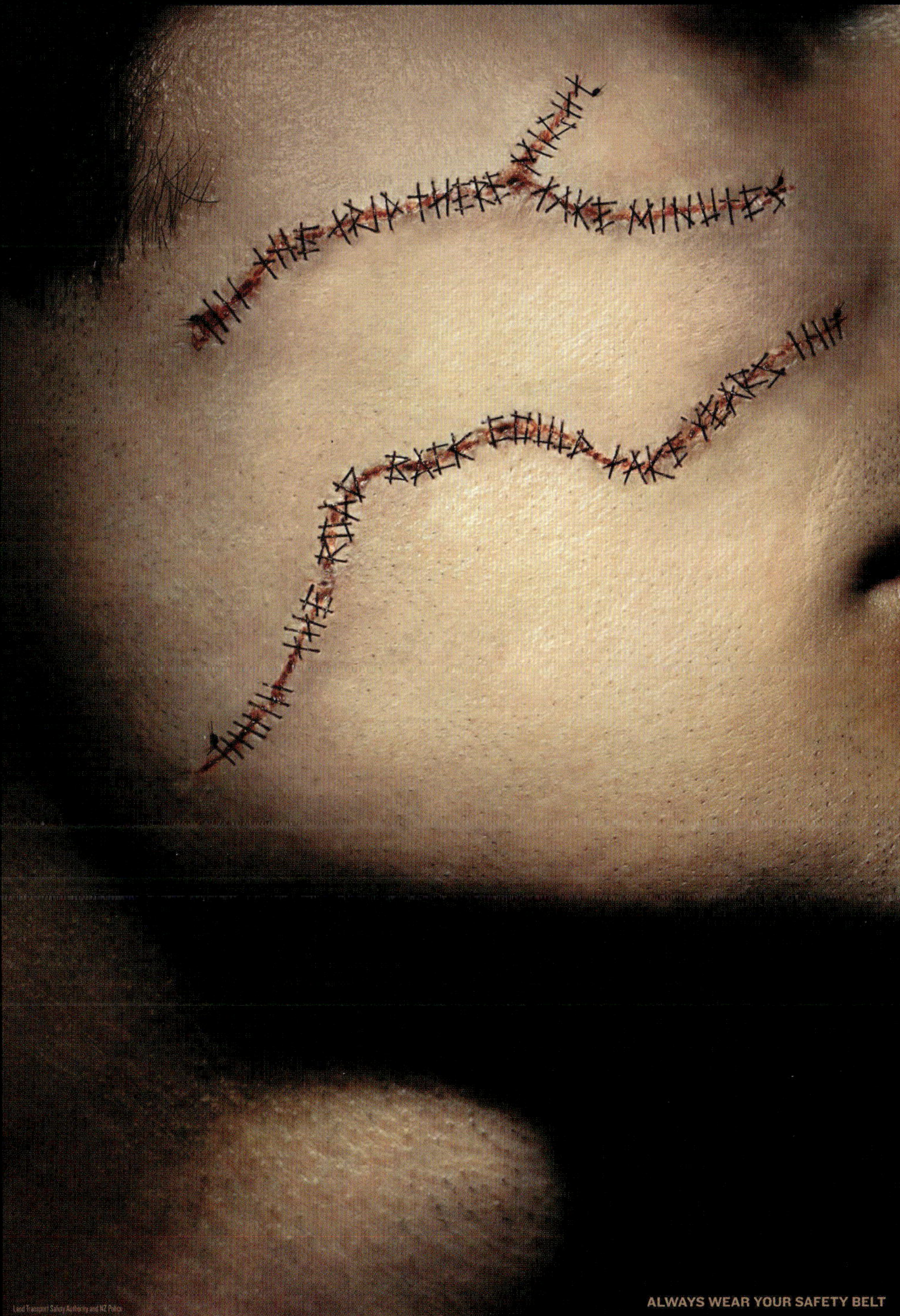
THE ROAD BACK COULD TAKE YEARS
Land Transport Safety Authority and NZ Police
ALWAYS WEAR YOUR SAFETY BELT

Nocturnes for an Only Daughter

In a town where no one locks the doors,
you crept down stairs in the night
to find the door locked,
and knew
that your mother believed in monsters too.

Text by
Olivia Macassey

Photographs by
Rachel Ahmad-Hall

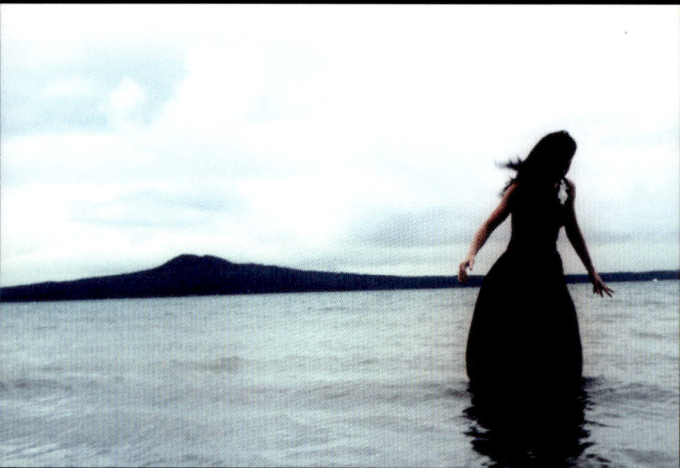

Green River

She played Chopin because she suited it; it
wasn't the other way round. One of
your Grandmothers killed herself,
but you like to think that she drowned.

You look like her underwater sometimes,
with green stretched over the bones of your face
you wave at me in slow motion before you run
out of air. The water
is always there;
it moves slowly
through its pools, it gently lines its walls,

it carefully traces the lips of swimmers, stops
at the places where the body is sealed. While
those places are there.

Your mother stood alone sometimes,
in a dark room. The white walls shone
though trees cast a deep shadow
over the roof. She felt
each breath enter her lungs
and leave again, heard the movement
of river through her night.

She played that part because she suited it;
but never the other way round!
your Grandmother who killed herself.
Her eyes are greener than river bends,
and rivulets run through her hair,

I like to say that she drowned.
The water is always there

Green Skin

Once, I dreamed that I sleep-walked
down past the tree line into prickly liquid of scrub
and through the animal path to the place –

and woke at home in a warm ray of relief.

Snow angel mud angel angel made of grass
water isn't water while it flows through your hands.

Here's something: the worst sort of bruise
doesn't show up for several days.

We were eating blackberries
on the side of the road, when she joined us,
our mouths stained with dust
she was smiling also – don't forget that.

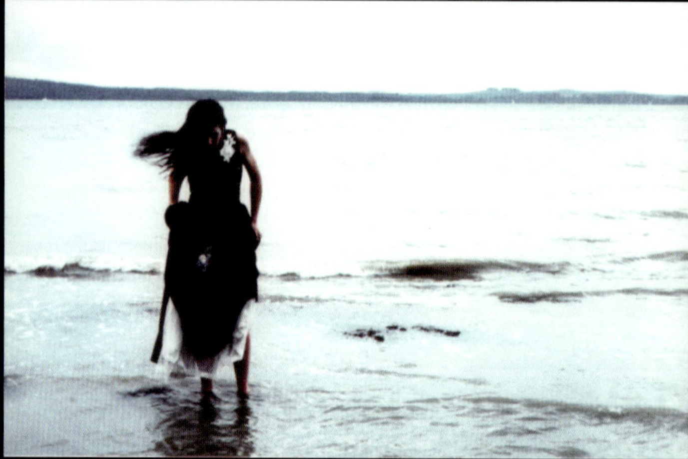

Muddy little no-wings with her borrowed dress
taught me how to find C in the white keys,
how to call horses and to hide in the creek bed
and the notes between nothing when the drunks stop breathing
and. start again and. start again

Here's another fact: he drew blood.
If you don't understand
we'll go through this point again.

Flax lines the driveway so
            you can't see the house.
Her eyes and the moon both looked like shells.

Mud girl, stick girl, woman made of grass:
I saw where you bled. And then I saw
leaves and twigs between the sheets
and my own muddy footprints which led
from the half open window with the curtain coming down
straight across the floor to this bed.

Manuka in Bloom

Ever since she explained the rata
to me – how it twines up as a vine
and replaces the older tree, in time –
I have loved it best, secretly,

a secret because
that woman was taller,
or perhaps for love of the other trees.

I see you feeling for tuatua
in the incoming tide
or swimming off the sand bar
in a moon clouded sea, and the green
sky stinging against your skin
how you were looking at him then, and

how we waited further up the beach
in a darkness smooth as sandworn rock
for your return.
You wound your salty arms
around me. But
how you had looked at him then!

And all the days are pale
since you have gone,

and the manuka flowers dim. My house
will fall in by the year, my strength shift
grain by grain from bones.
The black rock narrows in the gorge,

small leaves fall slowly
and the white petals fall, and the red.
The remembering sea wears away at me;
the water is always there.
Perhaps I was taller, or in the end
it was for love of the other tree.

Selected Photographs, 2003–2006
Yvonne Todd

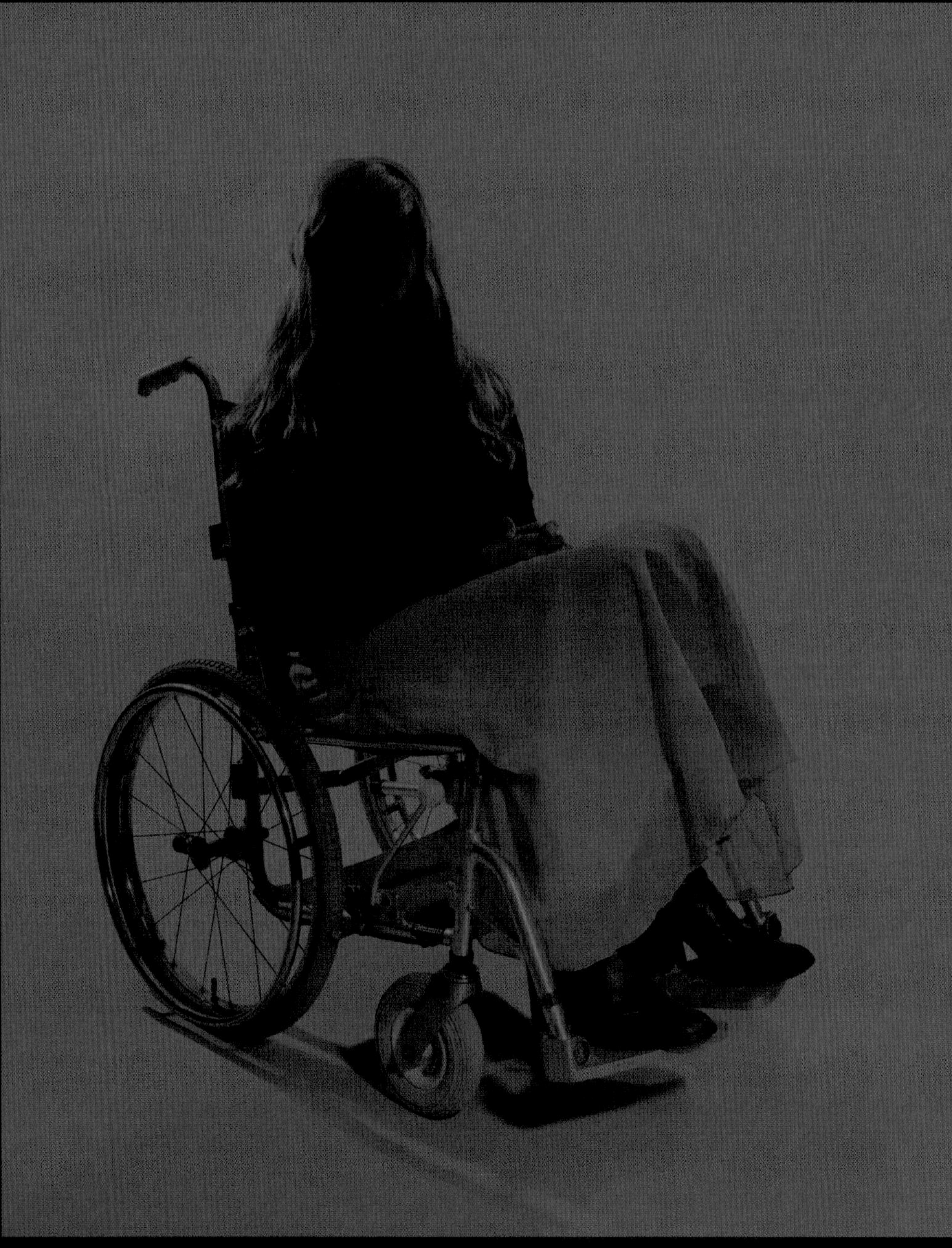

'Advancia' 2003, colour photograph, 43 x 34 cm

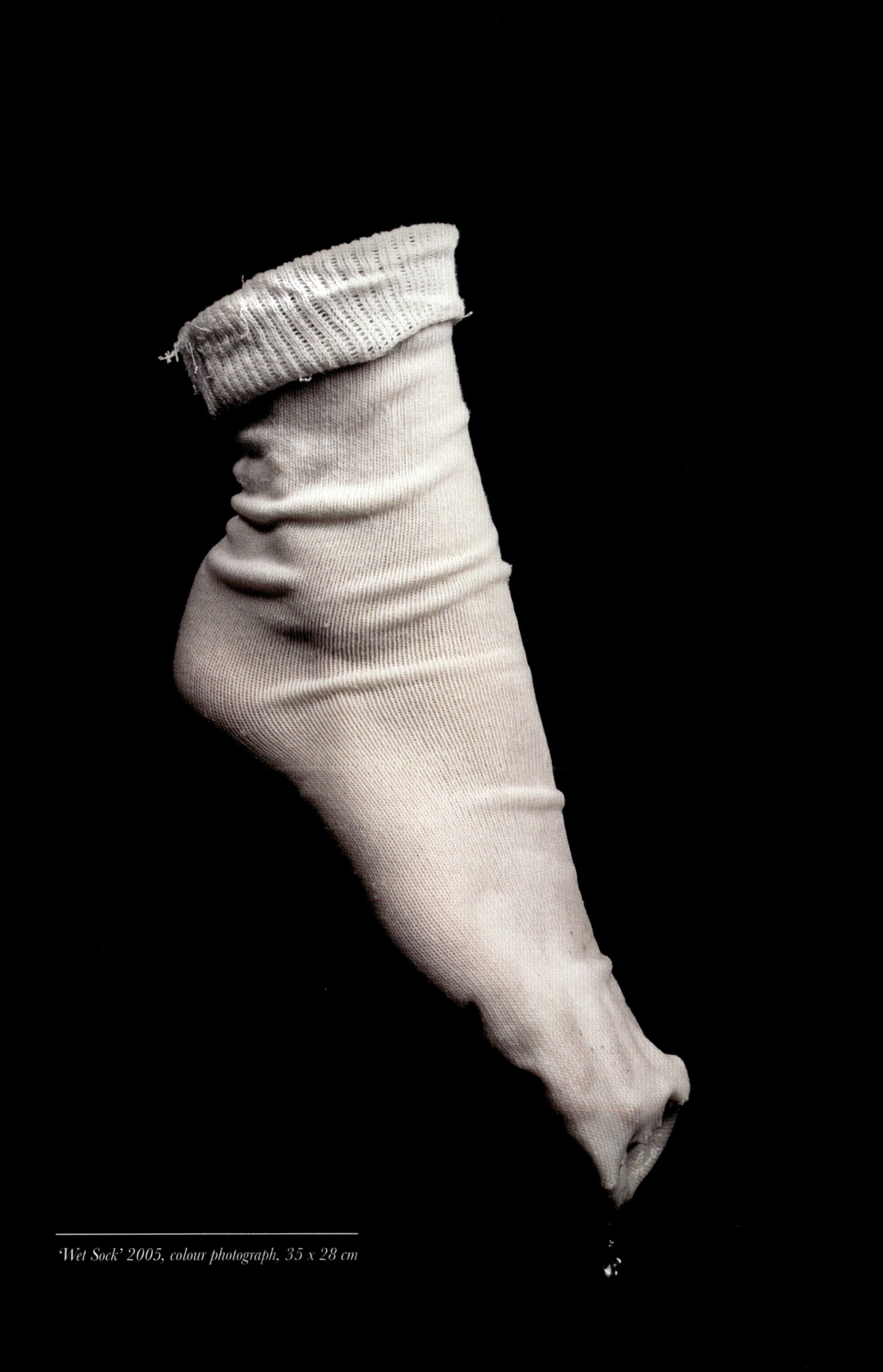

'Wet Sock' 2005, colour photograph, 35 x 28 cm

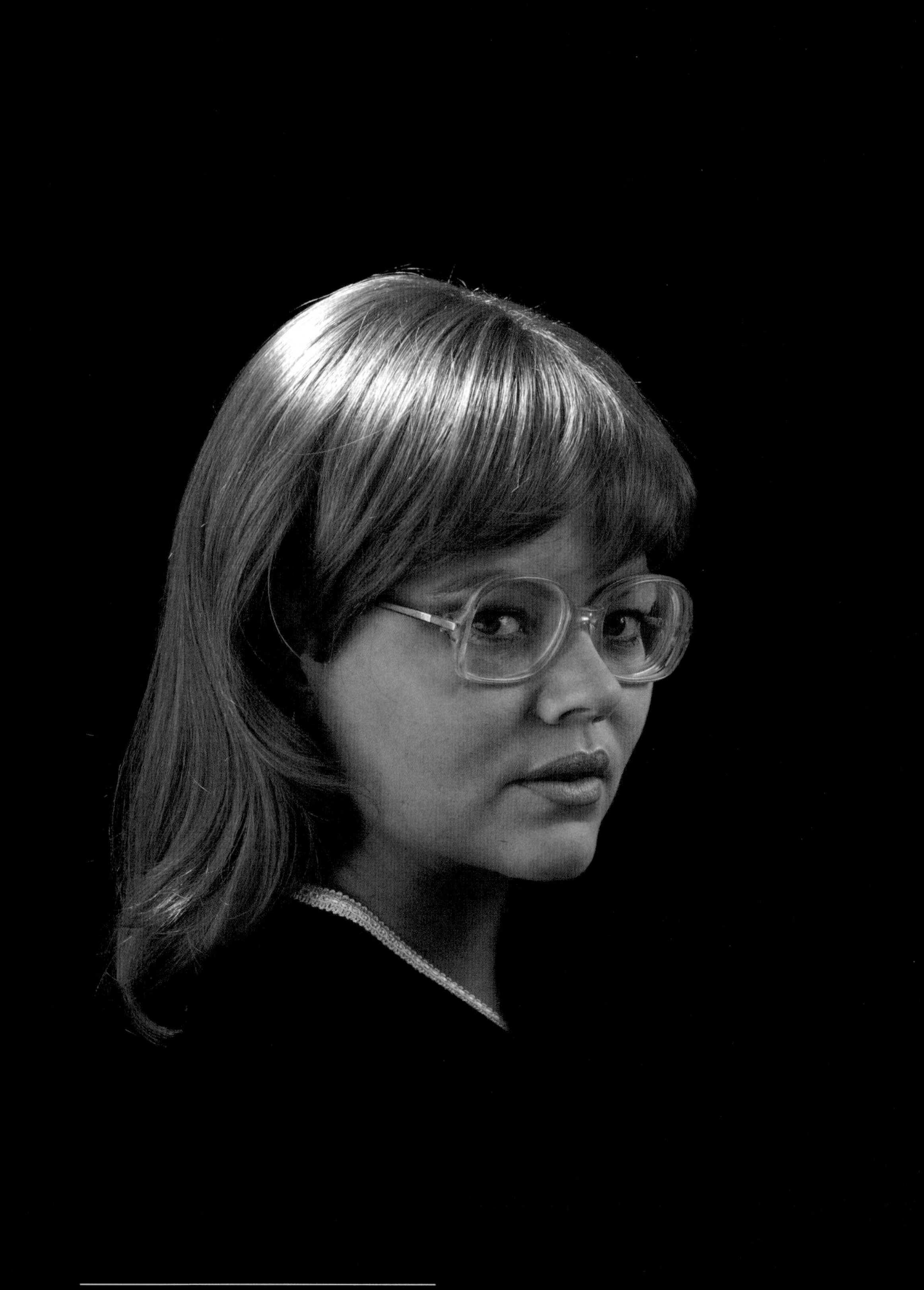

'Suchard' 2004, black & white photograph, 41 x 35 cm

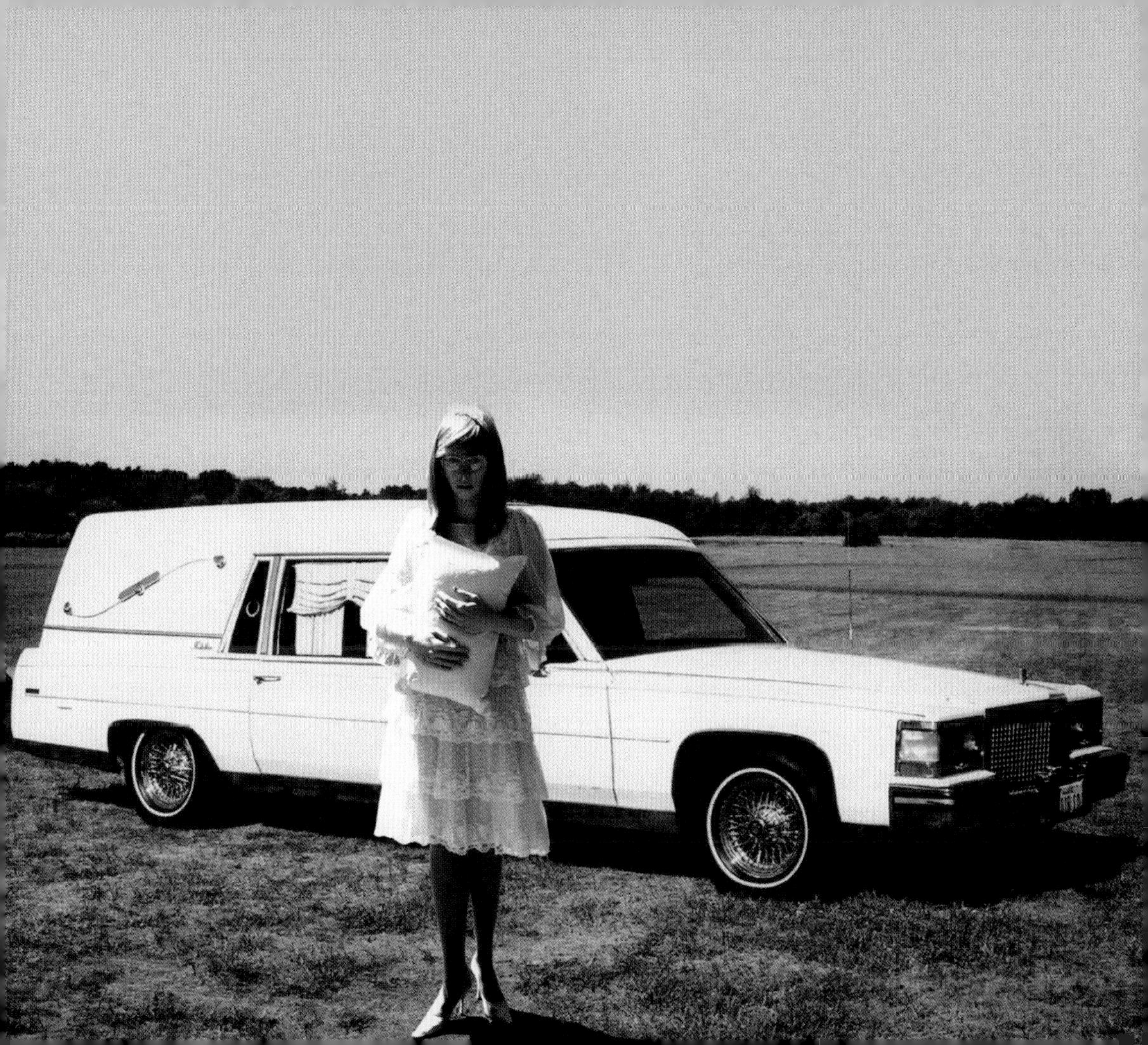

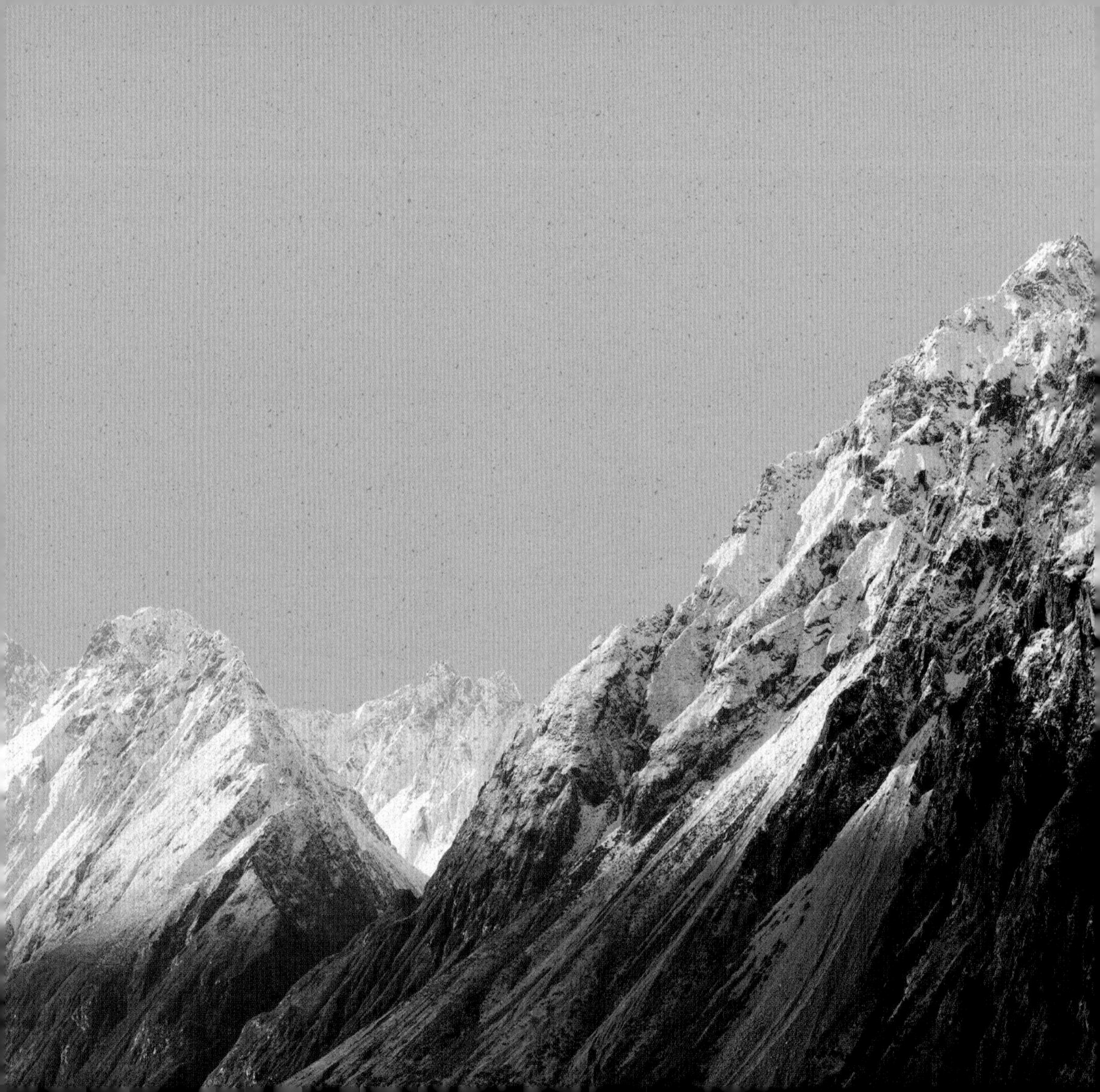

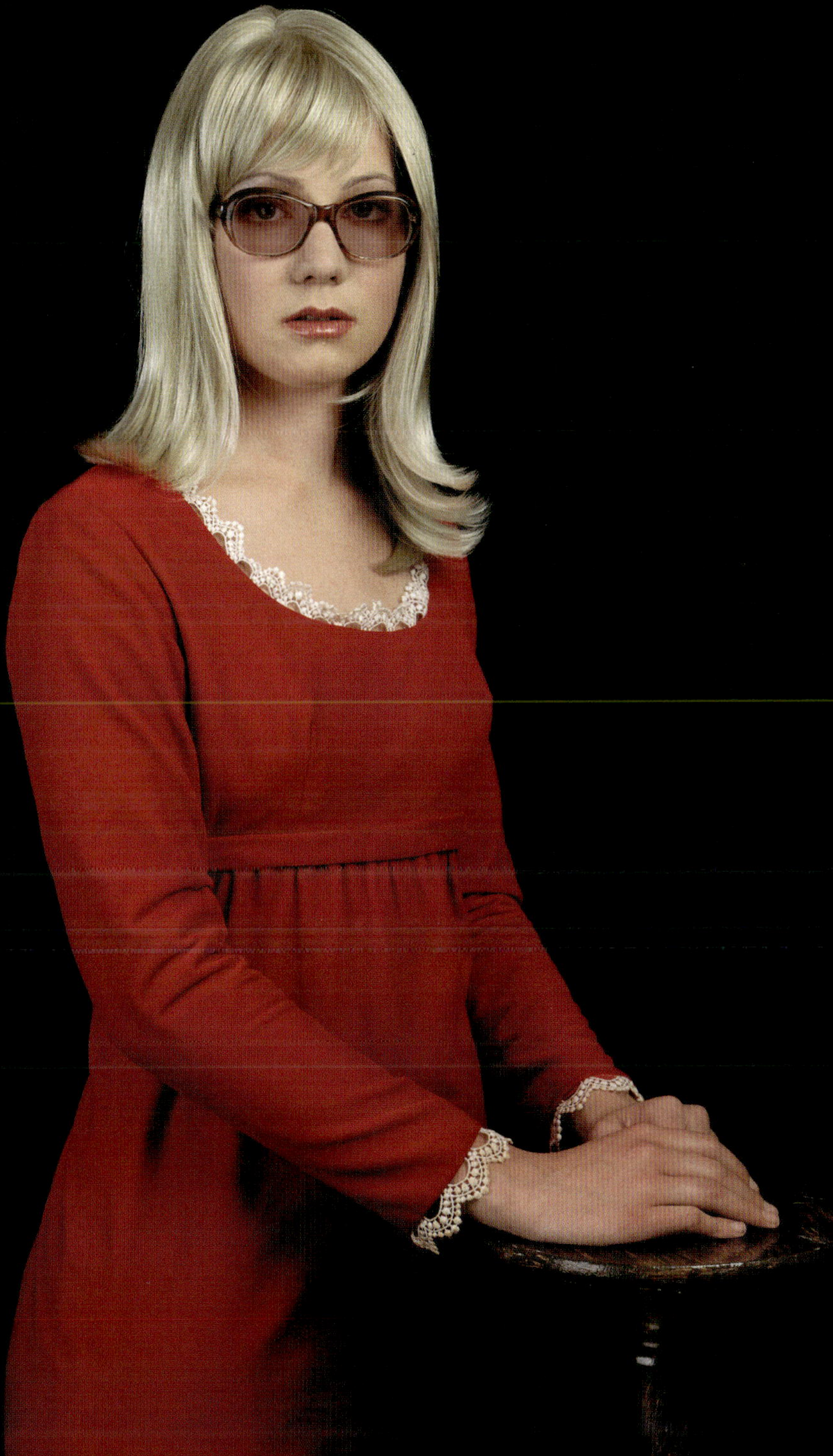

'The New Helen Keller' 2004, colour photograph, 120 x 95 cm

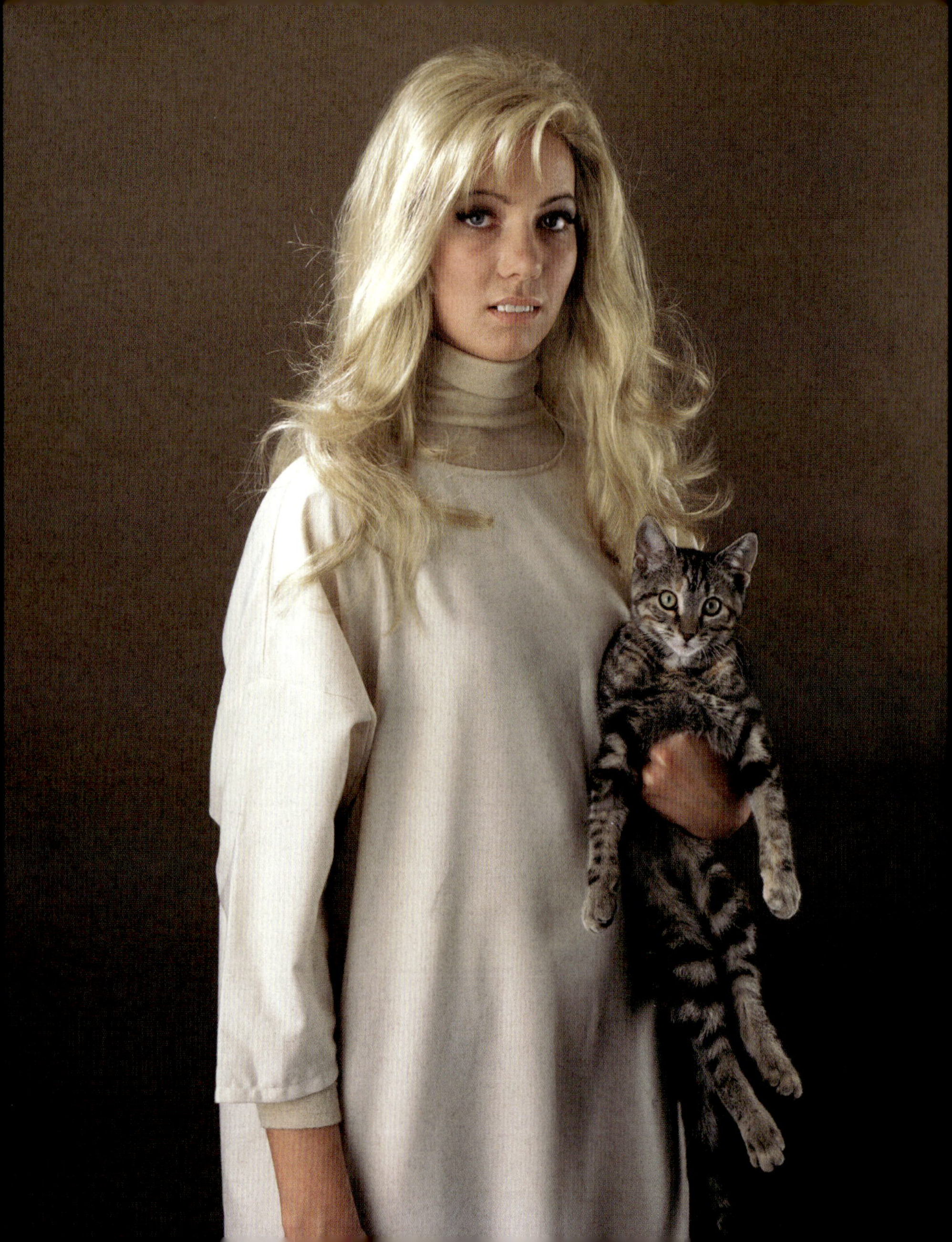

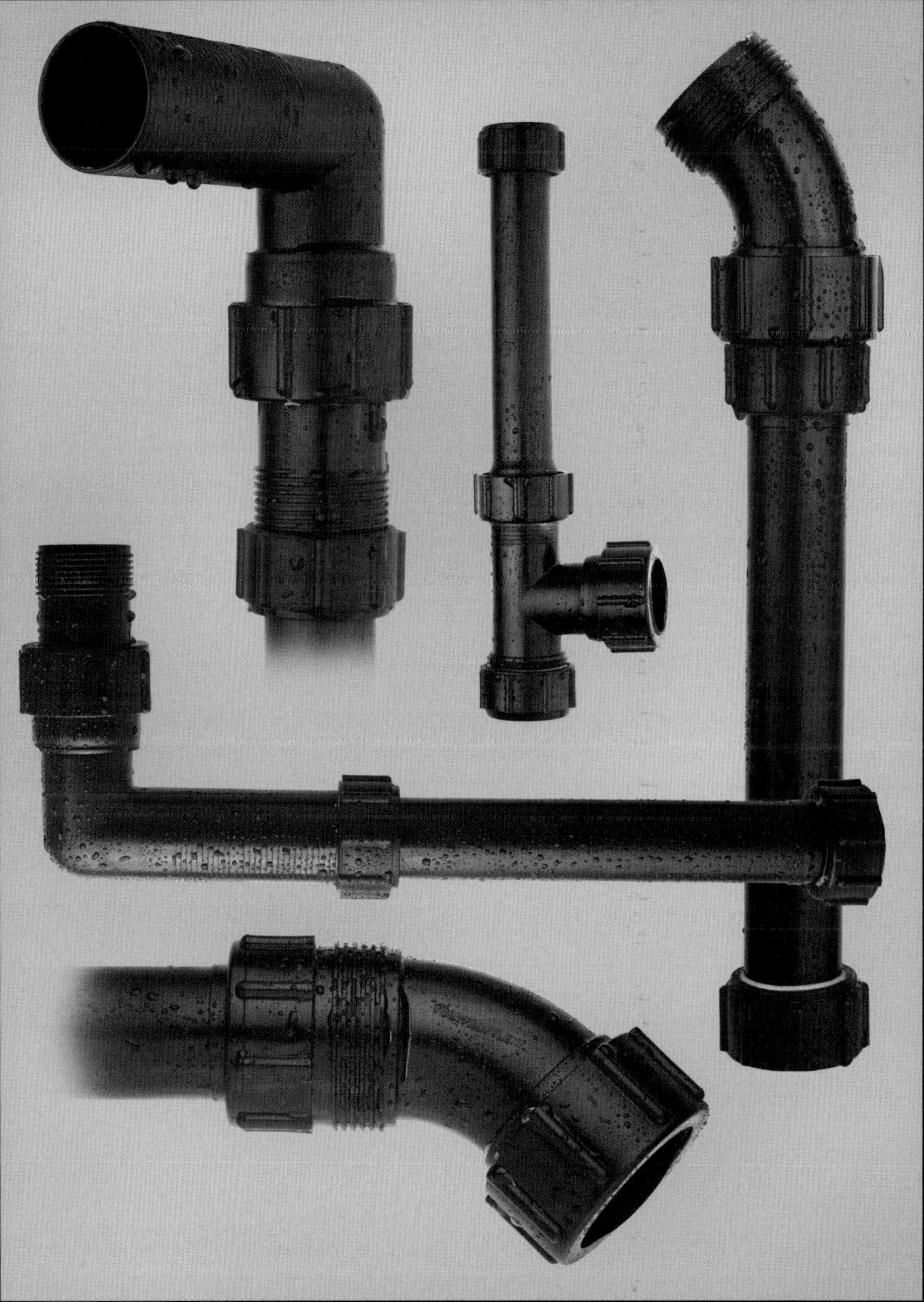

'Clammy Pipes' 2006, colour photograph, 90 x 66 cm

Misery: Art and Fashion

Text by
Misha Kavka

Images by
Misery

To enter the world of Misery is to develop a whole new appreciation for the word 'creepy'. When the artist talks about her work, 'creepy' recurs like a catchy refrain, heavy with appreciation and not infrequently accompanied by a giggle. It means dark and disturbing, certainly, but the kind of darkness that comes harnessed to innocence, arising from the latter's depths. Misery speaks of this recurring theme as 'the main thing I love: that cute, sweet innocence . . . bordering on something really psychotic, [on] wanting to kill and [on] death'.[1] There's a girlish sweetness to the artwork that embraces its opposite, savouring the morbid and perverse, sometimes with melancholic languor but more often with a sidelong evil grin that exposes some of the nastier fantasies that lie behind the façade of innocence. The backgrounds of this gothic world drip with reds and blacks and blues; awash with dark rain or blood or bubbles on the verge of popping, the space here is only as static as the girls are innocent – that is, not at all. To say, as Misery does of her work, 'I think that my art always shows the dark side', is a modest statement: in this world you find yourself revelling in the dark side with equal amounts of glee and horror. In fact, this is how the artist defines beauty, as the attempt to 'find a balance in between'.

The aesthetic of Misery – who earned her tag name as a 17-year-old in Auckland beginning to engage in graffiti and street art – provides a seemingly endless variety of twists on the little-girl theme. With their doll-like features, big heads on small bodies, and doleful eyes, these *manga*-influenced figures could/should be the height of cutsiness. But there is something too girly here, a hyper-femininity that overflows the boundaries of girliness: 'I like the girls to look pretty and to accentuate girliness but be doing creep things, boy things'. Right from the start, the eyes of these girls meet our gaze with discomfiting equanimity, but once we wrest ourselves away from their hypnotic pull we begin to notice the knives, tentacles, spiders and gnarled vines that make up their environment like lace tatted from unholy threads. Sometimes a girl is outright evil, like Fifi who holds a bloody knife in one hand and the tail of a dead fox in the other, while a pet sheep attached to her arm by a ribbon bears all the hallmarks of the abuse to which actual little girls subject their dolls and toys. More often, though, the mix of innocence and evil is more subtle, such as the Misery Bo-peep, whose upturned eyes seem

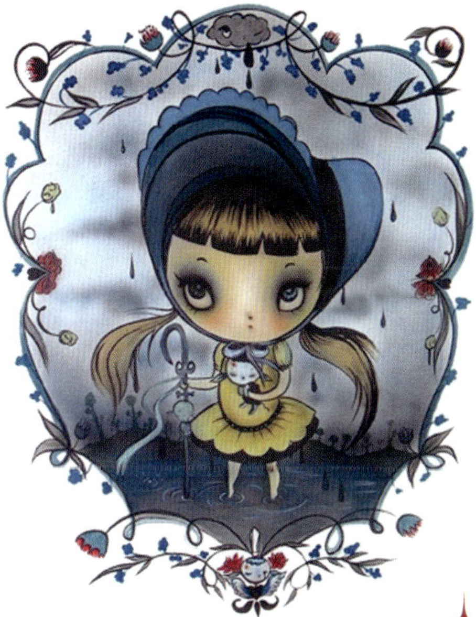

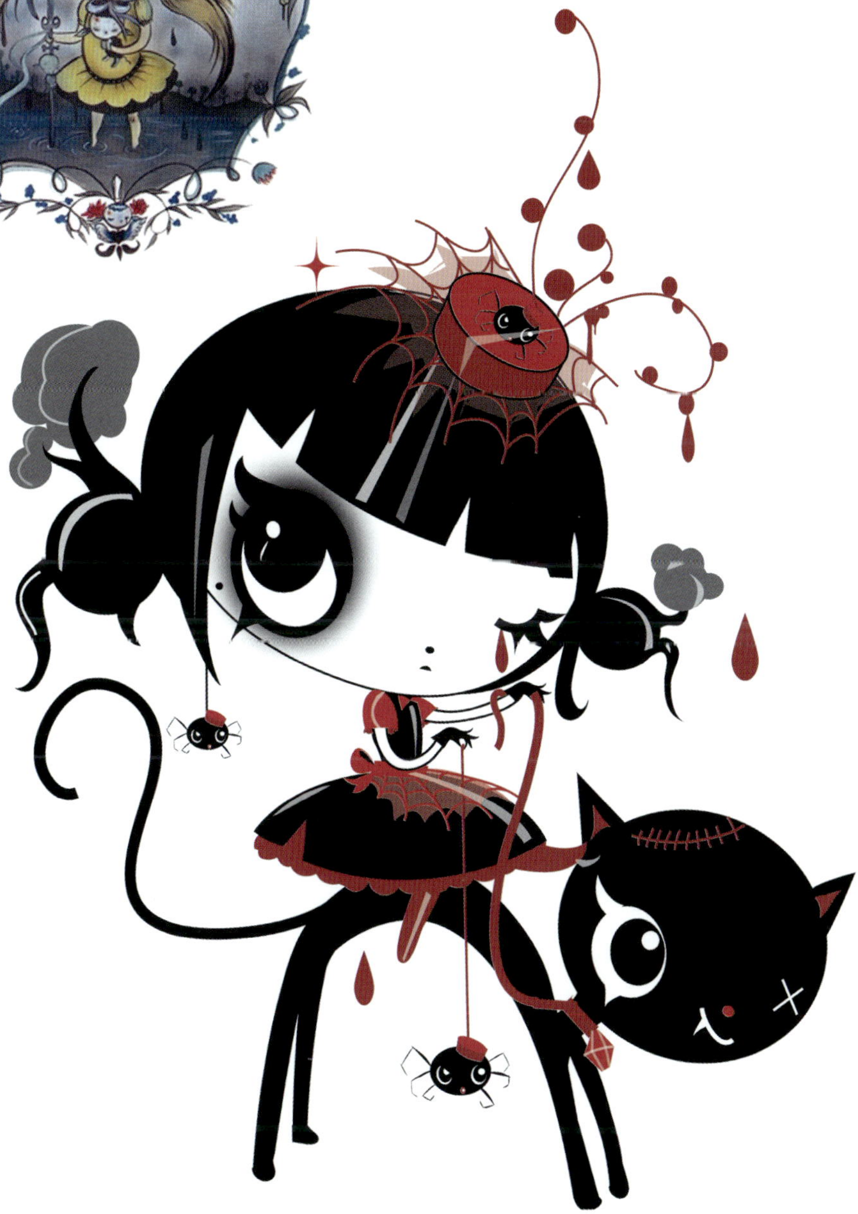

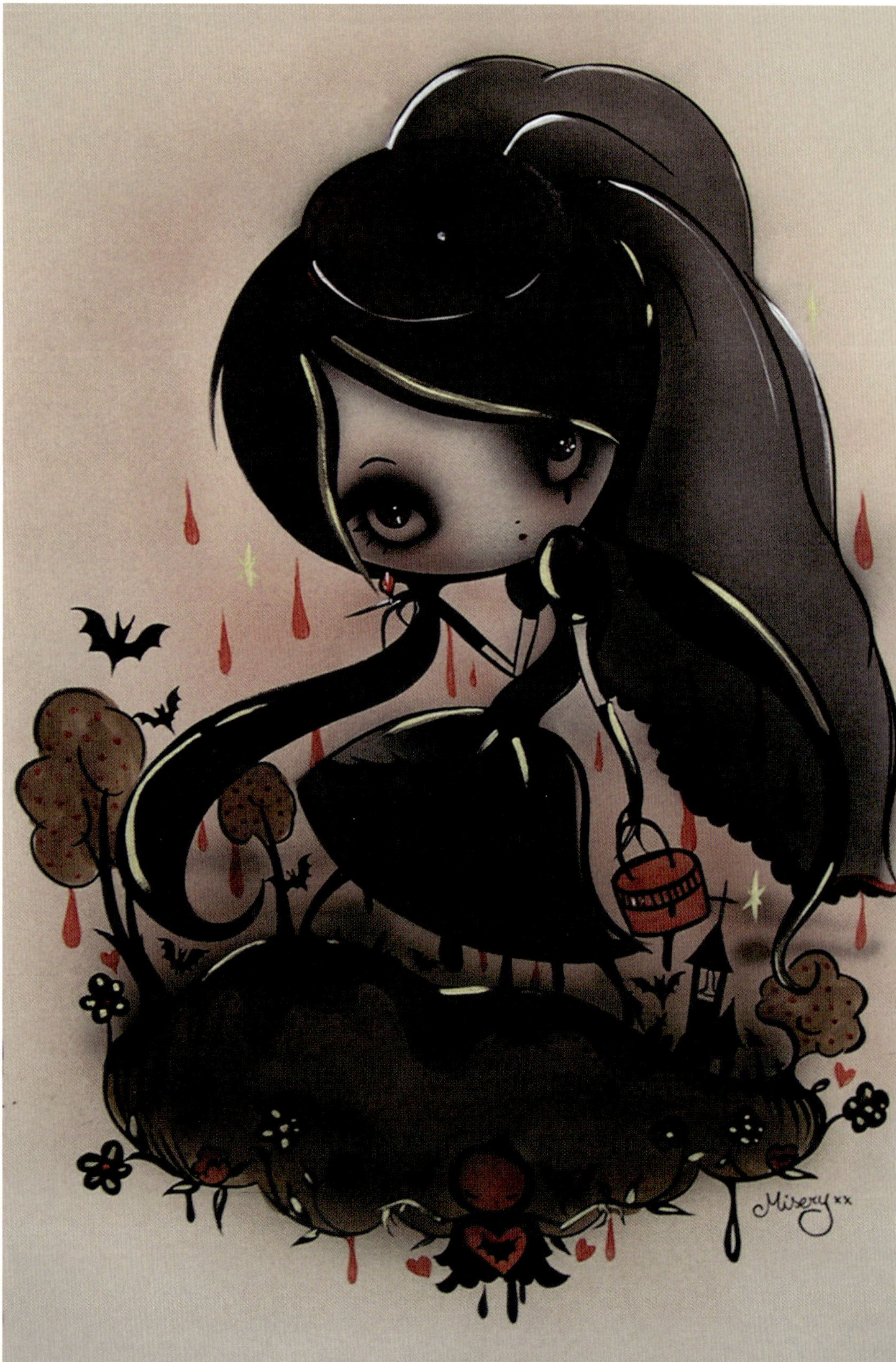
Misery xx

to plead helplessly for rescue from the flood in which she stands, distracting us from other rather disturbing details, such as the tiny, wounded sheep – perhaps already dead – that she holds in one hand or the crook decorated with skull and crossbones in the other. Over her head a winking raincloud squeezes black drops onto her bonnet, while at the bottom of the frame the face of the sheep reappears, this time crying a single bloody tear. Add to this the graze on Bo-peep's knee and our hearts go out to her – but who here is the victim, and who the perpetrator? Is there such a thing as an innocent wound, even on a little girl's knee?

Another range of Misery girls seems older than this nursery faction, and certainly more eroticised. With the same large heads now perched on slender, curving bodies, their almond-shaped eyes are far more knowing, seeking to cast a spell over the viewer while deflecting any attempt to be known themselves. They, too, come surrounded by gothic paraphernalia, by accoutrements from the dark side of innocence. In one, a squid girl sits dreamily under a parasol in a boat, cocking a raised eyebrow from a face surrounded by dark locks that wind their way into tentacles. In this melancholic blue-black world, where the frilly edging of the parasol matches the hair fringe of squid girl's face before resolving itself into the suction cups of her lock-tentacles, it is not so easy to decide whether the figure is innocent or menacing – just that she is quite definitely sexy. The same might apply for Miss Black Widow, slinking coyly across a churchyard in her widow's veil and weeds, accompanied in the background by bats that, for now at least, have left the church belfry. She faces us with Misery's signature combination of emotive appeal and blank bemusement, but as always whatever clues are to be had lie in the surrounding details. not just the bleeding sky or the beatific little devil at the bottom of the frame, but the obscenely large blood-red ring astride fingers so long and pointy that they appear more like a femme fatale's stilettos than the site of an erstwhile blushing bride's betrothal symbol. Again, our hearts – or something else – go out to her, even though the signs of evil should warn us well away.

Whether this bruised innocence recalls nursery tales or more adult *noir* fantasies, what all of these images have in common is a preoccupation with a femininity which – in a cross-over of high concept and high fashion – comes fully accessorised. No matter that the accessories might just as easily be a bloody knife and dead animal, or a rakish pillbox hat with matching handbag, or spider's-leg pigtails and a spiked bracelet, these icons of femininity wear their peculiar brand of innocence like any other fashion accessory: something to be mixed and matched in the process of dressing to kill. In this accessorising we see the clearest link between Misery's art and the Misery boutique, established as an outgrowth of the more heavily punk gothic Illicit, on Auckland's Karangahape Rd. With a window display in which large-headed Misery mannequins jostle for space with hyper-feminine dresses and shoes of the femme fatale era, the shop is reconfiguring the relationship between the gothic, femininity and fashion culture – three terms that have long been negotiating an embrace, but have never embedded themselves with such broad appeal across age groups and cultures.[2] For the artist, the boutique is a natural extension of the art, a sign of how she has been 'growing in [her] own way': 'I wanted to do a style of clothing that was more womanly and sexy, still dark but [that] catered for a more vintage 50s kind of look . . . There's all these other things that I want to make and want to do, and I felt that having my own shop for it would be the perfect home for just everything . . . make-up and shoes and bags and sunglasses, whatever'.

Beyond clothes and make-up, this accessorising artist is next venturing into toys, particularly – in a rather perverse closing of the circle – creating dolls out of the doll-like Misery figures, intended for women to collect and dress up in miniature Misery clothes. Like Barbies for grown-ups or the big-eyed Blythe dolls of the 60s and 70s that have recently made a come-back,[3] the artist gleefully envisions her customers embracing the perversities of girlhood and treating the dolls like twisted but inspiring alter egos: '[The Blythe dolls] are weird because they're . . . these cute dolls, but they make them sexy and womanly . . . There are women all over the world that are absolutely obsessive . . . they put their hair up and change their outfits. I hope people will treat mine like that, that would be so creepy'. From here, of course, it's just a short jump to the next stage of the enterprise, which involves creating Misery couture and a separate girlie streetwear label, before expanding into mini-Misery baby clothes. Fashion consumerism and the gothic don't mix, you say? Embrace the creepy possibilities of being female, counters Misery.

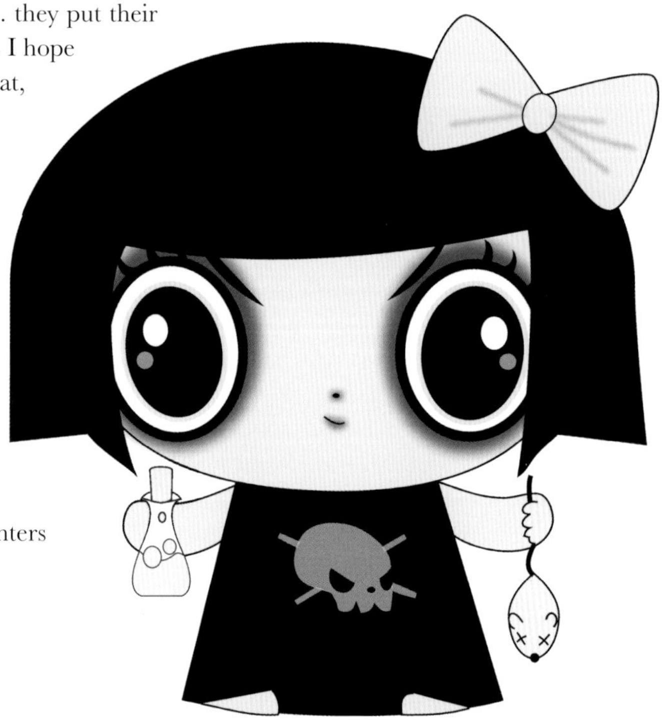

Don't Worry, Be Happy

Stephen Turner and Scott Wilson

Why worry?

New Zealand is a land of 'no worries', 'she'll be right', 'all good', and 'good thanks'. But the scary graphic realism of accidentsafe advertising asks us to watch out, to worry that 'she' might not be all right, and indicates, perhaps, a more true state of affairs. New Zealanders are either watchful and worried all the time, or, if not, we are told we should be because injury and death is all around, even in your own house: you could, as these public announcements so graphically demonstrate, fall down your own stairs (today). Scary accidentsafe adverts are not peculiar to New Zealand,[1] but the juxtaposition of imminent death with no-worries public culture is peculiar, a mixed feeling that produces the odd humour of a vernacular gothic.

Such public messages are not strictly adverts like other adverts, because they are not obviously trying to sell us anything. However, in order to get us to experience pain, to think about what the unwelcome experience of injury or death might be like – might *feel* like – accidentsafe messages use advertising tactics (some even masquerade as adverts, that is, before the unwelcome accident occurs and the 'advert' turns out to be a public message). These would-be adverts invite us to 'consume' injury and death – a threat we would ordinarily turn away from, or run from. We are constantly directed by advertising towards objects – things to have, to wear, to consume; in accidentsafe adverts, however, we are asked to avoid things – falling down stairs, off ladders, driving fast. Yet I am already consuming, in some sense, the 'object' of this advert, which is the accident it is telling me to avoid. And what's the pleasure of this? Why am I even watching? Not quite willingly I find myself vicariously participating in the experience of something I do not, cannot, possibly want, which is injury and death. What am I supposed to do with that?

Adverts produce new, unexpected, and attractive objects of desire. Such objects are partly desirable to the extent that other viewers, watching the same adverts, desire them, too; in desiring the same things, other people add to the cultural value of the objects of advertising. In this way consumer capitalism organises social desire. All those objects through which adverts shape and direct our desire will contain, more or less, the satisfaction generated by us consumers in the act of consuming them. However, the injury and death of accidentsafe adverts cannot be simply consumed, or contained (I am not going to go out and have an accident like I would go out and buy the product). Injury and death necessarily exceed what I can take pleasure in, what I can simply enjoy. So I worry, but, if I watch these adverts at all, I must still enjoy it at some level (the worrying). This makes our 'no worries' public culture somewhat perverse.

Public culture appears in accidentsafe advertising to be shaded by a worried counter-consumer culture. The next advert, you never know, might be an accidentsafe one. This is disconcerting, to say the least. Such advertising disturbs our trust in the visual pleasures of our consumer society. Ads aren't supposed to frighten us! Consuming the products they promote becomes unsafe, makes me insecure, vaguely worried (these ads make you think about accidents you could never imagine for yourself, for instance if you didn't own a car, or have any stairs in your house that you could fall down). Thus accidentsafe adverts insert something else – an unlocalised fear – into the ever-cheerful world of consumer advertising.

Nor is accidentsafe advertising, unlike accidents themselves, avoidable. Adverts and anti-advert public messages are as seamlessly mixed as are advertising and 'proper' programming. Television (and not just television) has gotten so artful that whole programmes now work, relatively painlessly, as adverts (viz. reality television devoted to buying or doing up your house, or getting a job with the Trump organisation). So adverts and accident messages, in order to make us watch – and not turn way – use the same codes. We expect to see something, well, unexpected, something that will make us look and laugh or cry, altogether something affecting. This is what we have learned to expect in a publicity-driven, which is to say advertising-dependent, society. In accidentsafe adverts the form this viewer-pleasure takes is horror and suspense (for instance, sometimes the accident we anticipate doesn't occur).[2] That is, the form that the spectacle of perverse public culture takes is gothic.

In our media-oriented social environment, public messages too must be spectacularised. Accidentsafe adverts must make a spectacle – in this case of injury and death. The spectacle or spectacularising of injury and death is the realm of the gothic. The gothic quality of such messages, at once aesthetic and excessive, makes the

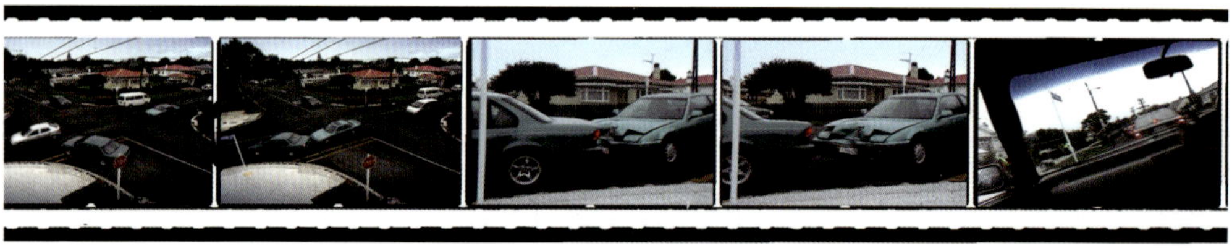

'Don't worry, be happy'
Television advertisement
(Land Transport NZ)

otherwise inaccessible experience of injury and death – how would we know how death feels? – watchable, and therefore, in some way, pleasurable. If anything distinguishes New Zealand-based accidentsafe advertising, it is this aesthetic quality.

There are certainly real reasons to worry about accidents, given accident statistics in New Zealand, and their personal and social cost.[3] No one would quibble with the amount of money spent on accidentsafe campaigns, which reduce personal suffering (from personal injury to loss of family, friends, workmates) as well as the social costs of injury and death.[4] And yet there is an excessive quality to local accidentsafe advertising that cannot be explained by the public concern to reduce the cost of accidents (including a national accident compensation scheme). Such advertising does not simply ask us to take care: it graphically, and sometimes sardonically, depicts the consequences of not doing so.

The black or bleak humour of the 'Don't Worry, Be Happy' advert, which overlays a sequence of car accidents at intersections with Bobby McFerrin's hit song, is particularly – peculiarly – haunting. If you don't immediately recognise, mute and turn away from the advert, you might find yourself silently humming or singing along to a sequence of perfectly executed accidents at intersections, including a woman being bowled by a car that doesn't stop quickly enough. Less successful and effective, perhaps, than the 'Don't do it' campaign – where, say, individual members of a whole community tell a man who has come out of his local pub not to get in his car – this ad is all the more watchable for its sheer excess in the piling up of accidents. However realistic its particular accident scenarios, their sheer repetition, with the addition of the catchy song, makes them highly watchable, even enjoyable (why are you still watching? with what kind of horror?). This advert seems to admit the pleasure that we are inclined to take in advertising – that we have learned to expect from it – even when it involves injury and death.[5]

Imagining injury and death

In the more visceral, most affecting accidentsafe adverts the use of heightened realism and vernacular speech – 'if you don't drink and drive, you're a bloody legend' – tries to shock us into greater awareness of the everyday possibility of injury and death.[6] Visual 'realism' is of

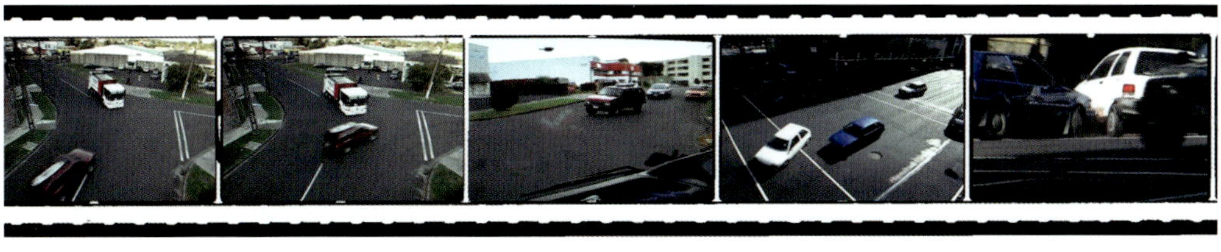

course a qualified term: one does not see people swearing, or slagging off the Prime Minister, on supposedly 'realistic' (i.e. hard-hitting) drama during primetime, nor does one see bodies being blown up (in a war zone) on the evening news. But difficulties of representing injury and death go beyond what constitutes televisual realism, and/or what the greater public will tolerate on screen. For no matter how artful, gripping or graphic the portrayal of real accidents is, 'death' is not exactly an experience. No one who has experienced death can tell us what 'it' is like, or feels like (because that person is dead). The 'experience' of death is in this sense unrepresentable. Yet this is what accidentsafe advertising asks us to imagine. A website supporting the Land Transport NZ's most recent campaign, for instance, asks us to imagine our mates killing us.[7]

Even though the *experience* of death, strictly speaking, is unrepresentable, this does not mean that injury or death is simply unimaginable; on the contrary, accidentsafe adverts make death an act of social imagination. If you cannot imagine your own death, a world without yourself in it, someone else can. And you can always imagine the accident of someone else's death (and wonder what that is like). So the response of others watching accidentsafe adverts makes your own death imaginable. Those others watching the same advert, those would-be consumers of the same things, add social value, meaning, or weight to accidents by experiencing the same advert (if not the accident itself, if not injury or death). In this way we can imagine pain in and through the mixed feelings of others without anyone who is watching necessarily knowing that pain themselves. And in this way the pain of injury and death caused by accidents is also social and shared – social pain.

The pain of injury and death is, then, imaginable though not strictly or properly representable (an image of my pain will be importantly different from the experience). Indeed, codes of representation in the media – given the demand for visual pleasure and a redemptive narrative of drama (restoring or putting to rights the social order) – work against the experience of the pain of accidents even when trying to express it. Accidentsafe advertising resorts to metaphor and to the conventional genre of the gothic to convey the 'reality' of death (to give us something of the 'experience', although truly what we are given is the *threat* of injury or death). The metaphor may

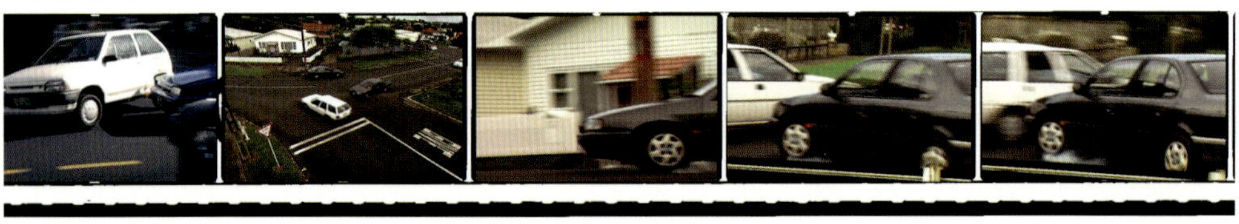

be relatively simple: an image of a razorblade with two windscreen wipers, a hammer and a nail (the car is the hammer, the pedestrian the nail), a can-opener cutting around a tin can (accidents cut into flesh this way).[8]

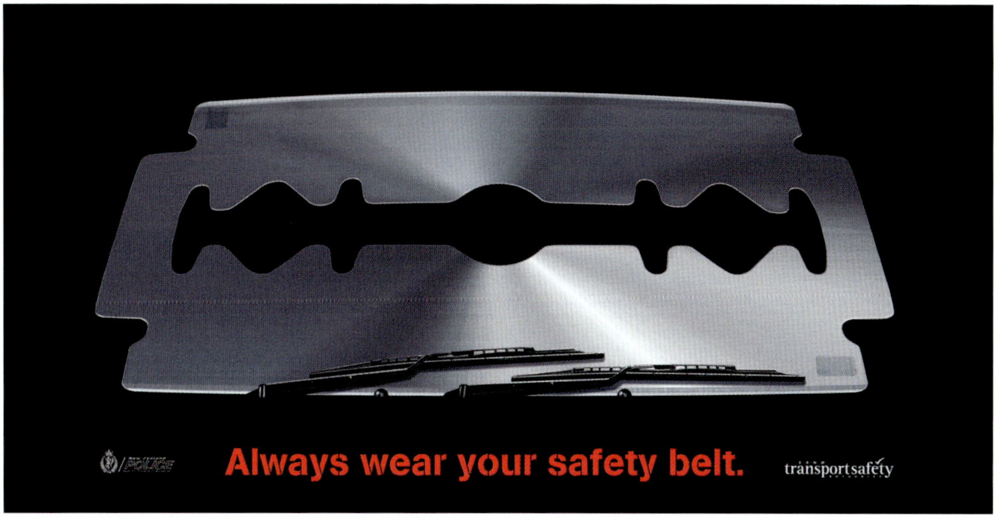

Razor blade windscreen (Land Transport NZ)

But such adverts aren't very affecting, and don't work terribly well. They are too cerebral, and don't seem scary enough. They lack people and flesh – the visceral content, if you can ever call dead or dying people 'content' – of horror/thriller/slasher films. Asked to 'take another look at intersections', what exactly do we see? A bunch of copybook, medieval-era barbarians. It is very difficult, when driving across an intersection, to actually imagine a bunch of fantasy-genre warriors (you merely see an oncoming car, or not, feel a wash of anguish, or not). The need to somehow represent the nearness to death, or to represent the threat of death, means that the gothic genre, with its panoply of figures (including hoary barbarians straight out of *Gladiator*), plays a significant role in public messages of this kind.

The social fact of death on roads is represented in accidentsafe adverts as a gothic haunting, whether in faces blanked out of photos – people once here and now gone ('every year, speeding drivers turn more of us into memories') – or in images of people killed in accidents who return from the dead to warn people of the dangers of speeding (in a 1990s British advertising campaign 'Kill your Speed'). One British ad asks you to imagine what it might be like to have died, and to return to your neighbourhood where life goes on without you. Again, it is others watching this advert that makes your own death conceivable, representable, to you.

This haunting sits oddly with the 'scientific' approach of a 2005

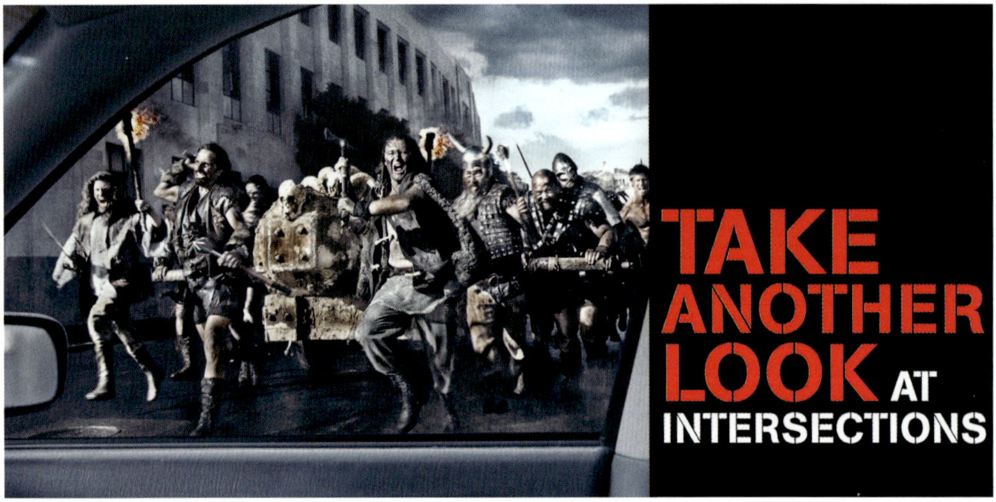

Barbarians (Land Transport NZ)

accidentsafe series. The typology of accidentsafe adverts runs from the fantastic, through the actual ('realistic') to the scientific (each, in another context, would require breaking down according to its own visual mode). But how can the fantastic and the scientific be part of the same public awareness campaign? In the scientific adverts, Dr Ian Johnston of Monash University in Australia explains the difference that five kilometres per hour makes at the point of collision; Dr John Olver, an Australian neuro-rehab physician, explains how the human body, unconstrained by a safety belt, is thrown around in a car like a pinball.[9] One may question these purely scientific explanations: there are a variety of contextual or situational factors in collisions that make five kilometres per hour one variable among others, including road conditions, visibility, the kind of road or intersection, the positioning of other traffic, and the behaviour of other drivers. But beyond the variables which might well have been added to these accounts of accidents, science cannot fully account for the social pain of injury and death, which seems to lie outside its domain.

In a world fully subjected to scientific explanation the gothic addresses the historical and social fact of death: why do people die needlessly? Where do they go? Are they still here? Such questions demand metaphysical as much as scientific explanation, and meet a psychological need. The incidence of death (on roads) may be susceptible to the analysis of physics or statistical quantification, but social pain is not. Roads themselves became 'gothic', pockmarked with crosses (driving past such crosses, the refrain 'don't worry, be happy' – as opposed to something more like 'bloody hell' – seems inappropriate, and positively ghoulish). The gothic imagery and even uncomfortable beauty of accident adverts tries to account for this existential cost over and above scientific explanation or statistical quantification. But it also generates the problem of taking pleasure in images of injury and death.

The mixed feeling of accidentsafe messages

That physics or statistics aren't adequate to social pain is perhaps why those adverts depicting the social cost of injury and death are the most intense and affecting. It's impossible for viewers to embrace the real pain of this loss. After all, it's most likely not my loss, my experience, and, anyway, why would I want to embrace, or even re-live, this loss. Don't I watch television, or respond to its messages, for some kind of pleasure, some reward or return? Insofar as they try to persuade by fear, such adverts push the gothic into hyper-realism, which I respond to as if I am watching a horror film. In other words, I *want* the thrill of someone being knocked down, which is not how the message is supposed to work.

Because they try to register pain, accident adverts twist the visual pleasure of advertising. They are asking you to 'buy' fear (to buy into fear). But how do we know that adverts which rely on inducing fear actually work? The message may well get across, accident rates may well be reduced, but we can't be sure that that is because people are responding to fear. What is clearer is that such adverts resort to excessively graphic or metaphorical imagery (an excess which tries to match an incalculable social pain) to get you to watch. But the social pain of accidents, which is unquantifiable and therefore impossible to absorb, tells us something about advertising itself. Thinksafe adverts in New Zealand[10] – adverts to do with accidents around the home – do not mimic other adverts without reason: a man who falls backwards off an unsecured ladder set against the upper level of his house starts by advertising the paint he is using as a product; a woman who stands on a child's toy and falls through a glass coffee table starts by advertising a ubiquitous fruit snack bar. These would-be adverts turn into accident adverts. This twist, or element of surprise, might make us afraid that any advert could have a similar horror ending, or they might make us want every advert to go this way.

Such 'anti-adverts' shade or cast a shadow over other adverts. They reveal how advertising shows us objects we are supposed to want, and how, in doing so, our sense of social pain is (ordinarily)

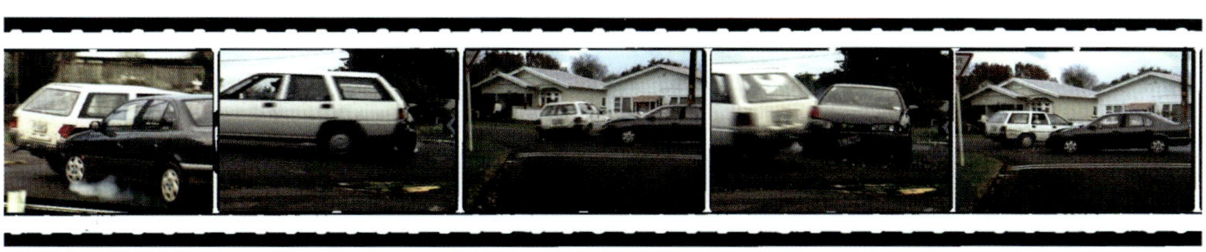

eclipsed. The deadness one experiences when watching a lot of advertising (or too much television) is just why one might yearn for a greater thrill, something more intense, more real, something that pierces all this easy, protective, and safe desire – the sponsored desire for this or that product. This might feel like the thrill, for instance, of someone being hit by a car, falling off a ladder, or crashing through a coffee table. In the film *Crash* (1997) David Cronenberg registers a contemporary deadness of feeling where sex, which stands for desire, or what I'm supposed to want, is never enough, partly because it is everywhere (thanks to advertising), and partly because sex, or whatever is associated with sex, is just what one is always supposed to want. Perhaps what we really want – more than sex or anything associated with it – is to *feel*, but not necessarily to feel good about something, or to have something that will make me feel good.

The model straddling a souped-up car has been disfigured by an accident so that we will find this image horrible. We are also meant to find horrible other accidentsafe adverts with scarred people. But given our predisposition to find images pleasurable (something trained, instilled, developed through a lifetime of watching media), one might find this image perversely appealing, perhaps more truly pleasurable because more intense, more thrilling, more real. What is 'real' here is not just the fact or rate of disfigurement by accidents,

Amputee (Land Transport NZ)

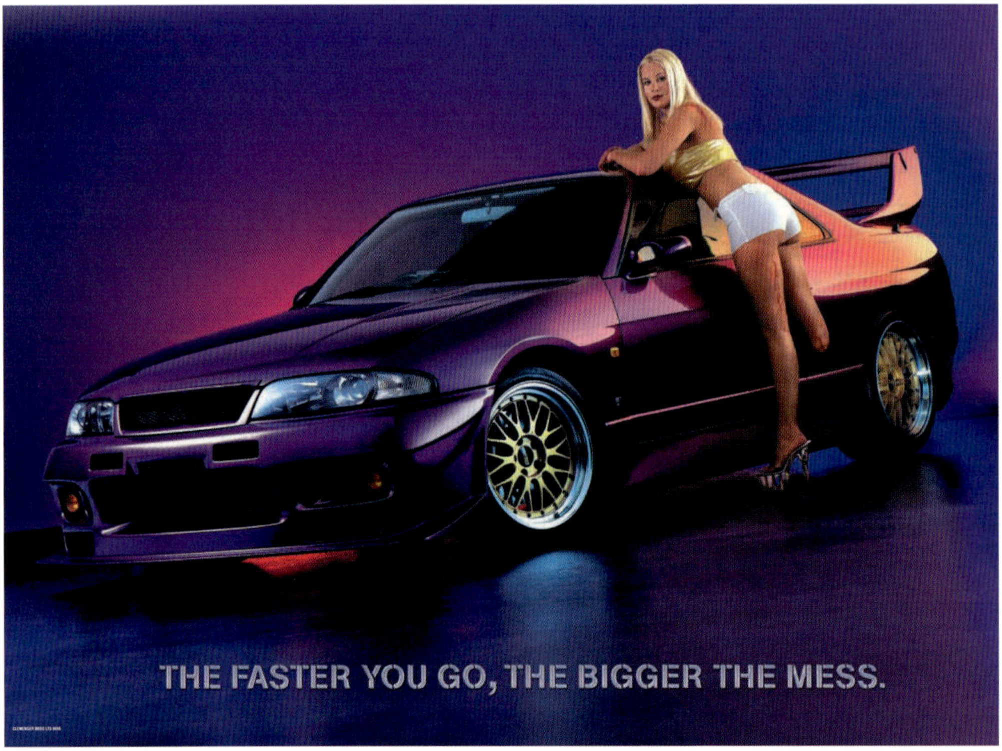

but the intense feeling – the painfully mixed pleasure – that this image induces. This is something of which we are ordinarily deprived by endless car + sex adverts, though the effect of this particular advert depends on the existence of all those other adverts, and other possible consumers who are watching and presumably desiring what the adverts advertise. Of course this mixed feeling is not something one can easily or ordinarily say, much less quantify (it is, after all, a mixed feeling). The public domain is about not having difficult, dodgy feelings of this kind, and yet these are feelings that our commercialised media actually animates, mobilises. The only way in which such worrisome feeling (because it is difficult, dodgy) can legitimately appear is in an ironic mode, which is perhaps no bad thing.

The intensity and difficulty of mixed feeling defines the vernacular gothic. That combination of deathrace driving (not just boy-racers) and 'no worries' public culture produces the bleak humour of 'don't worry, be happy'. The humour, or better, the irony of worry is vital to a healthy public sphere. A healthy society countenances the fact that people may be sick or depressed, and that they die, sometimes horribly. We do say 'no worries', or 'she'll be right', or 'it's all good', but in the context of accidents such sentiments contribute to social death, because they suggest a lack of any real feeling – a reflexive indifference, a fretful sameness. The sense that 'she' won't be alright is therefore highly aestheticised in accidentsafe advertising because it's not ordinarily easy to say. What is otherwise unsayable, what is strictly unrepresentable, feeds the local gothic. In this way oddly aestheticised or ironic adverts stave off social death and defray the social cost of accidents – the cost, deeper than ACC expenses, of a public culture of pretend social good (it's going well, really it is). Road deaths make a mockery of such pretence – there's every chance of dying on a New Zealand road – but there's also a mockery of death in such cartoon-like representations (just mind the barabarians, love).

Take another look at intersections

I don't need to look again at the woman being bowled over by a car, but I know I'm going to see it many times anyway. So how do I deal with this don't-look-now moment? The perverse pleasure of

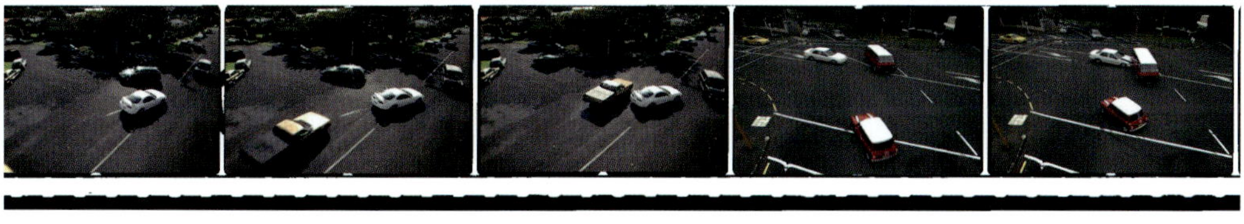

its repetition at least keeps death at bay; the advert produces, after all, some (mixed) feeling rather than the total absence of feeling. We aren't convinced that the fear of injury or death that this advert is trying to instill will make anyone drive differently, because the fear is necessarily coded as pleasurable. However, enjoyable accidental death – the bleak humour of 'don't worry, be happy' – may, perversely, have social value. There is something outlandish, excessive about local accidentsafe imagery. This is because social pain – something you kind of know, but can't easily say, or see – is actually unquantifiable, unrepresentable. So do buckle up, drive carefully, take another look at intersections, and enjoy your imagined death.

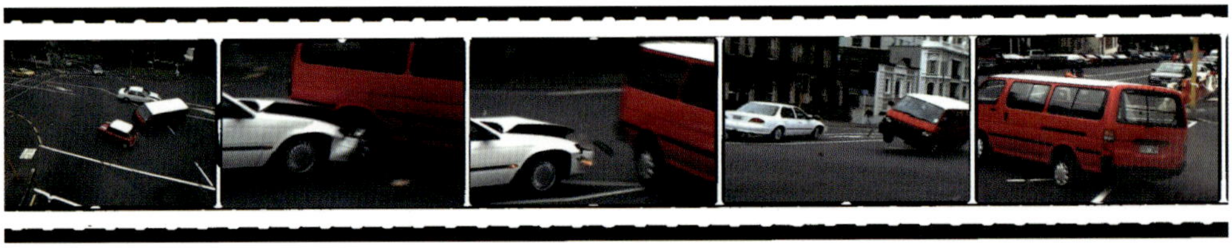

Afterword: How Gothic Is It?

Ian Wedde

Graf Orlok:	Is this your wife? What a lovely throat.
	Nosferatu, eine Symphonie des Grauens (F.W. Murau, 1922)

Warden:	The patient that came in yesterday is having a fit.
Van Helsing:	Which one?
Warden:	The one that bit the cow.
	Nosferatu: Phantom der Nacht (Werner Herzog, 1979)

Van Helsing:	Yes, I agree using garlic seems like nonsense, but I sense something evil and I must try everything to combat it. Evil will not disappear simply because we disapprove.
Dr John Seward:	But what is evil?
	Count Dracula (BBC TV, 1977)

Carl:	Here, take this.
	[*he hands Van Helsing a bag, then begins to fill it*]
Carl:	Rings of garlic … holy water … silver stake … crucifix …
	[*they pass two monks test-firing a Gatling gun*]
Van Helsing:	Why can't I have one of those?
	Van Helsing (Stephen Sommers, 2004)

> Not only does Sam Neill [in *Cinema of Unease*] provide interesting insights into what drives New Zealand's filmmakers, and the cultural background (or apparent lack of it!) they come from – it is also a brilliant piece of documentary film-making in its own right.
>
> Review comment by 'frodolives' 4 July 2002
> IMDb on-line movie database.

No laughing matter

There's a question that haunts the essays collected in this book. It resembles a more disorderly one that was present at the conference which preceded the book. Back then, I sometimes found myself trying to focus the question while looking at the tranquil, green landscape surrounding the Albany campus of Massey University north of Auckland. I was trying not to be distracted by the familiarly incongruous Tex-Mex architecture of the university's buildings, the drone of the northern motorway and a suite of light industrial buildings cresting a nearby hill. The ordinariness of these surroundings and not least their random sampling of a semi-bucolic Kiwi modernity seemed at first to be a distraction from the question I was trying to hear in order to attempt an answer. The question kept stumbling back and forth across a kind of grammatical tripper: how gothic is this? And then, how is this gothic? Even with my eyes shut to the distracting, fragmented modernity of the environs, even looking for the question within a darkened, internal place of thought, it kept stumbling. It wanted to be in both places at once. It wanted both places to be held by a single question.

Goth fashionistas (Barney, Pavement Magazine, 2004/05)

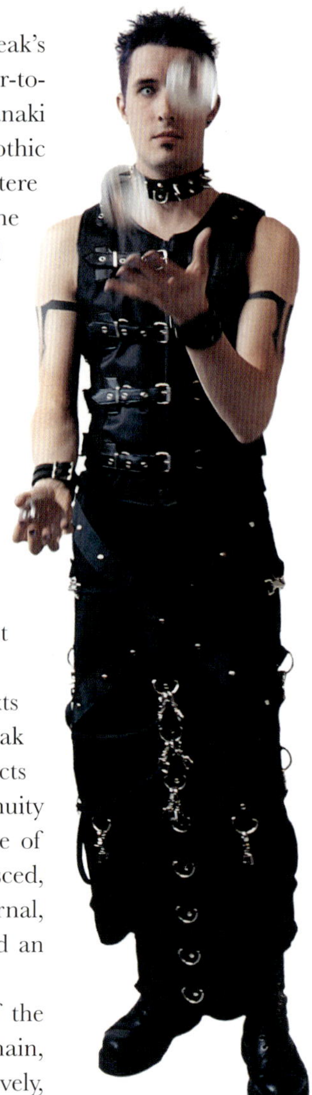

Soon, however, the surroundings, and not least the coffee break's plate of chocolate wheaten biscuits snacked upon by shoulder-to-shoulder scholars of gothic literary classics, aficionados of Taranaki Gothic, kohl-eyed goths, gothic dungeon clubbers, the neo-gothic storytellers of the movie *Scarfies*, goth fashionistas, and austere theorists of the uncanny, stopped intruding on my hunt for the phantom question and began, instead, to frame it. I reviewed the motley conference crowd, sometimes dabbing crimson jam from its lips, at home in the terracotta-roofed buildings that might, in a shape-shifted reality, have been the film set for the vampire lap-dance bar in the Quentin Tarantino/ Robert Rodriguez bloodsuck romp, *From Dusk Till Dawn* (with the incomparably uncanny Juliette Lewis). I took in the unnaturally green pasture, the unsafe screech of traffic on the northern motorway, the unwholesome, blankly shuttered profile of the light industrial buildings looming on the rise. I sensed an infection seeping not into these comfortably familiar surroundings from the gothic business of the conference, but into the conference from its homely milieu.

When, now, I read in Jennifer Lawn's introduction to these texts that it may, on their evidence, already be a given for us to speak of a New Zealand gothic 'as a mode, not a genre', that gothic acts on us as 'a shifting warp of the familiar', that it 'exposes the tenuity of the natural, scaled, domestic world', I remember the sense of uneasy displacement with which my stumbling questions coalesced, somehow, into a single one whose tension was between the external, defined materiality of genre taxonomies and etymologies, and an internal, uncertain, phantasmagoric unease.

It's a tension captured in Jack Ross's marginal annotation of the narrative gothic costumery of crown, ear pendants, neck chain, breast ornaments, girdle, clasps and loincloth as, respectively, walkman, dark glasses, gold cross, tank top, black jeans, watch-strap and G-string. It's there in Sarah Shieff's chillingly accurate suggestion that an appropriate homologue for Tourism New Zealand's original '100% pure' landscape might be *Lebensraum* – a gothic repositioning of the sublime as awe and terror before the Unnatural (with eugenic and racist undertones). It's there in Stephen Turner's and Scott Wilson's discovery of 'viewer-pleasure' in the horror of television accidentsafe advertising. It's certainly there in David Craig's identification of photography as a key medium of 'gothic modernism' – an exploitation of the uncanny effects of a seemingly empirical, realist science made to reveal spooks and, we might add, a link to the uncanniness of science that mesmerised Mary Shelley in 1818 when electricity was weird, new, modern, the future.

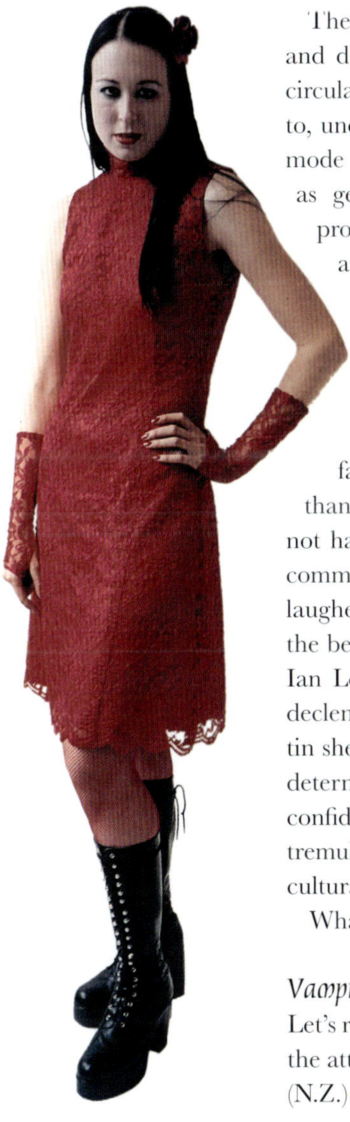

The uneasiness that the conference was looking for ways to out and document now, in these texts, appears as linked stages in a circular process. It begins with a precondition of, or predisposition to, uneasiness. It then employs 'the gothic' as an instrumentalising mode of production whose uneasy effects can be taxonomised as genres, histories, conventions, codes. These uneasy gothic products are, next, the causes of uneasy affects. Their uneasily affected subjects are returned to, or reinforced in, the uneasy predisposition with which the process began. It's eerie, it's inevitable – we're doomed.

But this is way too deterministic, even fatalistic. Applied to Misha Kavka's mordant plumbing of the mouldy domestic, for example, it would turn all of us into abject fatalists, the victims of rising, or is it creeping, damp – rather than the cheerfully accident-prone renovators we are. We may not have crashed through glass tabletops in our own accidentsafe commercials, but we've bashed our thumbs with hammers and laughed to tell the tale. As gothic fatalists, we'd be impervious to the belittling, even parodic, aspects of architectural history that, in Ian Lochead's account, can take European cathedrals through a declension from High Gothic through Gothic Revival to the little tin shed of the Naseby Athenaeum. As gothic determinists, or pre-determinants, we'd be without humour and we'd lack the cultural confidence that laughing at yourself sometimes discloses. Even the tremulous sniggers of uneasy provincials in the haunted houses of cultural subalternism.

What was the question?

Vampire Hobbits

Let's return to the quotations with which this essay began. Although the attentive credits-reader would have spotted Weta Workshop Ltd (N.Z.) well down the long list of Special Effects Companies involved in Stephen Sommers' comprehensively inclusive gothic camp spoof *Van Helsing* (2004) – Weta was responsible for making the miniature ship – this would hardly qualify the movie for inclusion in Sam Neill's and Judy Rymer's 1995 *Cinema of Unease: A Personal Journey by Sam Neill*, even had the latter been capable of looking into a gothic future for New Zealand film that would include the uncanny and gothic elements of the *Lord of the Rings* trilogy and *King Kong*, not to mention Glenn Standring's hugely successful video release *The Irrefutable Truth About Demons* (2000).

The 'apparent lack of' cultural background – surmised by the Hobbit-bitten 'frodolives' after viewing Sam Neill's and Judy Rymer's biomentary – wouldn't have explained why Neill and Rymer (thought they) detected such an uneasy undertow in postcolonial New Zealand culture in general and film culture in particular. What the film might have converted the zombie Frodofanatic to, however, is the rabid belief that New Zealand film is incapable of levity, parody, self-mockery, genre-awareness, or plain, simple fun.

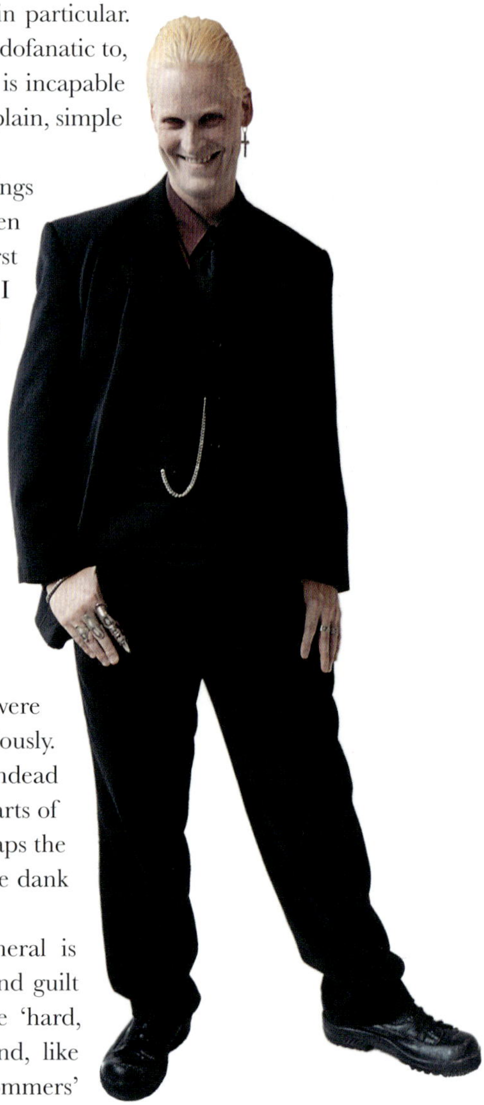

For several years I've walked or run most mornings through parts of Wellington's Mount Victoria green belt and it was here, during the filming of the first of Peter Jackson's *Lord of the Rings* trilogy, that I encountered Frodo and his companions cowering under the enhanced roots of old pines off to one side of the walking track. Long after all traces of the location equipment had been cleared away, I'd meet small parties of *Rings* devotees and tourists re-enacting the scene in which Frodo and his Hobbit mates hide from the gothically hooded dark riders. Many of the tourists had gone to some trouble to dress up in heavy cloaks reminiscent of *The Monk* and they were usually taking turns videoing each other. Some of the tourist Hobbits were laughing and hamming it up, but there were some who took the re-enactments very, very seriously. Sometimes, I'd meet Hobbit-location seekers and undead Dark Rider hunters wandering lost in the wrong parts of the green belt with their vague internet printout maps the wrong way up, and I'd have to redirect them to the dank cowering location.

Whether or not New Zealand culture in general is metonymically darkened by postcolonial unease and guilt (or whether, on the contrary, it is blinded by the 'hard, clear light' famously lampooned by Francis Pound, like Carl's vampire-blinding invention in Stephen Sommers'

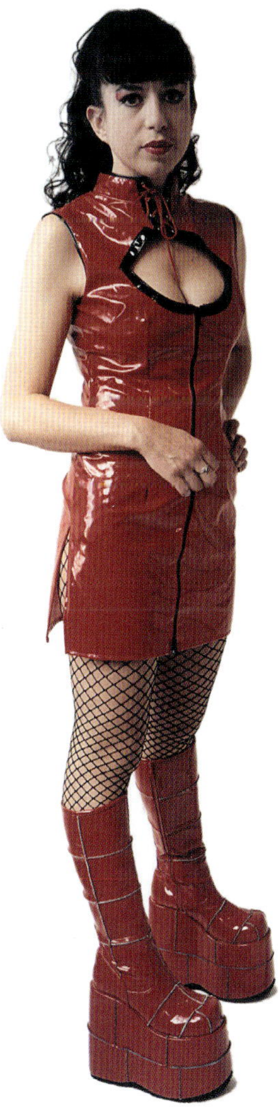

Van Helsing), this debate isn't, in the end, as productive or interesting as one that asks for evidence of confident mockery in the cultural production of 'unease'. 'Unease', after all, can be both an affect and a consumer experience: the former the more or less involuntary condition of a psychologised subject, the latter the more or less voluntarily desired commodity of a fully conscious thrill-seeker. Most of us are both – that's how it works. An audience's awareness and confidence – its *consciousness* – are easily found in evidence of its willingness to accept the conventions, the genres, the discourse models, of cultural products at face value: to conspire with the artist in knowing willingness to role-play, to accept the mode of informed spectatorial address described by Michael Fried[1] and exemplified in the disenchanted comment of a child recorded by the great American animator Chuck Jones: 'You don't *draw* Bugs Bunny, you draw *pictures* of Bugs Bunny'.[2] New Zealand audiences are no less saturated in the long, bloody history of hardcore gothic than audiences anywhere else and are no less susceptible to and able to play with the inevitable ironies, spoofs and camp-ups that such a sensational history of repetition and reproduction will inevitably generate. The demand-side and the supply-side feed, and feed on, each other: the culture of pastiche is vampiric by nature. The nourishment it provides has to be simultaneously familiar and fresh. It is hard, now, to look back at the folkloric founding intentions of F.W. Murnau's 'classic' *Nosferatu* and not be entertained by the historical process that has transformed Graf Orlock's 'What a lovely throat' into a joke – let alone keep a straight face at the 'one that bit the cow' dialogue in Murnau's most direct descendant, Werner Herzog's, 1979 *homage*, or at the muffled English common sense of Abraham Van Helsing's scepticism about the efficacy of something as trans-Channel as garlic to combat evil in the BBC's television version of 1977.

It seems highly improbable that the 'unease' detected in Sam Neill's and Judy Rymer's investigation of the dark side of New Zealand film culture could be attributed to the 'lack-of-cultural-background' idea with which the IMDb zombie Hobbit's thought has been infected, though provincial cultural uncertainty has certainly been the cause of humourlessness on more than one occasion. But nothing announces cultural confidence more loudly than the sound of loud, confident laughter as culture vampires feast upon the bodies of products for which they've developed an educated taste. Though ironic tastes for the camp, kitsch, spoof, pastiche and parody can go beyond a joke, the undying loop in which vampiric supply and demand satisfy each other is one sign of a healthy, well-fed 'cultural background'.

Some mornings, watching the by-now normal Hobbitic charades being enacted under dripping pines off the muddy Mount Vic track,

I had to remind myself of the components and structure of this cultural sport. The dark, sopping pines were in New Zealand and originated mostly from the Monterey Peninsula in California. The hill they covered had been renamed from Maori after an English queen. The characters they were impersonating derived from an English fantasy novel which recycled elements of mostly Scandinavian but also Germanic (and Gothic) myth after processing them through the mouli of xenophobic and racist British nationalism, Anglo-Catholicism and anti-Semitism – though, to be fair, very few viewers of the movies are going to be thinking this, let alone spotting Gollum for an anti-Semitic caricature. The gothic, too, has to live with the blithe consumption of its products by audiences who couldn't care less. The chilly, cowering Hobbit re-enactors were from many parts of the world, especially Asia, and seemed not to be locating the world of the film outside the film world in which it lived and prospered – though they were welcoming the chance to elide the supra-national and non-geocultural world of the film with one of its production locations. The hero of the film was its director and co-writer, the New Zealander Peter Jackson, and its support star was the special effects team of Weta Workshop Ltd. – the same that would subsequently provide Stephen Sommers' *Van Helsing* with its miniature boat. But the film was produced, financed and distributed by the American film industry, for which New Zealand existed only as the location preferred by its director and as the non-unionised labour force preferred by its American project managers. That notwithstanding, some of the film's spectacular mountainous scenery would be conflated at governmental level with the 2002 '100% Pure' Tourism New Zealand marketing campaign and with mountainous endorsements from Mastercard as key signifiers of New Zealand's (Pacific?) national identity – a sublime drawn uneasily between eugenic cleansing and awesomely unnatural deculturation. The Wellington City Council would co-opt the film's international success and revenue-earning clout to its 'Creative Capital' marketing campaign, adorning its airport with a gigantic facsimile of the über-gothic creature Gollum, though the city's useful contribution to a local film industry has been confined to the marketing opportunities of Red Carpet celebrations and cutting some slack in respect of location scouts. It has not run to venture capital, nor to themed shelter for the dripping Hobbit-fans once they'd come down off their dark mountain, or rent-a-hood services before they got themselves up there.

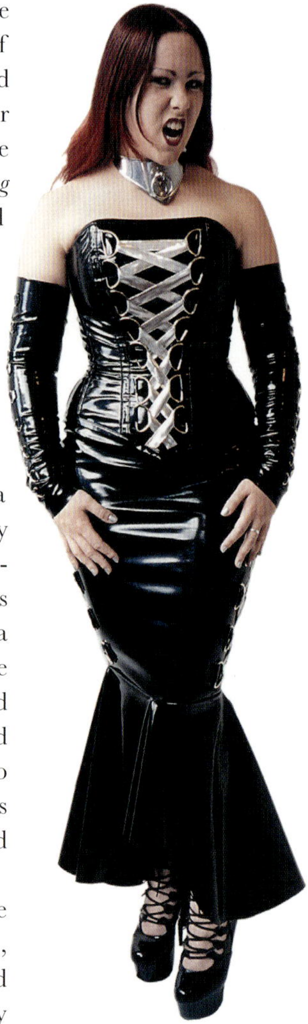

But this is how it works – it's all over the place. The confidence of a cultural idea and history as global and popular as 'the gothic', composed of equal parts of classic genres, spoofs, psychologised subjects at national and individual levels, fashions and tastes, uncanny cultural conditions and varieties of the sublime whose terrors are felt before spectacles of the awesomely unnatural rather than the majestically natural – such a confidently persisting, resourceful and undying idea is pretty much free of the provincial anxiety of the self-perceived underachiever.

Isn't it? Surely the 'unease' that might be attributed to either (or both) post-colonial malaise and guilt, and 'lack of' robust, spoofable cultural background, isn't the sort of unapologetic background that's made possible the edgy humour of *Bro'Town*? Which, surely, can only with extreme implausibility be co-opted to a 'gothic mode' as White Fear? The sprawling geocultural audience reach, global capital flows and complexly mediated and retooled narratives of *The Lord of the Rings*, encountered in miniature in a giggling huddle of drenched Japanese Hobbit role-players on the Californian hillside above my house in Wellington, New Zealand, altogether constitute a not-bad model from which to launch an inquiry into the gothic down-under that wants to know not, uneasily, 'are we up to it', but, confidently, 'how do we get up to it?' How gothic are we?

How gothic is it?

How we get up to antipodean gothic was the inquiry of the *Antipodean Gothic* conference from which this book has emerged. From time to time during the conference, while chasing my phantom question around the *From Dusk Till Dawn* setting, I thought about the German writer Walter Abish's 'detective story' *How German is It?* – not because his novel is a gothic one or because the conference had a detective-story (or even a whodunit) shape to it, but because, embedded in the novel's crafty appropriation of the detective genre, the question '*Wie Deutsch ist es?*' appears as an unforgiving, tireless, remorseless demand for answers: the sleuth-novel that won't stop and that will stop at nothing. The answers the novel's demanding in the guise of a hard-bitten detective who won't let go of his inquiry relate to the historically sinister vibration of the book's German title, *Wie Deutsch ist es?* And they're also succinctly captured in the novel's laconic epigraph by Jean-Luc Godard: 'What is really at stake is one's image of oneself'.

The haunted self-reflexivity of the German investigation (or denial) of what it was to be German in 1979 when Abish's book was published did, of course, reach back to an uneasy past in Nazism and, past that, also to the dark forests of bad-blood mythology, redemption and expiation, and the fresh re-issues of these narratives in the present. What the book's remorseless inquiry worries at is the tension between the involuntary unease of the culturally insecure or infected subject and the voluntary unease of the redemption-seeking role-player. It probes the degrees of self-consciousness and authenticity with which its subjects ask the question, 'How German is it?' It wants to know if its characters are aware of their 'spectatorial address', if they know that what they're looking at (in themselves, for instance, in 'one's image of oneself') is a 'picture of', or if it's *das Ding an sich*, the Kantian unknowable reality that haunts phenomenal experience – or if it's just the phenomenon that scares the living daylights out of them when they encounter it, when they encounter themselves. The quest of Abish's unforgiving novel is for identity – 'German' identity as well as self-image – defined in terms of its position along the continuum from haunted abject to ironic subject. Where, on that continuum, do the novel's characters locate themselves? Are the abject merely victims of history – infected by the sins of their fathers? Are the ironists cynical vampires nourishing themselves knowingly on the fresh reissues of old stories? How to be simultaneously disenchanted and ethically committed? How German is it to be abject, disenchantedly ethical, cynical? How is one to be those things in a 'German' way?

The inquiry 'how do we get up to antipodean gothic?' might be rephrased with more nuance as 'where do we find the antipodean gothic on a continuum from haunted abject to ironic subject?' Or, 'how gothic are we antipodeans when we are abject or ironic down here?' Or, 'how are we antipodeans to be those things in a "gothic" way down here?'

This has now, of course, become also a question about brand identity, a cultural tool whose influence has grown hugely since Walter Abish wrote *Wie Deutsch ist es?* in 1979. Now, in 2006, much cultural unease is generated here in New Zealand by the question, 'how excellent is it?' ('how excellent are we?') – a question that derives the authority of its inquiry from commodity marketing's version of the Jean-Luc Godard question about self-image. Excellence is attributable to products and is often best judged by brand strengths and successes – by the efficacy of brand values. Excellence is less frequently, and less smoothly, attributed to social processes and conditions. Excellence measures appearance, performance and desirability in a competitive or comparative present. It is less likely to be asked to, or be able to, measure social interiority, process and relevance within a sustainable history. Along with being reminded from time to time during the conference of the dry, precise, laconic humour with which Abish interrogated the 'values' of Germany in 1979, I was often reminded of the pseudo-seriousness with which brand values and identities are discussed a quarter-century later. This was because the conference itself, as you'd expect, represented in its registrants diverse 'brands' of the gothic and diverse points-of-view about which brands had the strongest values, that is, which were the most excellent. There were several academic brands whose values were derived from scholarship and taxonomic and/or etymological rigour. There were club brands whose values depended on the excellence of the leisure experience they provided – of the architecture, art direction, music, drugs and immersive risk-taking in gothic clubs. There were down-home brands – in New Zealand, the Ronald Hugh Morrieson version prevails – which saw value in the appropriation of luridly 'gothic' narrative tropes by giant-shadow-casting ripping yarns. There were brands defined by gender and sexual orientation and by their politicised values in feminist and queer estimations of excellence. Some brands announced their values through dress and fashion – how could you presume to gothic excellence if you weren't a goth? Gothic excellence manifested as a ghastly, waxy pallor on the surfaces of some artworks and as a brooding chiaroscuro in others whose *noir* colour-grading emphasised the carmine of lips and the impenetrable darkness of shadows. Urban camp values shared the same plate of chocolate-wheaten biscuits at morning coffee time as values derived from the investigation of a rural uncanny associated with ferality.

The question 'how gothic is it?' is by now being asked to answer to several measures of truth: 'how excellent is its brand?', 'how sustainable are its social conditions?', 'what are its cultural manifestations?', and 'what kind of ethical confidence does its self-analysis disclose?'

Smells uncanny

Carl: Why does it smell like wet dog in here?
Van Helsing: [*running past him*] Werewolf! (*Van Helsing*)

'The gothic' was certainly pungently present at the conference, in all its many guises. I'd naïvely come to the convention expecting my one presupposition to be endorsed, but it wasn't. My only defining thought about the gothic prior to being in its strongly marked presence had been that 'the gothic' in its classic manifestations such as Matthew Gregory Lewis's *The Monk* (1796), Mary Shelley's *Frankenstein* (1818) and Bram Stoker's *Dracula* (1897) was incompatible with humour – would tissue-reject humour – but that its later, antipodean (or, more probably, post-colonial) manifestations were all about humour – were, in fact, about the liberated piss-taking by post-colonials of imperial culture's sacred cows, especially the ones that went 'Mooo!' in the night. Nice theory. But while vampiric, post-colonial irony and a relish for fresh imperial cow were manifest at the conference, so were varieties of seriousness in which I began to see that 'the gothic' persisted as an unbroken, not-funny historical narrative from its psychoscientific frisson in Mary Shelley through Sigmund Freud's essay 'The Uncanny' of 1919 to contemporary vampirisms of blood products associated with pathogenic catastrophe, AIDS, ghoulish trafficking in human organs, the Undead of cloning, and the unnatural chimeras of transgenic mutation. It was clear that some of the serious, core questions asked by and in the gothic narrative were not going to die.

If we stay with this dead-serious spoor, we find that Mary Shelley's fascination with the life-creating energy of new-fangled electricity is decanted into the psychopathology of Freud's look at uncanny states of life such as the 'living doll' Olympia in Offenbach's *Tales of Hoffmann*, the same essay's succinct summary of 'the double' as a 'preservation against extinction'[3] and its inclusion of 'suspended animation' states such as epilepsy. The same life-and-death narrative appears almost unchanged in our own times in the uncannily beating heart cells cultivated in a Petri dish from stem cells,[4] or in the blubbing new-life-from-old sound of the uncannily onomatopoeic word 'Bellerophon', which is a contemporary 'double': at once the Greek hero who horse-whispered Pegasus and with the winged horse slew the monstrous transgenic Chimera; and the biotech software-assisted programme Bellerophon used to detect chimeric genetic sequences.

Think of Gollum as a gothic product nurtured in the Petri dish of racialism from stem cells of anti-Semitism.

Though less gothic in their disembodied, bloodless nature, digital Artificial Life (rather than Artificial Intelligence), or Alife, agents whose algorithms begin to have lives (and minds) of their own, may also be narrative descendants of Mary Shelley's prescient fascination with the unnatural science of life and the gothic mirror in which life and death look at each other and see themselves. Then fall in love with each other/themselves. Then have sex (with each other/themselves). Then spawn. *Liebestod.* Self-perpetuating digital babies. The technological sublime. Especially if we accept the ALife researcher Christopher Langton's hypothesis that life is a property of form not matter – of organ-isation (so to speak), not materiality.[5] Note to reader: this is not by any stretch of credulity an argument for Intelligent Design. God only knows what ID advocates would make of the idea that the software organ-isations of computers could 'come to life'.

Needless to say, the hauntings of fascist eugenics are what spook bioethics committees peering into the murky mirror of the human genome project, for example. If we're all nearly the same, what's the difference and how is it marked? Branded? Let's hope it doesn't come down to competitive 'excellence' and the values of national brands – to commodified versions of the question, 'How German is it?'

Maybe (I think) what we need more of are unsettling gothic stories, the ones about life and death and everything in between, that we can tell and listen to with varieties of Michael Fried's 'spectatorial address' from serious to camp and everything in between.

We'd benefit, too, from a gothic impetus to put the bite on one or two other sacred, nationalist cows (and let's not forget the cannibalism, Pacific-historical and post-immunosuppressant, that public culture continues to avert its eyes from). newzealandgenetics.com, for starters, the 'livestock improvement' subsidiary of Fonterra (formerly New Zealand Milk). In its logo, as in Fonterra's, a familiar landscape appears. It's what '100% pure' alps look like when logoised and lowered to the uncraggy horizons of pastureland. It reminds us that the sublime backcountry Nicholas and Caroline Chevalier spurred their horses towards when crossing the Taramakau River through massive forest giants in April 1866 would soon, under Nicholas's pencil and brush, become the picturesque vistas of marketable real estate – realty not reality – tufted with grassy fodder for the mossy cattle beasts the painter shrewdly imported to the scene from the Scottish Highlands. The Otago and Canterbury Provincial Councils paid his fees.

What the fees also bought – not the cheerfully enterprising Nicholas's fault – was a tradition in which the abject dissociations of a European sublime would be persistently co-opted to the pragmatic urgings of antipodean realty (the new reality). The glassy picture frame through which we view versions of the verdant vistas from Massey University's Albany campus is now, in its prime hilltop locations, usually organising our safe distance from haunted places. They are haunted by the ash of forests and the ghosts of Pacific Uruk-hai. Inhabiting these hauntings and histories, as Donna Haraway proposes, rather than viewing them, might be a gothic task – a liberating one, as Martin Edmond suggests in this book.

We could end, then, with a kind of answer to a kind of question. Leaving plenty of room for confident self-mockery of gothic pretension and compassion for gothic abjection, we can argue with Jacques Attali in *L'Homme nomade* (Fayard 2003) for displacement as the foundation of culture. If gothic is, as Jennifer Lawn suggests, more a mode than a genre, it may be more a mode of displacement than of any other condition. And as a mode of displacement it may be what jolts us, through laughter or horror or both at once, into the kind of cultural confidence that lives in its histories, not in spite of them. That chooses to be haunted as a necessary condition of consciousness. That doesn't turn up its nose at the smell of wet dog.

Notes

Introduction

1 Lydia Wevers, 'The Politics of Culture', in *Writing at the Edge of the Universe*, ed. Mark Williams (Christchurch: Canterbury University Press, 2004), p. 116.
2 Stuart Hall, cited in Ken Gelder and Jane Jacobs, *Uncanny Australia* (Carlton South, Vic.: Melbourne University Press, 1998), p. xi.
3 Throughout this text, uppercase 'Gothic' is used to describe recognised artistic and architectural movements, while lowercase 'gothic' is the more generic term.
4 Grant Shanks with Tahu Potiki, *Where No Birds Sing* (Christchurch: Shoal Bay Press, 1998), p. 22.
5 William Schafer, *Mapping the Godzone* (Honolulu: University of Hawai'i Press, 1998), p. 137.
6 Cited in Michael Fitzgerald, 'Southern Gothic: Karen Walker's Edgy Designs Reflect the Darker Tones of her Native New Zealand', *Time South Pacific*, 24 May 1999: 60.
7 Noel Virtue, *The Redemption of Elsdon Bird* (Auckland: Century Hutchinson, 1988), p. 29.
8 Patricia Grace, *Baby No-Eyes* (Auckland: Penguin, 1998), p. 83.

The Abandoned House

1 Merrilyn George, *Ohakune: Opening to a New World; a District History* (Ohakune: Kapai Enterprises, 1990).
2 Julia Millen, *Ronald Hugh Morrieson: A Biography* (Auckland: David Ling, 1996), pp. 35, 204.

Gothic Inversions And Displacements

1 Everett F. Bleiler, 'Introduction', *Three Gothic Novels: The Castle of Otranto by Horace Walpole, Vathek by William Beckford, The Vampyre by John Polidori, and a Fragment of a Novel by Lord Byron*, ed. Everett F. Bleiler (New York: Dover, 1996), xvi.
2 See Anne Williams, *Art of Darkness: A Poetics of Gothic* (Chicago: University of Chicago Press, 1995), xi.
3 See for example Ellen Moers, 'Female Gothic: Monsters, Goblins, Freaks', *New York Review of Books* 21, no. 5 (1974): 35–9; and Sandra Gilbert and Susan Gubar, *The Madwoman in the Attic: The Woman Writer and the Nineteenth-Century Literary Imagination* (New Haven: Yale University Press, 1979).
4 All this is given a nice but different spin (with forensic architectural photos) in Peter Wood, 'Bodies in Question – Domestic Crime Fiction – Domestic Crime Fact', *Pander* 9 (Spring 1999), rpt. http://www.thepander.co.nz/architecture/pwood9.php (accessed 3 March 2006).
5 See Nick Perry, *Hyperreality and Global Culture* (London: Routledge, 1998), pp. 4–23; and David Craig, 'Taranaki Gothic: Stalking the Grotesque in Provincial Art', in *Seppelt Awards Exhibition Catalogue* (Sydney: Museum of Contemporary Art, 1997).
6 Cited in Bleiler, 'Introduction', *Three Gothic Novels*, xvi.
7 Robert Storr, in Marie de Brugerolle, 'Disparities and Deformities: Our Grotesque. Interview with Marie de Brugerolle', *Flash Art* 37, no. 236 (May–June 2004): 75.
8 Michael Fitzgerald, 'Southern Gothic: Karen Walker's Edgy Designs Reflect the Darker Tones of her Native New Zealand', *Time South Pacific*, 24 May 1999: 60.
9 David Craig, 'Thin Topsoil: Queer Blokes, Moral Modernity and Real Estate Politics in New Zealand's Biggest Borough', in *Almighty Auckland?* ed. Ian Carter, David Craig and Steve Matthewman (Palmerston North: Dunmore, 2004), pp. 163–80.
10 Stuart Jeffries, 'The Joy of Concrete', *The Guardian*, 15 March 2004, http://society.guardian.co.uk/urbandesign/comment/0,11200,1169644,00.html (accessed 3 March 2006).
11 See Anna Miles, 'Gavin Hipkins', *Artforum* 38, no. 10 (Summer 2000): 196.
12 See David Craig, 'Taranaki Gothic and the Political Economy of New Zealand Narrative and Sensibility', *New Zealand Sociology* 20, no. 2 (2005): 18–40.
13 David Craig and Michael Stevenson, 'The Work of Art in the Age of Mechanical Provincial Reproduction', *Art New Zealand* no. 106 (February 2003): 62–65, 84.
14 See David Craig, 'If I can't wear my old Wrangler Shirt I'm not going', *Left Right Confusion in New Zealand Art: Michael Stevenson* (Auckland: Greg Flint Galleries, 1994).
15 Miles, 'Gavin Hipins', 196.
16 Bernard Smith, *Modernism's History* (New Haven: Yale University Press, 1998).

Ghost Painting

1 This text accompanied the exhibition of *Ghost Painting* at the Dunedin Public Art Gallery, 2000.

Out Of The Kitchen Sink

1 See Stephen Turner, 'Settlement as Forgetting', in *Quicksands: Foundational Histories in Australia and New Zealand*, ed. Klaus Neumann, Nicholas Thomas and Hilary Ericksen (Sydney: UNSW Press, 1999), pp. 22–37.
2 Linda Hardy, 'Natural Occupancy', in *Asian And Pacific Inscriptions: Identities, Ethnicities, Nationalities*, ed. Suvendrini Perera, *Meridian* 14, no. 2: special issue (1995): 213–28.
3 Hardy, 'Natural Occupancy', p. 214.

Corrugated Iron Gothic

1 See Michael McCarthy, *The Origins of the Gothic Revival* (New Haven: Yale University Press, 1987).

2 The classic history of the Gothic Revival is still Kenneth Clark, *The Gothic Revival: An Essay in the History of Taste* (London: John Murray, 1962). More recent studies include Christopher Brooks, *The Gothic Revival* (London: Phaidon, 1999) and Michael J. Lewis, *The Gothic Revival* (London: Thames & Hudson, 2002).

3 For a concise discussion of Pugin's architectural theory and the ideas of the Ecclesiological Society, see Roger Dixon and Stefan Muthesius, *Victorian Architecture* (London: Thames & Hudson, 1978), pp. 182–95.

4 William Scott, 'On Wooden Churches', *Ecclesiologist*, IX, no. lxvii (August 1848): 23.

5 On Old St Paul's see Margaret Alington, *Frederick Thatcher and St Paul's: An Ecclesiological Study* (Wellington: Government Printer, 1965). St Mary's Parnell is discussed in Ian Lochhead, *A Dream of Spires: Benjamin Mountfort and the Gothic Revival* (Christchurch: Canterbury University Press, 1999), pp. 173–80.

6 See Stefan Muthesius, 'The "Iron Problem" in the 1850s', *Architectural History* 13 (1970): 58–63; and Stefan Muthesius, *The High Victorian Movement in Architecture* (London: Routledge & Kegan Paul), pp. 197–202.

7 John Ruskin, *Seven Lamps of Architecture* (London: Smith, Elder and Co., 1849), ch. II, ix, p. 36.

8 See *Illustrated London News*, XXVI, no. 750, 30 June 1855: 652. On the Oxford Museum see Eve Blau, *Ruskinian Gothic: The Architecture of Deane and Woodward* (Princeton NJ: Princeton University Press, 1982); and Trevor Garnham, *Oxford Museum: Deane and Woodward* (London: Phaidon, 1992).

9 Francis Skidmore to Ecclesiological Society, in *Instrumenta Ecclesiastica* (London: John Van Voorst, 1856), commentary to plate LXXII.

10 Miles Lewis, 'The Corrugated Iron Aesthetic', *Historic Environment* 2, no. 1 (1982): 55.

11 James E. FitzGerald to Bishop Henry J.C. Harper, Private Correspondence, 14 August 1859. Cathedral Commission, Inward Correspondence, Christchurch Diocesan Archives, Christchurch.

12 For a detailed discussion of the Clock Tower, see Lochhead, *A Dream of Spires*, pp. 102–4.

13 See Robert C. Lamb, *Street Corner* (Christchurch: Caxton, 1967), pp. 37–42.

14 See Lewis, 'The Corrugated Iron Aesthetic', *Historic Environment* 2, no. 1: 49–64; Geoff Chapple, John Maynard, David Mitchell and Warren Viscoe, *Corrugated Iron in New Zealand* (Wellington: Reed, 1983); and most recently Stuart Thomson, *Wrinkly Tin: The Story of Corrugated Iron in New Zealand* (Wellington: Steele Roberts, 2005).

15 Hardwick Knight and Peter Coutts, *Matanaka: Otago's First Farm* (Dunedin: John McIndoe, 1975), pp. 38–45.

16 For a detailed study of Mountfort's career, see Lochhead, *A Dream of Spires.*

17 For the early architectural history of the hospital see R.M. Helms, 'Christchurch Hospital 1861–1876: An Architectural History', *Bulletin of New Zealand Art History* 11 (1990): 3–18. Mountfort's buildings are also discussed in Lochhead, *A Dream of Spires*, pp. 123–4.

18 Benjamin Mountfort to Bishop Andrew B. Suter of Nelson, Private Correspondence, 18 October 1884, Box 16, Diocesan Archives, Anglican Centre, Nelson.

19 The Colonial Hospital, now known as 'The Gables', still stands in Brooklands Park. See Frances Porter, 'New Plymouth Buildings', in *Historic Places of New Zealand: North Island,* ed. Frances Porter (Auckland: Cassell, 1979), pp. 179–81.

20 A.W.N. Pugin, *An Apology for the Revival of Christian Architecture in England* (London: John Weale, 1843), p. 42.

21 See Lochhead, *A Dream of Spires*, pp. 117–9. For a history of the Gaol see David Gee, *The Devil's Own Brigade: A History of the Lyttelton Gaol, 1860–1920* (Wellington: Millwood Press, 1975).

22 For a discussion of the early use of concrete in New Zealand building see Geoffrey Thornton, *Cast in Concrete: Concrete Construction in New Zealand, 1850–1939* (Auckland: Reed, 1996).

23 *Press*, 10 August 1872: 2.

24 See C.C. Burdon, *Dr A.C. Barker, 1819–1873: Photographer, Farmer, Physician* (Dunedin: John McIndoe, 1972).

25 See Don Hamilton and Rodney Wells, *The Buildings of Christ's College, 1850–1990* (Christchurch: Caxton Press, 1991), pp. 24–5 and 56. The former entrance door and gabled hood of the Synod Hall now forms a lych gate between Christ's College and the Christchurch Botanic Gardens.

26 Lois Galer, Jill Hamel and Linda Pears, *Historic Buildings of Otago and Southland* (Wellington: GP Books, 1989), p. 78.

27 Glenis Bowman and Rodney Wells, *In A Southern Churchyard* (Christchurch: Caxton Press, 1997)

28 St Alban's can be compared to the corrugated iron-clad churches in Tologa and Tokomaru Bays illustrated in Geoff Chapple et al., *Corrugated Iron in New Zealand*, pp. 2 and 50–1.

29 On Murcutt, see Philip Drew, *Leaves of Iron: Glenn Murcutt: Pioneer of Australian Architectural Form* (Sydney:

The Law Book Company, 1985) and Françoise Fromonot, *Glenn Murcutt: Buildings and Projects 1962–2003* (New York: Thames & Hudson, 2003).

30 See, for example, the beach house at Muriwai by Mitchell, discussed in E.M. Farrelly, 'Auckland Opposites', *The Architectural Review* 181 (July 1987): 48–52. See also David Mitchell, 'Dunnies should be made of tin', *Corrugated Iron in New Zealand*, pp. 23–35.

31 Peter Beavan, 'Country Living: Facing up to the Landscape', *New Zealand New Home Trends,* 8 no. 2 (1992): 22–9.

32 See, for example, Beaven's use of corrugated iron at Longbeach School, illustrated and discussed in Ian Lochhead, 'Learning From Longbeach: Peter Beaven's Award-Winning School', *Architecture New Zealand* (August 2001): 54–8.

33 See, for example, the Kilwinning Lodge in Lyttelton, where a classical façade of timber fronts a building faced with corrugated iron on the other three sides. See John Wilson, 'A Port Apart', in *Historic Buildings of New Zealand: South Island,* ed. Frances Porter (Auckland: Methuen, 1983), pp. 104–5.

34 Bill Millbank, Mark Amery and Philip Drew, *Jeff Thomson: Sculpture, 1992–2000* (Wellington: Bowen Galleries, 2000).

Underworlds Down Under

1 See, for instance, the documentary film *Cinema of Unease* (Sam Neill and Judy Rymer, 1995), which emphasises the isolation of characters in gothic and other dark films. Vincent Ward draws on this imagery in *Vigil*. *The Scarecrow* (Sam Pillsbury, 1982) takes Ronald Hugh Morrieson's comic gothic novel of the same name and shows the inward warping that can occur in isolated rural locations.

2 Maurice Gee, *Under The Mountain* (London: Puffin Books, 1982), p. 16.

3 Gee, *Under The Mountain,* p. 42.

4 Gee, *Under The Mountain,* p. 42.

5 Gee, *Under The Mountain,* p. 16.

6 Gee, *Under The Mountain,* p. 81.

7 Vincent Ward, 'A Dialogue with Discrepancy: Vincent Ward Discusses *The Navigator*', interview by Russell Campbell and Miro Bilbrough, *Illusions* 10 (1989): 9–14.

8 Vincent Ward with Alison Carter, Geoff Chapple and Louis Nowra, *Edge of the Earth: Stories and Images from the Antipodes* (Auckland: Heinemann Reed, 1990), p. 10.

9 Gee, *Under The Mountain,* pp. 157–8.

10 Gee, *Under The Mountain,* p. 84.

11 Gee, *Under The Mountain,* p. 152.

12 Gee, *Under The Mountain,* pp. 158–9.

Well-laundered Elves

1 See Kwame Anthony Appiah, 'Race', in *Critical Terms for Literary Study*, ed. Frank Lentricchia and Thomas McLaughlin, 2nd edn. (Chicago: University of Chicago Press, 1995), p. 277.

2 See, for example, Anderson Rearick III, 'Why Is the Only Good Orc a Dead Orc? The Dark Face of Racism Examined in Tolkien's World', *Modern Fiction Studies* 50, no. 4 (Winter 2004): 861–74.

3 J.R.R. Tolkien, *The Lord of the Rings: The Two Towers* (London: The Folio Society, 1977), p. 368. All references to Tolkien's *The Lord of the Rings* are to the three-volume Folio Society Edition. References to the film version are to the three-volume Special Extended DVD Edition (Roadshow Entertainment/New Line Cinema).

4 Tolkien, *The Two Towers*, p. 49.

5 Tolkien, *The Lord of the Rings: The Return of the King*, p. 300.

6 Tolkien, *The Two Towers*, p. 120.

7 See *The Lord of the Rings: The Fellowship of the Ring* (DVD), Appendices: 'Designing Middle Earth' and 'From Book to Script'. For a brief outline of Tolkien's debt to Wagner, see Alex Ross, 'The Ring and the Rings', *New Yorker*, 22 December 2003: 161.

8 Mary Douglas, *Purity and Danger: An Analysis of Concepts of Pollution and Taboo* (Harmondsworth: Penguin, 1970), p. 12.

9 Douglas, *Purity and Danger*, p. 15.

10 Cited in Douglas, *Purity and Danger*, p. 17.

11 Tolkien attributes Aragorn's phenomenal longevity entirely to the purity of his blood: 'I shall die …. For I am a mortal man, and though being what I am and of the race of the West unmingled, I shall have life far longer than other men ….' Tolkien, *The Return of the King*, p. 263. In the film, however, Aragorn is much less certain about the virtues he may have inherited through his race: 'I do not know what strength is in my blood', he says to the dying Boromir, 'but I swear to you that I will not let the white city [of Gondor] fall'.

12 *The Fellowship of the Ring* (DVD), Appendices: 'Weta Workshop'. Tolkien describes the Balrog – 'Durin's Bane' – simply as a 'dark figure streaming with fire'. It carries a whip, and appears to have wings. Tolkien, *The Two Towers*, pp. 372–6.

13 *The Fellowship of the Ring.* In the circumstances of their birth, their appearance and general demeanour, Jackson's Uruk-hai seem to owe a certain debt to the Golem. Golems – human-like beings made of clay – have their origins in the Kabbalah, which contains legends of adepts who could animate clay figures using specific ritual incantations. By the sixteenth century, the Golem had become a kind of super-hero: the legend of

the Golem of Prague tells how a golem created by a devout rabbi saved the Jewish community from a terrible pogrom. Golems have no will of their own and exist only to do their masters' bidding and hence are capable of great good; as supernatural beings, however, they also harbour the potential to do great harm. Both Jackson's Uruk-hai and Tolkien's Gollum may well have taken their first breaths in the Golem legend. For a brief, scholarly discussion of the origins of the golem, see Gershom Scholem, 'The Idea of the Golem', *On the Kabbalah and Its Symbolism* (New York: Schocken Books, 1965), pp. 158–204.

14 Douglas, *Purity and Danger*, p. 51.

15 See Douglas, 'The Abominations of Leviticus', *Purity and Danger*, pp. 41–57.

16 Tolkien, *The Return of the King*, p. 276. While this small detail is introduced simply as a sign of Gollum's 'otherness' and marks him as comically un-English in his tastes and habits, it is perhaps pertinent to note, in the light of the general tenor of Tolkien's representation of Gollum, that fish and chips were probably developed by Joseph Malin, a Jewish immigrant from Eastern Europe, who started selling fried fish with chips in his shop in London's East End in the 1860s. See Claudia Roden, *The Book of Jewish Food* (Harmondsworth: Penguin, 1996), p. 100.

17 Tolkien, *The Two Towers*, p. 230.

18 Bram Stoker, *Dracula* (Harmondsworth: Penguin, 1979), p. 47. Jonathan's diary entry for 12 May. Interestingly, swarming, creeping and sniffing are all likely to be richly suggestive motifs for the gothic imagination. Douglas's structuralist model might suggest that these are anomalous behaviours in terms of an idea of the properly unitary human subject: insects and reptiles swarm and creep; dogs sniff. They are therefore likely to produce a pollution-reaction of revulsion.

19 Tolkien, *The Two Towers*, pp. 309–10.

20 Tolkien, *The Return of the King*, p. 236.

21 Tolkien, *The Return of the King*, p. 279.

22 For a discussion of New Zealand as Middle Earth which foregrounds the problematic position of Maori, see Stephen Turner and Misha Kavka, '"This Is Not New Zealand": An Exercise in the Political Economy of Identity', in *Studying the Event Film: The Lord of the Rings*, ed. Sean Cubitt, Thierry Jutel and Harriet Margolis (Manchester: Manchester University Press, forthcoming 2007). On Jackson's appeal to environmentalist values in producing the trilogy, see Allan Phillipson, 'Dollarman vs *The Lord of the Rings*: The Battle of Nature and Progress', *World Literature Written in English* 39 (2002–3): 18–37.

23 *The Fellowship of the Ring* (DVD), Appendices: 'Cameras in Middle Earth'.

Misery: Art and Fashion

1 All quotations are taken from an interview with the artist, conducted 3 May 2006.

2 Of her transition from having a screen-printed range of clothing in the Illicit store to opening her own boutique next door, Misery says, 'When I was with Illicit, it was mostly Asian kids [because my work] is really like Japanese culture; they really love the big eyes and the dark goth girls. And heaps of teenage girls [came who] were punk and goth. Then when the boutique opened, the customer base broadened immediately; it was amazing. I think that putting in that pink, girlie environment brought all sorts of different people in. Now it's huge: girls come in with their mums, and their mums love it and they buy stuff as well'.

3 See 'blythe history', http://www.thisisblythe.com (accessed 10 July 2006).

Don't Worry, Be Happy

1 See, for example, the United Kingdom's *Think Road Safety* website (http://www.thinkroadsafety.gov.uk); and Australia's *Road and Traffic Authority* advertising archive (http://www.rta.nsw.gov.au/roadsafety/advertisingcampaigns/index.html).

2 There are two predominant forms this teasing can take. The first, seemingly common in Australia, leads with the complete advertisement and then follows with truncated versions, each delivering a different closing message over the same images (see 'Heaven and Hell', *Road and Traffic Authority*, http://www.rta.nsw.gov.au/roadsafety/downloads/tvc/countryspeedingtvc_dl1.html [accessed 5 January 2006]), while the second, common in New Zealand, tends to favour a more traditional type of tease. With the *Can You Trust Your Mates?* campaign we are treated to innocuous images of how one can't trust one's friends (the mid-party 'downtrow'; the pre-shaken beer can; the cellophane over the toilet), leading us into the final betrayal: the drunk driver. *Can You Trust Your Mates?*, http://www.canttrustmates.co.nz (accessed 5 January 2006).

3 For a complete overview of this country's accident and injury statistics, see 'ACC Injury Statistics 2005', *Accident Compensation Corporation Inc.*, http://www.acc.co.nz/wcm001/idcplg?IdcService=SS_GET_PAGE&nodeId=8070&ssSourceNodeId=4249 (accessed 9 June 2006).

4 According to the *Land Transport NZ* website, 'to support the road safety campaign, the Government provides funding of approximately $9.5 million per year for advertising. This funding supports a $150 million Police strategic enforcement programme

and is divided over the speed, drink-driving, failure to give way at intersections and safety belt campaigns'. 'Funding', *Land Transport Safety Authority*, http://www.landtransport.govt.nz/advertising/campaign.html (accessed 5 January 2006).

5 No surprise, then, that the 'Don't Worry, Be Happy' campaign has received a number of complaints to the Advertising Standards Authority, all of which make note of the way the use of this 'happy tune trivialised the serious consequences of road accidents and it [the advert] should be shown at a time when children were not watching'. In response, the Chairperson of the Appeals Board noted that 'the song "Don't Worry, Be Happy" had been used in a satirical manner, to emphasise that careless disregard for road rules would not result in "happy" outcomes but serious accidents and injuries.' 'Decision 03/3/02 – Land Transport Safety Authority', *Advertising Standards Authority Inc.*, http://www.asa.co.nz/decisions/FULL/D03302.rtf (accessed 9 June 2006).

6 According to the *Land Transport NZ*, '[t]he vernacular in each advertisement is targeted to its specific audience so they can relate to it, e.g., the rural alcohol advertisement uses the tagline "If you don't drink and drive, you're a bloody legend". The word "legend" is the everyday language that this audience tends to speak'. 'How do you decide what language to use in your advertising?', *Land Transport Safety Authority*, http://www.landtransport.govt.nz/advertising/faq.html (accessed 5 January 2006).

7 On the website of the *Can You Trust Your Mates?* campaign, you can type in your mate's name and his, or her, age and get a character synopsis: Typing in 'Scott' delivers: 'Scott's a joker, he's the guy who put apples in your microwave to see how long it would take for them to explode ... Sure Scott's a mate, but don't trust him with your eyes closed. One guy woke up with no eyebrows, shaving cream down his pants and a dick on his face. So when Scott says he's driving and offers you a ride, make sure he's sweet – because if he's pissed, you're screwed'. Typing in 'Stephen' delivers: 'On April the first you might get a call from the Army, confirming your enlistment. The Navy and Air Force will ring soon after, and as you hang up the phone for the third time, you'll probably be able to hear Stephen laughing from next door. Constantly finding new ways to get you in trouble, he's a real funny guy. But when he's had a few drinks then offers you a ride, it's no laughing matter – because if he's pissed, you're screwed'. *Can You Trust Your Mates?*, http://www.canttrustmates.co.nz. (accessed 5 January 2006).

8 Examples of these are available at the Land Transport NZ advertising archive (http://www.landtransport.govt.nz/advertising/archive.html).

9 Indeed, the Land Transport NZs most recent speed-related campaign, 'High Rise', compares incremental increases in speed over the limit with the distance one would have to fall in order to sustain the same damage. The 'High Rise' ad sits uncomfortably alongside these more scientific ads: each of the cars is suspended above a Wellington street and, as we crane up past each of them (90 kilometres equals falling from the first floor; 110 kilometres equals falling from the fifth floor), we notice that each car in turn holds only a single (male) driver, until the final car (120 kilometres equals falling from the ninth floor) in which a wife and two children peer nervously past the driver. 'High Rise', *Land Transport NZ*, http://www.landtransport.govt.nz/advertising/archive.html (accessed 5 January 2006).

10 See 'Slips, trips and falls', *Accident Compensation Corporation*, http://www.acc.co.nz/wcm001/idcplg?IdcService=SS_GET_PAGE&ssDocName=wcm001893&ssSourceNodeId=4047 (accessed 9 June 2006).

Afterword

1 Michael Fried, *Absorption and Theatricality: Painting and Beholder in the Age of Diderot* (Berkeley, CA: University of California Press, 1980).

2 Cited in Jacqueline Millner, 'Patricia Piccinini: Love in the Time of Intelligent Machines', *Artlink* 21, no. 4 (December 2001): 42–7.

3 Sigmund Freud, 'The Uncanny', *The Standard Edition of the Complete Psychological Works of Sigmund Freud,* ed. and trans. James Strachey, Vol. 17 (London: Hogarth Press, 1957), pp. 219–52.

4 Conversation with the artist Patricia Piccinini (February 2006).

5 Christopher Langton was the founding Editor of the *Artificial Life* journal (MIT Press) and a founder of the Swarm Corporation, a company providing multi-agent computer simulation tools.

Contributors' Notes

Chris Braddock is Associate Professor and Chair of St Paul St Gallery at the School of Art and Design, Auckland University of Technology. He completed a Bachelor of Fine Arts from the University of Canterbury and studied at the École Nationale Supérieure des Beaux-Arts in Paris. In 1989 he completed a Master of Arts from London's Courtauld Institute of Art in Byzantine Mosaics. His work *Votive Mutations*, exhibited at Gow-Langsford Gallery in 1998, marked a turning point in his work around themes of the body, fetishism, minimalism, ornamentation and Catholicism. Braddock is represented by Galerie Römerapotheke in Zurich and Roger Williams Contemporary in Auckland.

This project enabled a shift in my sculptural practice from referencing bodies, with materials like silicon, to inscribing real bodies and working with people's histories and stories. I'm grateful for the models' enthusiasm and trust which was crucial in creating images of this intimacy and religiosity.

David Craig teaches Social Theory and Public Policy in the Department of Sociology at the University of Auckland, and writes at the intersection of political economy, institutions and policy, and the arts and culture. Recent books include *Development Beyond Neoliberalism* (Routledge, 2006), co-written with Doug Porter, monographs on child poverty and local government partnerships in New Zealand, and *Almighty Auckland?*, co-edited with Steve Matthewman and Ian Carter. He has nearly finished co-writing (with Alan Rodgers-Smith) a Taranaki gothic novel, *The Dairie Queene*.

'Gothic Inversions' grew out of my long fascination with NZ provincial reception and domestication of other people's forms, narratives and other ways of seeing the world: both sharp modernist/masculinist perspectives and their domestic dark sides. The photographers discussed here, it seemed to me, got at these issues in three different but related ways.

Martin Edmond has published three unclassifiable books, with a fourth, *Luca Antara*, due from Adelaide-based East Street Publications in November 2006. He has also collaborated on a number of screenplays, including Leon Narbey's much-loved *Illustrious Energy*. He lives freelance in Sydney.

The King Country in the 1950s was so remote that past and future seemed contemporary, while the present inhabited some other dimension altogether. I've tried, among other things, to evoke that timeless dislocation of people and circumstance in this essay.

Elizabeth Hale has co-edited *Marvellous Codes: The Fiction of Margaret Mahy* with Sarah Fiona Winters. She is currently working on a further editing project on Maurice Gee, with Lawrence Jones. She received her PhD from Brandeis University in Massachusetts, and now lectures in English Literature and Critical and Creative Writing at the University of New England, Australia.

I had not visited Auckland before reading Under the Mountain. *To this day, the city is shaped for me by that novel: when I visit now, I cast nervous glances at Rangitoto and wonder if I'll see the Wilberforces sliding by. Perhaps that is why the city seems profoundly gothic.*

Mark Jackson is Associate Professor of Design and Coordinator of PhD Studies in the School of Art and Design at Auckland University of Technology as well as Head of Research in the School. He is also Faculty Head of Postgraduate Studies in the Faculty of Design and Creative Technologies at AUT. Prior to this he has held lecturing positions at the Faculty of Architecture, University of Adelaide and at the Sydney College of the Arts, University of Sydney. He has had a number of film and video works exhibited internationally. His current research focus is on ethics and design cultures.

My involvement in this project stems in part from ongoing collaboration with Christopher Braddock, who was initially invited. The gothic has particular intrigue for its partial legacy in nineteenth-century Romantic aesthetics and for the manner whereby it is capable of extolling evil as the harbinger of progress and salvation of humanised technology.

Misha Kavka teaches Film, Television and Media Studies at the University of Auckland. She has written numerous articles on reality television, New Zealand film, gothic cinema, feminist studies and queer theory. At present, she is completing a book on the affective appeal of reality television.

Whether family home, suburban house or bach, the desire for a new life in a new country is troubled by the very processes of settlement which were meant to make paradise inhabitable. I experience the shadow of the gothic in New Zealand every time something creeps back up out of the kitchen plughole.

Jenny Lawn lectures in English and Media Studies at Massey University's interdisciplinary School of Social and Cultural Studies, Auckland. She has published articles on New Zealand gothic in *New Literatures Review*, *Journal of New Zealand Literature*, *Australasian-Canadian Studies* and *The Listener*.

I guess I would call myself a cultural Calvinist, not by faith but by upbringing and mentality. I'm fascinated by the way in which social proprieties breed particular gremlins of deviance and shame.

Ian Lochhead teaches Art History at the University of Canterbury. He has published extensively on nineteenth- and twentieth-century New Zealand architecture and has a particular interest in the Gothic Revival in New Zealand. His book, *A Dream of Spires: Benjamin Mountfort and the Gothic Revival*, was published by Canterbury University Press in 1999.

I have always been fascinated by the ways in which New Zealand architects and builders have adapted imported building traditions to suit local conditions, and the way in which the Gothic Revival was re-interpreted here exemplifies the ways in which the new environment transformed inherited European styles into something that is uniquely our own.

Olivia Macassey's first collection of poems, *Love In The Age of Mechanical Reproduction*, was published in 2005 (Titus). Her work has also appeared in magazines such as *Poetry New Zealand, Brief, Magazine, Craccum, Tongue in Your Ear*, and on the nzepc website. She is currently a doctoral candidate at the University of Auckland.

This poem spans several places and times: suburban Auckland, colonial Invercargill, the mysteries of my childhood on the Coromandel Peninsula. As I was writing, Rachel Ahmad-Hall showed me her photographs. They reminded me of some things which I've been haunted by for a long time.

Mary Paul is a Senior Lecturer in English in the School of Social and Cultural Studies at the Auckland campus of Massey University. Her last book, *Her Side of the Story* (1999), was a critical and cultural study on Mansfield, Mander and Hyde. In 1998 she designed the first gothic paper to be taught at a New Zealand university, including local texts alongside the classics. This paper led on to the Antipodean Gothic Conference organised with Jenny Lawn and Misha Kavka in 2002.

I am interested in the tensions between monsters within and monsters without in relationship to social and material changes in NZ culture. Haunting goes on, from Robin Hyde's reaction to stifled households – 'Our city had doorways, too many shut' – to Olivia Macassey's: 'In a town where no one locks the doors/ you crept down stairs in the night/ to find the door locked/ and knew/ that your mother believed in monsters too'.

Jack Ross has published two books of poems and four of fiction, most recently *The Imaginary Museum of Atlantis* (Titus, 2006). He has also edited several anthologies, including – with Jan Kemp – the spoken-word collection *Classic New Zealand Poets in Performance* (Auckland University Press, 2006). He teaches Academic and Creative Writing at Massey University's Auckland campus.

I wrote these poems while working as a language teacher in my hometown Auckland. The place appeals to me more and more the darker and stranger it becomes. It's as if the city is gradually growing into its own face, the face that was always waiting underneath.

Sarah Shieff teaches New Zealand Literature and Cultural History, Contemporary Jewish writing and Gothic Fiction at the University of Waikato. She edits the *Journal of New Zealand Literature* and convenes the University of Waikato's programme in New Zealand Studies. Her most recent book is *Talking Music: Conversations with New Zealand Musicians* (Auckland University Press, 2002). She also writes about contemporary New Zealand fiction.

Although J.R.R. Tolkien's epic The Lord of the Rings *was not published until the early 1950s, Middle Earth was the imaginative product of the 1930s. Unsurprisingly, then, Tolkien's narrative is structured in overtly racial terms: 'goodies' are mostly white and baddies are largely dark or deformed. I was interested to find out what happens to that now-unfashionable racism in Peter Jackson's version of the saga. How much of it could the films jettison or rework, given that without it the conflicts which drive the narrative would evaporate like morning mists over Lothlorien? And what bearing might the New Zealand locations have on the story as it moves through its tropes of purity, degeneracy and race?*

Yvonne Todd's most recent exhibition was *Blood, in its Various Forms* at Ivan Anthony Gallery, Auckland (August 2006). Her book of new photographs, *Dead Starlets' Assoc.* is to be published late 2006 as part of a short residency at the Institute of Modern Art, Brisbane, Australia. Yvonne Todd is represented by Ivan Anthony, Auckland and the Peter McLeavey Gallery, Wellington.

I've always favoured the grim and pathetic. I find cheerful things boring.

Stephen Turner teaches in the English Department at the University of Auckland. He has published on issues of indigeneity and settlement in *Arena, Cultural Critique* and *JNZL*, and in the anthologies *Quicksands: Foundational Histories in Australia* and *Television in New Zealand: Programming the Nation.* He is currently completing a book on the 'broken history' of Aotearoa/ New Zealand.

In a world fully subjected to scientific explanation the gothic addresses the historical and social fact of death: Why do people die needlessly? Where do they go? Are they still here? Such questions demand metaphysical as much as scientific explanation, and meet a psychological need.

Ian Wedde's most recent books are *Three Regrets and a Hymn to Beauty* (Auckland University Press) and *Making Ends Meet: Essays and Talks 1992–2004* (Victoria University Press). A new novel, *The Viewing Platform,* will be published by Penguin in September 2006.

I wrote this chapter in response to the others in the book and to the conference that came before it, but coincidentally while working my way around the gothic territories of stem cell research, Artificial Life and Artificial Intelligence, cross-braided somehow with some morose reflections on the dark side of the '100% Pure New Zealand' campaign. In New Zealand, it may be the haplessly 'unnatural' Dolly who ruminates our gothic for us.

Scott Wilson is a PhD student with the University of Auckland, writing a formal exploration of the films of David Cronenberg. He has taught extensively, focusing on the major theoretical approaches to film analysis.

The way a society attempts to discipline its subjects says a great deal about both its intentions and its fears. These advertisements contain within them a deep ambivalence about their own central concern, not least because they must catch our attention even as they repel us. My only other qualification to write this comes with my involvement in two serious car crashes – both fascinating, neither my fault.

Bibliography

Accident Compensation Corporation. 'ACC Injury Statistics 2005'. *Accident Compensation Corporation.* http://www.acc.co.nz/wcm001/idcplg?IdcService=SS_GET_PAGE&nodeId=8070&ssSourceNodeId=4249 (accessed 9 June 2006).

_____. 'Slips, Trips and Falls Campaign'. *Accident Compensation Corporation.* http://www.acc.co.nz/wcm001/idcplg?IdcService=SS_GET_PAGE&ssDocName=wcm001893&ssSourceNodeId=4047 (accessed 9 June 2006).

Advertising Standard Authority, Inc. 'Decision 03/3/02 – Land Transport Safety Authority'. *Advertising Standard Authority, Inc.* http://www.asa.co.nz/decisions/FULL/D03302.rtf (accessed 9 June 2006).

Alington, Margaret. *Frederick Thatcher and St Paul's: An Ecclesiological Study*. Government Printer: Wellington, 1965.

Attali, Jacques. *L'homme nomade*. Paris: Fayard, 2003.

Beaven, Peter. 'Country Living: Facing up to the Landscape'. *New Zealand New Home Trends* 8, no. 2 (1992): 22-29.

Blau, Eve. *Ruskinian Gothic: The Architecture of Deane and Woodward 1845–1861.* Princeton, NJ: Princeton University Press, 1982.

Bleiler, Everett F. 'Introduction'. In *Three Gothic Novels: The Castle of Otranto by Horace Walpole, Vathek by William Beckford, The Vampyre by John Polidori, and a Fragment of a Novel by Lord Byron,* edited by Everett F. Bleiler, v-xl. New York: Dover, 1996.

Bowman, Glenis and Rodney Wells. *In a Southern Churchyard.* Christchurch: Caxton Press, 1997.

Braddock, Christopher. *Sanitate.* Dunedin: Dunedin Public Art Gallery, 2005.

Brooks, Chris. *The Gothic Revival.* London: Phaidon, 1999.

Brugerolle, Marie de. 'Disparities and Deformities: Our Grotesque. Interview with Marie de Brugerolle'. *Flash Art* 37, no. 236 (2004): 75.

Burdon, C. C. *Dr A.C. Barker, 1819–1873: Photographer, Farmer, Physician.* Dunedin: John McIndoe, 1972.

Cain, Stephen, ed. *Antipodean Tales: Stories from the Dark Side.* Wellington: IPL Books, 1996.

Calder, Alex. 'Unsettling Settlement: Poetry and Nationalism in Aotearoa/New Zealand'. *REAL: Yearbook of Research in English and American Literature* 14 (1998): 169–72.

Cambridge Camden Society. *Instrumenta Ecclesiastica.* London, 1847; second series, London: John Van Voorst, 1856.

Chapple, Geoff, John Maynard, David Mitchell and Warren Viscoe. *Corrugated Iron in New Zealand.* Wellington: Reed, 1983.

Clark, Kenneth. *The Gothic Revival: An Essay in the History of Taste.* London: John Murray, 1962.

Clark, Trish and Wystan Curnow, eds. *Pleasures and Dangers: Artists of the '90s.* Auckland: Moet & Chandon New Zealand Art Foundation/Longman Paul, 1991.

Craig, David. 'Taranaki Gothic and the Political Economy of New Zealand Narrative and Sensibility'. *New Zealand Sociology* 20, no. 2 (2005): 18–40.

_____. 'Thin Topsoil: Queer Blokes, Moral Modernity, and Real Estate Politics in New Zealand's Biggest Borough'. In *Almighty Auckland?*, edited by Ian Carter, David Craig and Steve Matthewman. Palmerston North: Dunmore, 2004: pp. 163–180.

_____. 'Taranaki Gothic: Stalking the grotesque in Provincial Art'. *1997 Seppelt Awards Exhibition.* Sydney: Museum of Contemporary Art, 1997.

_____. 'If I can't wear my old Wrangler shirt I'm not going'. In *Left Right Confusion in New Zealand Art: Michael Stevenson.* Exhibition catalogue. Auckland: Greg Flint Galleries, 1994.

Debord, Guy. *The Society of the Spectacle.* New York: Zone Books, 1995.

Dixon, Roger and Stefan Muthesius. *Victorian Architecture with a Short Dictionary of Architects.* London: Thames & Hudson, 1978.

Douglas, Mary. *Purity and Danger: An Analysis of Concepts of Pollution and Taboo.* Harmondsworth: Penguin, 1970.

Drew, Philip. *Leaves of Iron: Glenn Murcutt: Pioneer of an Australian Architectural Form.* Sydney: Law Book Co., 1985.

Eden, Dorothy. *An Important Family*. London and Auckland: Hodder & Stoughton; New York: Morrow, 1982.

Farrelly, E.M. 'Auckland Opposites'. *The Architectural Review* 181 (July 1987): 48-52.

Fitzgerald, Michael. 'Southern Gothic: Karen Walker's Edgy Designs Reflect the Darker Tones of her Native New Zealand'. *Time South Pacific*, 24 May 1999: 60.

Frame, Janet. *Scented Gardens for the Blind*. Christchurch: Pegasus; London: W.H. Allen, 1962.

Freud, Sigmund. 'The Uncanny'. In *The Standard Edition of the Complete Psychological Works*, edited and translated by James Strachey, Vol. 17. London: Hogarth, 1957, pp. 219–52.

Fried, Michael. *Absorption and Theatricality: Painting and Beholder in the Age of Diderot*. Chicago and London: University of Chicago Press, 1980.

Fromonot, Françoise. *Glenn Murcutt: Buildings and Projects 1962–2003*. New York: Thames & Hudson, 2003.

Galer, Lois, Jill Hamel and Linda Pears (Historic Places Trust). *Historic Buildings of Otago and Southland*. Wellington: GP Books, 1989.

Garnham, Trevor. *Oxford Museum: Deane and Woodward*. London: Phaidon Press, 1992.

Gee, David. *The Devil's Own Brigade: A History of the Lyttelton Gaol, 1860–1920*. Wellington: Millwood Press, 1975.

Gee, Maurice. *In My Father's Den*. 1972. Auckland: Penguin Books, 2004.

_____. *Under the Mountain*. London: Puffin, 1982.

Gelder, Ken. 'J.R.R. Tolkien and Global Terrorism'. In *Popular Fiction: The Logics and Practices of a Literary Fiction*, London: Routledge, 2004, pp. 142–57.

_____ and Jane Jacobs. *Uncanny Australia: Sacredness and Identity in a Postcolonial Nation*. Carlton South, Vic.: Melbourne University Press, 1998.

Gilbert, Sandra and Susan Gubar. *The Madwoman in the Attic: The Woman Writer and the Nineteenth-Century Literary Imagination*. New Haven: Yale University Press, 1979.

Gilman, Charlotte Perkins. *The Yellow Wallpaper*. London: Virago, 1981.

Goldie, Terry. *Fear and Temptation: The Image of the Indigene in Canadian, Australian and New Zealand Literatures*. Kingston, ON: McGill-Queen's University Press, 1989.

Grace, Patricia. *Baby No-Eyes*. Auckland: Penguin Books, 1998.

Griffiths, Richard D. *Darkness, Death and Distortion: A Sociological Examination of Moral Panic Theory and the Gothic Subculture*. Doctoral Thesis: The University of Auckland, 2005.

Hamilton, Don and Rodney Wells. *The Buildings of Christ's College, 1850–1990*. Christchurch: Caxton Press, 1991.

Hardy, Ann. 'The Return of the Taniwha: The Re-spiritualization of Land and Film in Aotearoa'. *British Review of New Zealand Studies* 14 (2003/4): 87–104.

Hardy, Linda. 'Natural Occupancy'. In *Asian & Pacific Inscriptions*, edited by Suvendrini Perera. Special issue *Meridian* 14, no. 2 (1995): 213–28.

Hebley, Diane. *Power of Place*. Dunedin: University of Otago Press, 1998.

Helms, R.M. 'Christchurch Hospital 1861–1876: An Architectural History'. *Bulletin of New Zealand Art History* 11 (1990): 3–18.

Hitchcock, Jane Maree. 'Inflections of the Gothic in New Zealand Film'. Masters Thesis: Massey University, 1998.

Ihimaera, Witi. *Woman Far Walking*. Wellington: Huia, 2000.

Jeffries, Stuart. 'The joy of concrete'. *The Guardian*, 15 March 2004. http://society.guardian.co.uk/urbandesign/comment/0,11200,1169644,00.html (accessed March, 2004).

Johnson, Mike. *Dumb Show*. Dunedin: Longacre Press, 1996.

Kavka, Misha. 'The Gothic on Screen'. In *The Cambridge Companion to Gothic Culture*, edited by Jerrold Hogle, Cambridge, UK: Cambridge University Press, 2002, pp. 209–28.

Kidman, Fiona. *Mandarin Summer*. Auckland and Exeter: Heinemann, 1981.

Knight, Hardwicke and Peter Coutts. *Matanaka: Otago's First Farm*. Dunedin: McIndoe, 1975.

Knox, Elizabeth. *Daylight*. Wellington: Victoria University Press, 2003.

Kouka, Hone. *Waiora*. Wellington: Huia, 1997.

Lamb, Robert C. *Street Corner: A Study to Mark the Thirtieth Anniversary of the Founding of the Caxton Press*. Christchurch: Caxton Press, 1967.

Land Transport New Zealand. 'Advertising Archive'. *Land Transport New Zealand Authority*. 9 December, 2005. http://www.landtransport.govt.nz/advertising/archive.html (accessed 5 January 2006).

_____. 'Advertising: Frequently Asked Questions'. *Land Transport New Zealand Authority*. 19 November, 2005. http://www.landtransport.govt.nz/advertising/faq.html (accessed 5 January 2006).

_____. *Can You Trust Your Mates?* 22 September, 2005. http://www.canttrustmates.co.nz (accessed 5 January 2006).

_____. 'The Road Safety Campaign'. *Land Transport New Zealand Authority*. 19 November,

2005. http://www.landtransport.govt.nz/advertising/campaign.html (5 January 2006).
Lawn, Jennifer. 'From the Spectral to the Ghostly: Postcolonial Gothic and New Zealand Literature'. *Australian-Canadian Studies* (Forthcoming).
_____. 'Vampires Don't Wear Shorts'. *NZ Listener*, 13 August 2005: 36–37.
_____. '*Scarfies*, Dunedin Gothic, and the Spirit of Capitalism'. *Journal of New Zealand Literature* 22 (2004): 124–40.
_____. 'Domesticating Settler Gothic'. *New Literatures Review* 38 (Winter 2002): 46–62.
Lewis, Michael J. *The Gothic Revival*. New York: Thames & Hudson, 2002.
Lewis, Miles. 'The Corrugated Iron Aesthetic'. *Historic Environment* 2, no. 1 (1982): 49-64.
Lochhead, Ian. *A Dream of Spires: Benjamin Mountfort and the Gothic Revival*. Christchurch: Canterbury University Press, 1999.
_____. 'Learning From Longbeach: Peter Beaven's Award-Winning School'. *Architecture New Zealand* (July/August 2001): 54-58.
Loos, Adolf. 'Ornament and Crime'. In *Programs and Manifestoes on 20th-Century Architecture*, edited by Urlich Conrads. Cambridge, MA: MIT Press, 1970, pp. 19-24.
McCarthy, Michael. *The Origins of the Gothic Revival*. New Haven: Yale University Press, 1987.
Miles, Anna. 'Gavin Hipkins'. *Artforum* 38, no. 10 (Summer 2000): 196.
Manhire, Bill. 'Picnic at Woodhaugh'. *What to Call your Child*. Auckland: Godwit, 1999.
Matthews, Philip. 'Local Infections: New Zealand Horror'. *Landfall* 201 (May 2001): 183–87.
Millbank, Bill et al. *Jeff Thomson: Sculpture, 1992-2000*. Wellington: Bowen Galleries, 2000.
Millner, Jacqueline. 'Patricia Piccinni: Ethical Aesthetics'. *Artlink* (2001).
Mitchell, Tony. 'Vincent Ward: The Eloquence of Isolation'. *Art New Zealand* 30 (1984): 36–39.
Mitchell, W.J.T. ed. *Landscape and Power*. Chicago: Chicago University Press, 1994.
Moers, Ellen. 'Female Gothic: Monsters, Goblins, Freaks'. *New York Review of Books* (1974). Rpt. in *Frankenstein: A Norton Critical Edition*, edited by J. Paul Hunter, New York: Norton, 1996, pp. 214-24.
Morrieson, Ronald Hugh. *The Scarecrow*. Sydney: Angus & Robertson, 1963.
_____. *Came a Hot Friday*. Sydney: Angus & Robertson, 1964.
Mulgan, John. *Man Alone*. London: Selwyn & Blount, 1939.
Muthesius, Stefan. 'The "Iron Problem" in the 1850s'. *Architectural History* 13 (1970): 58–63.
_____. *The High Victorian Movement in Architecture*. London: Routledge & Kegan Paul, 1972.
Perry, Nick. *Hyperreality and Global Culture*. London: Routledge, 1998.
Porter, Frances, ed. *Historic Places of New Zealand: North Island*. Auckland: Cassell, 1979.
_____. *Historic Buildings of New Zealand: South Island*. Auckland: Methuen, 1983.
Pugin, A.W.N. *An Apology for the Revival of Christian Architecture in England*. London: John Weale, 1843.
Rearick III, Anderson. 'Why Is the Only Good Orc a Dead Orc? The Dark Face of Racism Examined in Tolkien's World'. *Modern Fiction Studies* 50, no. 4 (Winter 2004): 861-874.
Road and Traffic Authority, Australia. *Advertising Campaigns*. 25 May 2004. http://www.rta.nsw.gov.au/roadsafety/advertisingcampaigns/index.html (5 January 2006).
Road and Traffic Authority, Australia. *Country Speeding Television Advertisements*. 3 June, 2004. http://www.rta.nsw.gov.au/roadsafety/downloads/tvc/countryspeedingtvc_dl1.html (5 January 2006).
Roden, Claudia. *The Book of Jewish Food*. Harmondsworth: Penguin, 1996.
Ross, Jack. *Nights with Giordano Bruno*. Wellington: Bumper Books, 2000.
_____. *Trouble in Mind*. Auckland: Titus Books, 2005.
Rudd, Tracy Jean. *In Despair of Subculture: An Analysis of Auckland City's Gothic Subculture*. Masters Thesis: The University of Auckland, 1998.
Ruskin, John. *Seven Lamps of Architecture*. London: Smith, Elder, and Co., 1849.
Schafer, William. *Mapping the Godzone*. Honolulu: University of Hawai'i Press, 1998.
Scott, W. 'On Wooden Churches'. *Ecclesiologist* IX (1849): 14–27.
Shanks, Grant with Tahu Potiki. *Where No Birds Sing: Tales of the Supernatural in Aotearoa*. Christchurch: Shoal Bay Press, 1998.
Shelton, Ann. *Redeye*. Auckland: Rim Publishing, 1997.
_____. *Public Places*. Auckland: Rim Publishing, 2003.
Simpson, Peter. *Ronald Hugh Morrieson*. Auckland: Oxford University Press, 1982.
Smith, Bernard. *Modernism's History*. New Haven: Yale University Press, 1998.
Stoker, Bram. *Dracula*. Harmondsworth: Penguin, 1979.
Te Awekotuku, Ngahuia. *Ruahine: Mythic Women*. Wellington: Huia, 2003.
Thornton, Geoffrey. *Cast in Concrete: Concrete Construction in New Zealand, 1850–1939*. Auckland: Reed, 1996.

Thomson, Stuart. *Wrinkly Tin: The Story of Corrugated Iron in New Zealand*. Wellington: Steele Roberts, 2005.

Tolkien, J.R.R. *The Lord of the Rings*. London: The Folio Society, 1977.

_____. *The Hobbit*. London: Harper Collins, 1995.

Turner, Stephen. 'Settlement as Forgetting'. *Quicksands: Foundational Histories in Australia and New Zealand*, edited by Klaus Neumann, Nicholas Thomas and Hilary Ericksen. Sydney: UNSW Press, 1999, pp. 22-37.

_____ and Misha Kavka. '"This Is Not New Zealand": An Exercise in the Political Economy of Identity'. In *Studying the Event Film: The Lord of the Rings*, edited by Sean Cubitt, Thierry Jutel, Barry King and Harriet Margolis. Manchester: Manchester University Press (forthcoming).

Tyler-Smith, Sam. '"Quardle oodle ardle wardle doodle": The Fear of Madness in the Face of the New Zealand Landscape'. *Push* 2, no. 4 (Oct. 2004): 10–17.

UK Department for Transport. *THINK! Road Safety Website*. 3 January 2006. http://www.thinkroadsafety.gov.uk (5 January 2006).

Upritchard, Francis. *Doomed, Doomed, All Doomed*. Auckland: Artspace, 2005.

Van Hout, Ronnie. *No Exit Parts 1 & 2*. Wellington: Ronnie van Hout and Hamish McKay Gallery, 2003.

_____. *I've Abandoned Me*. Dunedin: Dunedin Public Art Gallery, 2003.

Virtue, Noel. *The Redemption of Elsdon Bird*. Auckland: Century Hutchinson, 1988.

Votive: Sacred & Ecstatic Bodies. Exhibition catalogue. Wellington and Dunedin: Adam Art Gallery and Dunedin Public Art Gallery, 2002.

Walpole, Horace. *The Castle of Otranto: A Gothic Story*. London: Oxford University Press, 1969.

Ward, Vincent with Alison Carter, Geoff Chapple and Louis Nowra. *Edge of the Earth: Stories and Images from the Antipodes*. Auckland: Heinemann Reed, 1990.

_____. 'A Dialogue with Discrepancy: Vincent Ward Discusses *The Navigator*'. Interview by Russell Campbell and Miro Bilbrough. *Illusions* 10 (March 1989): 9–14.

Wedde, Ian. *Symmes Hole*. Auckland: Penguin, 1986.

Williams, Anne. *Art of Darkness: A Poetics of Gothic*. Chicago: University of Chicago Press, 1995.

Williams, Mark, ed. *Writing at the Edge of the Universe*. Christchurch: Canterbury University Press, 2005.

Wood, Peter. 'Bodies in Question – Domestic Crime Fiction – Domestic Crime Fact'. *Pander* 9 (Spring 1999). http://www.thepander.co.nz/architecture/pwood9.php (accessed January 2006).

Filmography

Apocalypse Now. Dir./ Prod./ Scr. Francis Ford Coppola. United Artists, 1979.

Braindead. Dir. Peter Jackson. Prod. Jim Booth. Scr. Peter Jackson, Stephen Sinclair and Fran Walsh. WingNut Films/ Avalon-NFU Studios/ NZ Film Commission, 1992.

Cinema of Unease: A Personal Journey by Sam Neill. Dir./Scr. Sam Neill and Judy Rymer. Prod. Paul Jalfon, Grant Campbell. BFI/ NZ Film Commission/ NZ on Air/ TV3 Network Service/ Top Shelf Productions, 1995.

Crash. Dir./Prod./Scr. David Cronenberg. Alliance Communications Corp./ RPC/ TMN/ Téléfilms Canada, 1996.

Crush. Dir./Scr. Alison Maclean. Prod. Bridget Ikin. Avalon-NFU Studios/ Hibiscus Films/ NZ Film Commission/ NZ on Air, 1992.

Heavenly Creatures. Dir. Peter Jackson. Prod. Jim Booth. Scr. Peter Jackson and Frances Walsh. Fontana Films/ Miramax/ NZ Film Commission/ WingNut Films, 1994.

Heart of the Stag. Dir. Michael Firth. Prod. Don Reynolds and Michael Firth. Scr. Neil Illingworth. New World Enertainment, 1983.

Jack Be Nimble. Dir./Scr. Garth Maxwell. Prod. Jonathan Dowling and Kelly Rogers. NZ Film Commission, 1993.

In My Father's Den. Dir./Scr. Brad McGann. Prod. Trevor Haysom and Dixie Linder. T.H.E. Film/ Little Bird, 2004.

Kitchen Sink. Dir./Scr. Alison Maclean. Prod. Bridget Ikin. Hibiscus Films, 1989.

The Locals. Dir./Scr. Greg Page. Prod. Steve Sachs. Rocket Pictures, 2003.

The Lord of the Rings: The Fellowship of the Ring. Dir./ Prod. Peter Jackson. Scr. Fran Walsh, Philippa Boyens and Peter Jackson. New Line Cinema/ WingNut Films, 2001.

The Lord of the Rings: The Two Towers. Dir./Prod. Peter Jackson. Scr. Fran Walsh, Philippa Boyens, Stephen Sinclair and Peter Jackson. New Line Cinema/WingNut Films, 2002.

The Lord of the Rings: The Return of the King. Dir./Prod. Peter Jackson. Scr. Fran Walsh, Philippa Boyens and Peter Jackson. New Line Cinema/ WingNut Films, 2003.

Mr Wrong. Dir. Gaylene Preston. Prod. Robin Laing and Gaylene Preston. Scr. Gaylene Preston, Graeme Telley and Geoff Murphy. Preston Laing Productions, 1984.

The Navigator: A Mediaeval Odyssey. Dir./Scr. Vincent Ward. Prod. John Maynard. Arena Film/Film Investment Corp. of NZ, 1988.

Nosferatu, eine Symphonie des Grauens. Dir. F.W. Murnau. Prod. Enrico Diekmann and Albin Grau. Scr. Henrik Galeen. Jofa Atelier Berlin Johannisthal/ Pran-Film GmbH, 1922.

Nosferatu: Phantom der Nacht. Dir./Prod./Scr. Werner Herzog. Société des Etablissements L. Gaumont/ Werner Herzog Filmproduktion, 1979.

Perfect Creature. Dir./Scr. Glenn Standring. Prod. Tim Sanders. Darclight Films/NZ Film Commission/Perfect Creature Ltd./Roc Media/Sensible Films/Spice Factory Ltd., 2006.

Perfect Strangers. Dir. Scr. Gaylene Preston. Prod. Robin Laing. Gaylene Preston Productions, 2002.

The Piano. Dir./Scr. Jane Campion. Prod. Jan Chapman. Australian Film Commission/CiBy 2000/ NSW Film and TV Office, 1993.

Rain. Dir./Scr. Christine Jeffs. Prod. Phillippa Campbell. Rose Road and Communicado, 2001.

The Scarecrow. Dir. Sam Pillsbury. Prod. Robert Whitehouse. Scr. Michael Heath and Sam Pillsbury. National Film Unit/TVNZ,1982.

Scarfies. Dir. Robert Sarkies. Prod. Lisa Chatfield. Scr. Robert Sarkies and Duncan Sarkies. Nightmare Productions, 1999.

Sweetie. Dir. Jane Campion. Prod. John Maynard. Scr. Gerard Lee. Arena Films/NSW Film Corporation/Australian Film Commission/ Australian Television Office, 1989.

Trial Run. Dir./Scr. Melanie Read. Prod. Don Reynolds. NZ Film Commission, 1984.

Van Helsing. Dir./Scr. Stephen Sommers. Prod. Stephen Sommers, and Bob Ducsay. Carpathian Films/ Universal Pictures/ Stillking Films/The Sommers Company, 2004.

Vigil. Dir. Vincent Ward. Prod. John Maynard. Scr. Vincent Ward and Graeme Tetley. John Maynard Productions, 1984.